Choosing the "Right"

The Rise and Repercussions of Republican Politics in the LDS Church

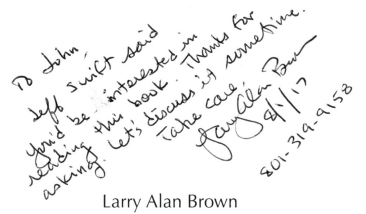

To John,

Jeff Swift said you'd be interested in reading this book. Thanks for asking. Let's discuss it sometime. Take care,

Larry Alan Brown

9/1/17

801-319-9158

Larry Alan Brown

ISBN number 978-0-9990367-0-9

Published by
ProcessProud Publishing
5406 West 11000 North
Suite 103–124
Highland, UT 84003-8942
larry@processproud.com

Cover design by Scott Filipiak
Cover design ©2017 Larry Alan Brown
Edited by Debbie Harrison
Design and layout by Erin Willder
Index by Sandra Thorne

Printed in the United States of America

To Tammy

Contents

Introduction

Members of the Church of Jesus Christ of Latter-day Saints, also known as Latter-day Saints, LDS or Mormons, are among the most generous, caring and faithful people in the world. Surveys have consistently found that the people of Utah (who are predominantly but not exclusively LDS) have volunteered more time and resources to their churches and other nonprofit organizations than the people of any other state. Mormons in other states and other nations also have a reputation for their devotion to Christian principles and good works in their communities. They place great value on unity, conformity, fellowship, community service, healthy democratic processes and bringing the gospel of Jesus Christ to all the peoples of the world.

But there are, as with any distinct and tight-knit group of people, aspects of Mormon culture and its members' social and political beliefs that have proven problematic. In many such cultures, especially a religious minority with a history of persecution and exclusion from mainstream society, members often believe their strength and protection depend on its members thinking and acting with a single mind. Nonconformity is often seen as a crack in the collective armor and is, consciously or unconsciously, strongly discouraged.

One of the more visible means by which Latter-day Saints are largely expected to conform is to demonstrate loyalty to a common conservative political ideology. An overwhelming 70 percent of Mormons in the U.S. are registered Republicans or lean toward the GOP. LDS Democrats, or those who lean left, make up 22 percent.[1] Many Republican members

---

1 "A Deep Dive into Party Affiliation," *Pew Research Center*, April 7, 2015, at http://www.people-press.org/2015/04/07/a-deep-dive-into-party-affiliation/ (accessed August 3, 2015).

suspect LDS Democrats of being, to some degree, not fully compliant with Church doctrine. Most of the time, Democrats in the Church keep their social and political beliefs to themselves to avoid having their faithfulness and patriotism questioned, no matter how subtly. They are particularly anxious to keep a low profile during partisan political campaigns and elections. Except for a hardy few, LDS Democrats, particularly in Utah, will avoid putting up a Democratic candidate's yard sign or gluing a bumper sticker on their car to avoid drawing attention to what may be considered their nonconformist views. Some have been openly criticized for their political leanings in their ward congregations.

Why is it important to focus on the striking imbalance in party affiliation among Latter-day Saints? It's because the near-automatic allegiance to Republican dogma by a vast majority of Church members causes unintended and troubling consequences. It fosters an environment in which feelings are hurt and member unity can be weakened, which, of itself, would be ample reason not to let political ideology become a de facto test of faith. But the imbalance also manifests itself in many other ways that can tarnish the reputation of the Church and its mission. It makes it more difficult for LDS missionaries to bring the gospel of Jesus Christ to all peoples in the world. It undercuts the Church's determined effort to gain acceptance into mainstream American society. And it erodes the principles of good government where significant concentrations of Mormon Republicans vote for political candidates based solely on their party label rather than qualifications.

One example of how member unity is jeopardized by cultural and political prejudice took place in my local LDS ward (a congregation roughly equivalent to a Catholic parish) as I took part in a high priest group meeting in October 2008. The hotly contested presidential race between Democrat Barack Obama and Republican John McCain was in its final weeks. During the gospel lesson, a fellow high priest cracked a negative joke about Democrats, eliciting a ripple of laughter. A second brother, unable to resist the temptation to score a few laughs himself, blurted out a caustic follow-up joke. Louder laughs. A third man in the meeting, apparently hoping to trump his fellow jokers, piled on with yet another derogatory comment. Unable to stand it any longer, I jumped to my feet and shouted, "I'm a Democrat!" The brethren laughed even harder, assuming I had joined in the fun. But they soon realized I was truly offended. "When you can be nonpartisan, I'll come back!" I shouted, and stormed out of the room.

My reaction, in hindsight, is not one that I'm particularly proud of. But I believe it underscored an important gospel point about having tolerance toward those with whom we disagree. To their credit, each of the contrite comedians called me after the meeting and apologized. To this day, we remain genuine friends in the gospel and good neighbors. With or without their apologies, I would not have stayed away from the Church as I threatened to do in a fit of pique. My faith and testimony are built on the rock of the gospel, not on personalities or insensitivities. For the same reason, practically all Mormon Democrats I know are faithful and active in the Church despite having had their social and political values come under the scrutiny of their fellow Church members.

My experience is not an isolated one. Based on decades of firsthand accounts and observations, I'm confident that most LDS Democrats in the U.S. have experienced some expression of bias by Republican members. Sermons from the pulpit, comments during Sunday School lessons and insinuations at social events, sometimes expressed teasingly and, at other times, openly critical, make many Mormon Democrats feel that the strength of their faith is being questioned.

It appears that the gravity of the situation has not gone unnoticed by LDS Church authorities. In recent years, they have increasingly taken actions that could be interpreted as an effort to persuade Latter-day Saints to migrate away from an aggressive strain of Republican conservatism that is sometimes at odds with Church teachings. LDS leaders appear to be trying to influence Church members and their lawmakers to moderate their social and political values, the kind of moderation that has been long supported by Democrats in the Church. The leaders' efforts have mostly taken the form of official Church announcements and unprecedented intervention in the legislative process, particularly regarding controversial social issues such as gay rights and undocumented immigration. Specific instances of these announcements and interventions are covered in later chapters.

A host of prominent Mormons, both Democrats and Republicans, whom I interviewed during my research, also expressed concern that the political biases of an overwhelming majority of Latter-day Saints who are loyal to the GOP is resulting in negative ramifications for the Church. The personal experiences and observations of those I interviewed support the belief that threats to the Church caused by the extreme imbalance between Republicans and Democrats are real. Those I interviewed include a former Republican Utah governor, a GOP Speaker of the Utah House of Representatives, current and former senior members of the Utah Legislature, history and political science professors, newspaper columnists, highly respected campaign operatives of both major parties, a nationally renowned Mormon author and historian, senior education, business and legal professionals and current and past candidates for local, state and federal offices.

A convert to Mormonism of over 40 years, my faithful activity in the Church gives me an intimate insight into the qualities, aspirations, biases and fears of my fellow Mormons. Also, I'm no stranger to the political arena. For two decades, I have volunteered countless hours to civic causes. I have served as a city council member, planning commissioner and a member of the parks and recreation commission at the municipal level. In addition, I have assisted in the campaigns of more than a dozen candidates for the county commission, state legislature and Congress.

This book is written to appeal to a broad audience — politically moderate Mormons (Republicans, Democrats and Independents alike) who range from having little-to-no involvement in the political arena to those who qualify as armchair partisans and even political junkies, and to readers who are not members of the LDS Church but would like to get an intimate glimpse into an important facet of Mormon culture.

The book is divided into three parts. Part 1 (Chapters 1–4) focuses on the historic forces that led to the rise of Republican ideology in the Church as well as the belief by many Mormon Republicans that their political ideology is synonymous with the gospel of Jesus Christ. These chapters examine how this belief emboldens, in most cases unintentionally, LDS Republicans to question whether a Church member can be both a Democrat *and* a good Mormon. Part 1 also shows how this bias results in hurt feelings, alienation and even the defection of some LDS Democrats from the Church. In Part 2, I devote five chapters

(Chapters 5–9) to a comparison of Republican and Democratic attitudes toward the poor and how their needs should be met. Why have I dedicated so much of the book to this topic? It's because much of Mormons' spiritual progression depends on how much compassion they have for the destitute and how much they are willing to sacrifice for them. It explores the differences between Democrats and Republicans in the Church with regard to their feelings toward the disadvantaged, whether the poor are to blame for their own circumstances, whether private charities alone have the capabilities to serve their needs or if the nation needs tax-funded government anti-poverty programs. Part 3 (Chapters 10–13), identifies what a healthy democracy should look like. It examines how the monolithic voting habits of Republicans in the Church, especially where Mormons make up an influential percentage of a state's population (such as Idaho, Arizona, Wyoming, Nevada, and, of course, Utah), have undermined the democratic process in the form of prolonged one-party rule, noncompetitive elections, unaccountable politicians and unchecked extreme behavior by lawmakers that reflects negatively on the Church. Since Utah has the highest number of Latter-day Saints in the nation in terms of percentage of population, I use the state and its social and political culture and institutions to illustrate how an immense and perpetual Republican advantage continues to foster these unfortunate characteristics. Part 3 also introduces the concept of the "a la carte candidate," one whose qualifications for office, not party label, should determine his or her suitability for public service.

Readers who are not familiar with LDS culture and terminology may wonder why the book's title shows the word "Right" in quotation marks. "Choose the Right" is a song title and a much-used phrase in the Church. It represents the Christian principle that one should always do the right thing in God's eyes no matter how contrary it might seem to peer pressure and the prevailing secular behavior in the world. The quotation marks are intended to give the word a double meaning that implies that it can also refer to right-wing politics. So the phrase, when considered within the overall context of the book, is meant to suggest that a preponderance of LDS Republicans believe that their choice to live a gospel life is synonymous with choosing to support a Republican political ideology.

The overall purpose of the book is to shed light on and suggest remedies for the unintended consequences of having an overwhelming majority of Mormons in the U.S. affiliate with a single political ideology. It's not an attempt to persuade Church members to change political affiliation. Nor does it suggest all Republican values are problematic or that all Democratic ones are desirable. Instead, my intent is to help Latter-day Saints become more sensitive to how the huge majority's near-universal loyalty to the GOP is actually weakening values they hold most dear: member unity, a strong missionary program, acceptance into mainstream American culture, charity for the poor, and a robust democratic process. Finally, my aim is to invite Mormon Republicans to take a closer look at the beliefs of LDS Democrats and their political candidates and how a more tempered, balanced distribution of political power among the members of the Church would help improve its image and its capability to carry out its mission. If I have succeeded in stimulating a constructive, fruitful and mutually respectful dialogue in that regard, I will have achieved my purpose.

Appendices

The reader is invited to visit the appendices at the back of the book before proceeding to Chapter 1. *Appendix A: Basic Political Terms,* provides definitions of words that are commonly used in the political arena and will make it easier to understand the concepts presented in the book. *Appendix B: Interchangeable Words,* lists several words and their substitutes that I use to avoid excessive repetition.

Part 1

Chapter 1

A Rising Tide of LDS Conservatism

"If you don't know the past, you can't understand the present and plan properly for the future."[1]

— *Chaim Potok,*
American novelist

Without a basic knowledge of LDS Church history, it would be easy for Latter-day Saints today, as they look around at the dominance of Republican Party ideology among Church members, to assume that it has always been this way, a constant since the founding of the Church. It would be easy to conclude that Heavenly Father ordained values that are more closely aligned with the modern-day Republican Party than those of the Democratic Party, that the gospel and Republican ideology are essentially one and the same. But unless Latter-day Saints view the evolution of the Church and its culture through the lens of history, including how it has been intertwined with American history, they may not understand that God is not a respecter of persons *or* political parties. They would not know that the extraordinary supremacy of the GOP in the Church is a recent phenomenon relative to its more than 185-year history and is not ordained of God. They would not have the context to grasp why LDS General Authorities have consistently taught that all political parties have many values

---

1   Chaim Potok, *Davita's Harp*, New York: Ballantine Books, 1985, pp. 11–12.

and candidates that are consistent with the gospel of Jesus Christ. Conversely, all parties have some values not in harmony with God's laws. Most importantly, Latter-day Saints would not be fully aware of why having a massive Republican advantage in the Church has tainted the Church's image and its capability to fulfill its mission. The intent of this chapter is to provide a glimpse into history and the perspective this history gives, for Mormons to understand that the ascension of the GOP in the Church is neither mandated nor preferred by Heavenly Father.

The Saints' Saga in a Growing America

The forces that led to the overwhelming domination of Mormon culture by a conservative Republican ideology cannot be understood without first examining how the Church's unique evolution took place within the grander tide of the nation's historical growing pains.

Founded by Joseph Smith in 1830, the Church and its members endured persecutions, forced evacuations, and an epic exodus from upstate New York, through Ohio, Missouri, Illinois and, in 1847, to an expansive Mexican-controlled region, a part of which would later be renamed the Utah Territory. They were relieved to finally be outside U.S. jurisdiction, the laws of which had done little to protect them. But their relief was short-lived. In 1848, the U.S. seized control of Utah and the surrounding territories after winning the Mexican-American War.

Once again under U.S. jurisdiction, the Saints' practice of plural marriage became the defining issue that fanned the flames of anti-Mormonism nationwide. Democrats in Congress did not like plural marriage but tolerated it because they were more concerned about restricting federal power and preserving states' rights. Republicans, on the other hand, condemned the practice and, playing to the American public's anti-Mormon passions, laid plans to abolish it.[2] The Republican majority passed the Edmunds-Tucker bill in 1887 that disincorporated the Church and did away with the Perpetual Emigration Fund that had been used to bring converts from Europe to the Salt Lake Valley.[3] Not

---

2 Jonathan D. Moyer, "Dancing with the Devil: The Making of the Mormon-Republican Pact," PhD Dissertation: University of Utah, 2009, p. 55.

3 Ibid. pp. 61–62.

surprisingly, a vast majority of Latter-day Saints reviled the GOP and affiliated with the Democratic Party.

In the space of only a few years, however, Republicans in Washington realized they needed Mormon cooperation. The GOP was anxious to elect more representatives to Congress to counter the Democratic Party's electoral gains in the South. Their strategy was to grant statehood to western territories in exchange for a commitment from territorial leaders that they would influence voters to deliver a Republican delegation to Washington.[4]

For its part, the Church needed Utah to become a state to be able to freely elect its own governors and legislatures, a freedom not enjoyed by territories which were forced to accept governors and bureaucrats appointed by the federal government. Church authorities embarked on an intensive campaign to convert Mormon Democrats to the GOP. They sent envoys to outlying settlements to convince Latter-day Saints that they could be Republicans and still be good Church members (quite the opposite of today). Not all Church leaders agreed. The campaign caused division in their ranks with many remaining opposed to adopting Republicanism.[5] Nonetheless, the political conversion of Church members was successful enough that, contingent on outlawing plural marriage and demonstrating political diversity, Utah was granted statehood in 1896. From that time forward, the Republican label and ideology has gained traction in Utah and the Church, albeit with ups and downs, until the GOP has reached its present dominant position.

Riding the Wave of American History

The extraordinary history of the Mormon Church left a deep imprint on its evolution to the political right. But its evolution has been influenced at least as much by the powerful economic, political and social upheavals that have shaken America from the 1930s through the present day. The Great Depression, World War II, the Cold War and the ongoing "culture wars" that emerged in the 1960s were instrumental in the development of a strong conservative ideology, not only in

---

4   Ibid, pp. 73–75.
5   Ibid, pp. 111–115.

the LDS Church, but also in many other faiths. An overview of these major upheavals will serve to shed light on this evolution.

The Great Depression

Republicanism in Utah, as in most of the country, fell out of favor during the Great Depression of the 1930s. Americans blamed Republican President Herbert Hoover for being out of touch with the common workers who were suffering under the severity of the economic collapse. They felt he had not done enough to engage the resources of the federal government to mitigate extreme unemployment, poverty, and hunger.[6]

Utah was especially hard hit. By 1933, its unemployment rate had risen to 35.8 percent, fourth highest in the country. Utahns joined a strong majority of Americans who, in a landslide, voted Republicans out of office and elected Democrat Franklin D. Roosevelt to the White House. Roosevelt's New Deal anti-poverty programs put Utahns back to work building public works and other projects, about half of which are still standing in the state. Utah got more New Deal help than most states, receiving seven dollars of assistance for every tax dollar the state sent to the federal government.[7] In other words, the hardships faced by Utahns during this trying time were alleviated by compassionate Democratic social programs, not the tight-fisted Republican fiscal policies that were largely blamed for the Depression in the first place. It seems that subsequent generations of Utahns have forgotten this lesson, given how conservatives in the Church today generally condemn New Deal programs as the genesis of today's anti-poverty programs.

The Cold War

The Great Depression lifted when the U.S. entered World War II, creating millions of well-paying industrial jobs to support the war effort. But just a few years after the end of the war, the darkness of the Cold

---

6   History.com Staff, "Herbert Hoover," *History.com,* 2009, at http://www.history.com/topics/us-presidents/herbert-hoover (accessed April 16, 2015).
7   John S. McCormick, "The Great Depression," *Utah History Encyclopedia,* at http://historytogo.utah.gov/utah_chapters/from_war_to_war/thegreatdepression (accessed December 2, 2014).

War descended on the world. The era lasted approximately from 1948, with the Soviet blockade of allied-controlled West Berlin, until 1991, when a declining Soviet Union collapsed during the tenure of President Boris Yeltsin.[8] It was called the "age of anxiety," a time marked by a dangerous three-sided standoff between the U.S., Soviet Union, and Communist China. It was exacerbated by the threat of military conflict in addition to proxy "shooting wars" in Korea and Vietnam. Americans' fears were heightened by the brutal crushing of rebellious states by the Soviet Red Army in Europe. The massive buildup of nuclear arsenals by the three emerging powers triggered a pervasive fear that radioactive mushroom clouds might one day explode over the major population centers of the world. It was a time when the Republican Party began to regain its strength as it persuaded much of the U.S. population, especially religious Americans, that it was the best party to protect them against the communist threat.

A Call to Christian Action

Even though a great majority of Americans had turned to the Democratic Party to raise Americans out of dire poverty during the Great Depression, many religious denominations, including the Latter-day Saints, began shifting their allegiance to the GOP during the Cold War.

The person considered most responsible for yoking American politics to religion at the start of the Cold War was the Reverend Billy Graham. In 1949, he was a little-known 30-year-old Southern Baptist preacher from North Carolina when he took his Christian revival crusade to Los Angeles. The timing of his campaign couldn't have come at a more auspicious moment. The Soviets exploded their first atomic test bomb just two days before the start of Graham's eight-week appearance. A mere six days later, the world learned that Mao Tse-tung's Red Army had overrun mainland China, subjugating a fifth of the world's

---

8 Quintard Taylor, Jr., Scott and Dorothy Bullitt, "United States History: Timeline: Cold War," *University of Washington History Department,* at http:// faculty.washington.edu/qtaylor/a_us_history/cold_war_timeline.htm (accessed January 19, 2015).

population under his control and establishing yet another powerful communist state that was openly hostile to the United States.[9]

Graham responded to the crisis by providing comfort and encouragement to Americans, beseeching them to accept Jesus Christ as their Savior and protector from the evil of godless communism. "We cannot stand the tremendous strain and stress of future days in our battle with communism unless we have a spiritual revival!" he preached. "I believe today that the battle is between communism and Christianity!"[10] It was Graham's call to action that thrust religion to the forefront of American politics, fused faith with patriotism, and launched his meteoric rise to the pinnacle of religious and political influence.

During this tense era, Americans flocked to houses of worship in record numbers. Putnam and Campbell point out that between 1945 and 1950, the annual construction costs to build new churches climbed at an unprecedented rate. In 1945 the cost was $26 million. A year later it had surged to $76 million and by 1950 the outlay was $409 million. A Gallup poll in 1952 found that an all-time high of 75 percent of Americans said religion was very important to them. The expense of constructing houses of worship continued unabated when, in 1960 alone, it was estimated to have grown to over a billion dollars.[11]

The Republicans Court Religion

The Republican Party seized on the paranoia that swelled the churches and turned it to political advantage. During the presidential campaign of 1952, Democratic candidate Adlai Stevenson faced an opponent whose patriotic credentials were unquestioned. Republican candidate and World War II hero General Dwight D. Eisenhower sought to differentiate the GOP from the Democratic Party by positioning the GOP

9   Grant Wacker, "Watershed: Los Angeles 1949," *Christian History Institute,* Issue 111, at https://www.christianhistoryinstitute.org/magazine/article/ watershed-los-angeles-1949/ (accessed December 3, 2014).

10   "God in America: 'The Soul of a Nation,'" *Public Broadcasting System,* October 11, 2010, at http://www.pbs.org/godinamerica/transcripts/hour-five.html (accessed February 5, 2013).

11   Robert D. Putnam and David E. Campbell, *American Grace: How Religion Divides and Unites Us,* New York: Simon and Schuster, 2010, p. 87; and Mark Silk, *Spiritual Politics: Religion and America since World War II,* New York: Simon & Schuster, 1988, p. 38.

as the strongest patriotic and religious citadel against communism. Mark Silk, author of *Spiritual Politics: Religion and America since World War II*, writes that Eisenhower referred to spiritual strength as "the matchless armor" against the forces of Godless tyranny and oppression. Stevenson was forced to counter by emphasizing that the Democratic Party was just as committed as the Republicans in opposing communism. That the Democrat had to make a special case that his party was just as patriotic and religious as the GOP, demonstrated the extent to which the Republicans had outmaneuvered the Democrats and put them on the defensive.[12] The bonds between the Republicans and religion began to grow tighter.

McCarthy and the Mormons

It could be argued that Mormon migration to the political and religious right gained further momentum during the widespread hysteria that spawned the communist witch-hunts of 1950–1954. Firebrand Wisconsin Republican Sen. Joseph R. McCarthy and his allies in Congress pledged, during what was to become known as the "Red Scare," to purge what they were certain was a subversive nest of high-ranking traitors in the U.S. military, government, education, Hollywood, and industry. McCarthy abandoned any pretense of constitutional due process while using fear and intimidation to hound and blacklist suspects, almost always without evidence, to turn colleagues and neighbors against one another and ruin careers.[13]

Indeed, some U.S. citizens were found to be Soviet sympathizers. But there was no evidence that suggested that more than a few individuals were guilty of espionage. It appeared the vast majority of McCarthy's alleged suspects were guilty of no more than being members or associates of members of communist-leaning organizations, most of which had had their roots in the Great Depression. At that time, many Americans became disillusioned with the failure of capitalism to prevent the economic catastrophe and were attracted to the

---

12   Mark Silk, *Spiritual Politics: Religion and America since World War II,* New York: Simon & Schuster, 1988, pp. 87, 90.

13   History.com staff, "Red Scare," History.com, 2010, at http://www.history.com/topics/cold-war/red-scare (accessed December 4, 2014).

promise of communist ideology. A considerable number had quit the organizations over a decade before McCarthy came on the scene but were still persecuted and even fired from their jobs if their names were found on old mailing lists or they associated with friends or family whose patriotism was considered questionable.[14]

Thousands of mainstream Protestant clerics also fell under suspicion of colluding with communist-friendly organizations. In 1953, the chairman of the House Un-American Activities Committee said the panel was considering an investigation of ministers who had belonged to groups that promoted "peace, international understanding, and social justice," groups that the U.S. Attorney General, without evidence, placed on a list of alleged subversive communist fronts.[15]

The Red-baiting of clerics took on a new intensity when J.B. Matthews, a right-wing theologian, was hired by McCarthy to head his powerful Permanent Sub-Committee on Investigations. Matthews published an article in *The American Mercury* entitled "Reds and Our Churches" in which he wrote, "the largest single group supporting the communist apparatus in the United States today is composed of Protestant clergymen." He named, without proof, eight Episcopal bishops and several others and claimed that at least seven thousand (clergy) were "[Communist] Party members, fellow-travelers, espionage agents, party-line adherents, or unwitting dupes" of the communist movement whose primary objective was the complete destruction of the Judeo-Christian civilization. Matthews' allegations stirred up a public uproar which prompted a majority of the subcommittee to demand that a reluctant McCarthy fire Matthews.[16]

Perhaps the real motivation behind smearing Protestant clerics, many of whom were openly critical of McCarthy's tactics, was to frighten their congregations into removing them from the pulpit. With a friendlier cadre of preachers on his side, McCarthy would have been able to declare that he had the support of religion, a claim he had

---

14   Wendy Wall, "Anti-Communism in the 1950s," *The Gilder Lehrman Institute of American History,* April 2012, at http://www.gilderlehrman.org/history-by-era/fifties/essays/anti-communism-1950s (accessed March 6, 2015).
15   Mark Silk, *Spiritual Politics: Religion and America since World War II,* New York: Simon & Schuster, 1988, p. 88.
16   Ibid, pp. 89–90.

already been making in an attempt to bolster the credibility of his crusade.[17]

One can imagine how the targeting of clergymen must have alarmed the leaders of the LDS Church. They could not have been blamed for turning up the volume of their Republican-friendly convictions to remove any doubts about their patriotism and anti-communist fervor. Besides naturally despising communism as a totalitarian philosophy hostile to religion, LDS leaders were well-aware that it had been only 54 years since Utah gained statehood. The Church still suffered from the distrust and prejudice from its territorial days when it resisted the American public's demand that it abandon plural marriage and theocratic rule. The Church also could not afford to alienate a growing pool of prospective converts by having its controversial past dredged up anew, another reason to distance Mormons from the Democratic Party.

LDS Church President David O. McKay defended McCarthy and his methods before eventually changing his mind. In *David O. McKay and the Rise of Modern Mormonism*, co-authors Gregory A. Prince and Wm. Robert Wright quoted McKay as telling his counselors and the Quorum of the Twelve that "the Communistic influence is being exerted there [in Washington, DC] to lessen the influence of men [such as Sen. McCarthy] who would ferret out the enemies in the high places of our government." Prince and Wright continued, "As the summer of 1954 wore on, however, and the extent of McCarthy's improprieties became evident, McKay switched sides on the issue."[18] It stands to reason that rank-and-file Mormons would have followed McKay's lead, both before and after he distanced himself from McCarthy. In any case, it would seem that the McCarthy era as a whole and the GOP's intensified claim to be the anti-communist party would have further strengthened the bond between the Church's leaders and members and the Republican Party.

The influence of another high Church official further instilled in the LDS faithful that Republican values were synonymous with the

---

17   Ibid, p. 90.

18   Gregory A. Prince and Wm. Robert Wright, *David O. McKay and the Rise of Modern Mormonism*, Salt Lake City: The University of Utah Press, 2005, p. 284.

gospel and patriotism. Nearly 14 years after the Senate-censured Senator McCarthy ended his reign, LDS Apostle Ezra Taft Benson, who would later become president of the Church, continued to praise McCarthy and his fight against senior officials in the U.S. government whom Benson said were communists engaged in subversion in the guise of the Civil Rights movement of the 1960s.

In an address at BYU on May 21, 1968, Benson condemned high government officials for conspiring to incite "an overthrow [of democratic government with] an uprising of the socialist government in our nation." In the same speech, he aimed his displeasure at the U.S. Supreme Court Justices, whom he labeled as "traitors" allegedly for making decisions that encouraged civil disobedience and allowing the communists to get a foothold in American society. "Today, by court edict, a person is allowed to advocate and convince others of the duty and necessity to overthrow the government by force and violence," he charged.[19]

Elder Benson used the power of the pulpit at General Conferences, BYU and other highly public events to press his political views. His high station as an apostle and credibility as a former two-term Secretary of Agriculture in the Eisenhower cabinet gave him a tall platform from which to condemn liberals and Democrats as communist surrogates, as did Senator McCarthy before him. His partisan positions, along with his ascendancy to prophet and president of the Church in 1985, helped persuade many U.S. Mormons to equate political conservatism with LDS doctrine. In an insular, tight-knit Mormon culture that is designed to transmit values from generation to generation, it's not surprising that Elder Benson's strident conservative principles would continue to have currency among the members of the Church today, old and young.

The Culture Wars

Prior to the 1960s, most arguments between Democrats and Republicans focused mainly on economic, domestic and international issues.

---

19   Ezra Taft Benson, "The Book of Mormon Warns America," May 21, 1968, *BYU Speeches,* at http://speeches.byu.edu/index.php?act=viewitem&id=1619 (accessed December 12, 2012).

But the emergence in the early 1970s of a host of emotional social issues, such as extramarital sex, abortion, women's rights, same-sex marriage and undocumented immigration, divided the nation and further stretched the gap between liberals and conservatives, particularly religious conservatives. In what came to be known as the "culture wars," liberals took a more permissive stance while conservatives viewed such permissiveness as the decay of traditional moral values and began their long fight to preserve them.

There were many causes that contributed to the loosening of moral norms and the erosion of respect for authority, especially among the increasingly alienated and bitter youth that set the stage for the culture wars. Among them was the prolonged, bloody Vietnam conflict and the Watergate scandal that brought down the presidency of Richard M. Nixon. Another factor was the rapid modernization of the nation's transportation system, including breakthroughs in automotive, air and rail technology as well as a rapidly expanding interstate highway system. In turn, the availability of convenient transportation gave Americans the mobility to break away from their traditional hometowns and the de facto community policing of cultural and moral conduct that came with living close to extended family and friends.

Conclusion

The evolution of Mormons from their early affiliation with the Democratic Party to a commanding preference for Republican conservatism today is the product of the singular history of the Mormon Church and its inexorable absorption into the wrenching economic, military, political and social upheavals of 20th century American history. The American people, including Mormons, overwhelmingly entrusted the leadership of the nation to the Roosevelt-led Democratic Party and its New Deal anti-poverty social programs during the Great Depression. Also, they fervently put their faith and trust in Roosevelt as Commander-in-Chief of the armed forces, a role in which he mandated the expansion of U.S. manufacturing capacity to rush weapons and supplies to the troops, and ordered the launching of the military strategy that ultimately doomed the nation's enemies in World War II.

But once the economic and immediate military threats to the nation subsided, the GOP outmaneuvered the Democratic Party in convincing many Americans, especially a growing population of religious Americans, that the conservative values of the GOP made them more patriotic, militarily aggressive and better able to protect the U.S. from Cold War threats than Democrats. It's a belief that persists in the minds of conservatives today. The GOP's courtship of religious Americans during the Cold War began the process of equating patriotism to religiosity. It inspired a burgeoning population of religious Americans to claim loyalty to the GOP.

Nowhere is this loyalty more evident than in the LDS Church, where it appears that many of the 70 percent of its members view their conservatism as much an act of faith as a political preference. There is evidence that this striking imbalance is undermining the image of the Church—its efforts to forge a strong sense of belonging for its members, its appeal to prospective converts, its intent to align with the Lord's admonition to succor the poor, and its promotion of a healthy democratic process in places where Mormons have a strong political influence.

Chapter 2

Is the Gospel Conservative?

> *"I find some wisdom in liberalism, some wisdom in conservatism, and much truth in intellectualism – but I find no salvation in any of them."*[1]
>
> — *Dallin H. Oaks, Member of the Quorum of the Twelve Apostles, Church of Jesus Christ of Latter-day Saints*

I believe a vast majority of Latter-day Saints would testify that Republican conservative social and fiscal values are essentially the same thing as the gospel of Jesus Christ and that these values explain why they are Republicans. Those laudable values include hard work and self-sufficiency, a pro-business environment, patriotism, a strong defense, living within a balanced budget, opposition to abortions of convenience, and the precedence of individual rights. But it is inaccurate for Latter-day Saints to believe that the Republican Party has exclusive ownership over those values. Even a cursory reading of the scriptures, including modern-day revelations from LDS General Authorities, shows there are at least as many values embedded in the scriptures that are the hallmark of Democratic beliefs. They include putting a high priority on serving and succoring the poor (it appears the Lord does not specify whether support for the poor must come only from voluntary means or also from civil governments). Democrats also believe in responsible stewardship over the environment, labor laws to protect workers, a

---

1 Dallin H. Oaks, "Criticism," *Ensign,* February 1987, at https://www.lds.org/ensign/1987/02/criticism?lang=eng (accessed January 19, 2015).

high priority on educational funding, and a reverence for the common good, all principles a loving God would endorse.

In reality, LDS Democrats and Republicans share just about all the values listed above. For example, every faithful Mormon Democrat I know, or whose stories I know, opposes abortions of convenience. That is, faithful Church members of both political parties, (with the exception of some far-right members who do not allow for any exceptions and far-left ones who allow for too many), are in alignment with Church teachings that abortions are justified only in the case of incest, rape or preservation of the health or life of the mother. Nearly every devout LDS Democrat I know or have heard about strongly advocates what I refer to as "affordable compassion," the implementation of government anti-poverty programs within a balanced budget. One can go down the list of spiritual values and find the same reality — Latter-day Saints of both parties who are active in the gospel mostly agree on the same things. But it is in the prioritization of funding and the implementation of their shared values where Church members of both major parties often differ.

So, is the gospel essentially the same thing as Republican ideology? Does it negatively impact the reputation of the Church and its worldwide mission if 70 percent of Latter-day Saints in the U.S. insist it is? Does it threaten member unity and, sometimes, even the salvation of Church members? Does it undermine the Church's efforts to portray itself as a compassionate mainline American religion? It is the purpose of this chapter to provide evidence and examples of how Mormon Republicans perpetuate, much of the time unwittingly, the misbelief that many Democrats in the Church are, to some extent, not as much in harmony with the gospel as they should be. And to encourage a reevaluation of this misbelief.

Laying Claim to the Gospel

Prominent Latter-day Saints disagree on whether or not the gospel is inherently Republican in nature. "I don't think there is anything intrinsic in Mormonism that leads towards the right-wing of American conservatism," says Dr. Richard Lyman Bushman, Professor Emeritus of History at Columbia University, a renowned LDS scholar of American and Mormon history and author of the critically acclaimed biography *Joseph Smith: Rough Stone Rolling.* "You can make a case in either direction," he says. "What happens is, once you find yourself favoring a certain political party, then you search around in your doctrinal principles and find things to support it. So you have this sense that you are harmonious with the Church and the political side."[2]

Doug Foxley, a Salt Lake City attorney who has served as a campaign manager and consultant for many high-profile Republican political candidates in Utah, does not share Bushman's view that Mormons pick and choose scriptures to justify their political affiliation. Instead, Foxley supports the notion that Church doctrine today is conservative, and, therefore, a better fit [than progressives, also known as liberals] with the Republican Party. "I think the doctrine from the 1830s to the 1890s was fairly progressive [and liberal]," said Foxley, an avid student of Mormon history. "I think it is . . . not as progressive today as it was in its beginnings."[3]

Foxley contended that conservative Republican ideology and Mormon doctrine today go hand-in-hand. "Do most people who are active members of the LDS Church tend to be conservative? Yes, they do," he said. "They are very pro-family, live within [their financial] means, [and] don't go into debt. Those [principles] that have been enunciated from the pulpits in General Conferences and priesthood meetings are pretty conservative doctrines."[4] Foxley's observation could be interpreted by LDS Democrats that they don't embrace the same pro-family and fiscal responsibility values as strongly as Republicans do.

But LDS Democrats insist they are just as devoted to gospel principles as Republicans are. When asked if one can find elements of the gospel of Jesus Christ in the tenets of both major parties, Foxley acknowledged, "Sure you can. If you listen to a Democratic national convention, one of their underlying tenets is the concept of compassion and caring. If those aren't Christian values, I don't what Christian

---

2   Richard Lyman Bushman, interviewed by author, August 1, 2012.

3   Doug Foxley, interviewed by author, July 12, 2011.

4   Ibid.

values are."[5] Here, even though Foxley is a Republican, he acknowledges there are good Christian values in both parties.

It is obvious God does not favor one political party or philosophy over another. Rather, He intends for His mortal children to wrestle with and agonize over where they should stand on the issues and candidates of their time regardless of party label. He has, through His leaders on earth, repeatedly let it be known that gospel principles can be found in the values of various political parties and their candidates. He urges Church members to study, ponder and act on the issues and candidates of the day. It seems certain He never intended His gospel to be co-opted by any party.

Another prominent Mormon who spread the word that the gospel is conservative is Paul Mero, then-president of the Sutherland Institute, an influential right-leaning public policy think tank in Salt Lake City. In an article in the *Deseret News,* he said that the LDS Church is built on conservative values. He told a group of college Republicans at the University of Utah that "I'm a conservative because I'm a Latter-day Saint. Explicit in this claim is that there is a strong relationship between Mormonism and conservative intellectual thought." Mero told his audience that the just governance of a free society is dependent upon conservative principles. "Authentic conservatism, at its core, [is] a cluster of prioritized values or principles that enable men to govern justly in a truly free society," he said.[6] By equating Mormonism with conservatism, and defining conservatism as the bedrock of a free society, Mero implied a strong, natural connection between Mormonism, conservatism and a strong America. The implied flipside of Mero's argument is that progressive, liberal ideals, and the Democrats who espouse them, are detrimental (or at least not helpful) to the strengthening of freedom in America or the mission of the LDS Church.

Widely known Mormon intellectuals also promote the idea that conservative Republican political ideology is synonymous with Mormon doctrine. One such Church member was the late W. Cleon Skousen, a prolific lecturer, writer and professor at the LDS Church-owned

---

5   Ibid.
6   Wendy Leonard, "Sutherland President Ties Religion, Politics," *Deseret News,* November 19, 2009, p. A13.

Brigham Young University. He was a highly esteemed intellectual whom Latter-day Saints and, indeed, non-Mormon members of the religious right, looked to as their ideological compass. In his 1981 book, *The Five Thousand Year Leap*, Skousen invokes the Founding Fathers as his authority to condemn government anti-poverty programs. He portrays the recipients of public assistance as lazy, undeserving welfare cheats who live the good life at the expense of hard-working citizens. To illustrate his view, he features a drawing in his book that shows a fat, lecherous man with an evil grin representing the government who is taking money out of the back pocket of an unsuspecting, hard-working, shovel-wielding man and handing it over to a smiling man wearing a bag of golf clubs on his shoulder. He says the devious goal of the welfare state was to create an "equal distribution of goods."[7]

What Skousen neglects to mention is that evidence has overwhelmingly proven that public anti-poverty programs are essential to providing the bare necessities of life for those in need, much less a bag of golf clubs. His claim that the nation's capitalistic system is being destroyed by a government-mandated distribution of income and goods to the poor at the expense of the wealthy, is exposed as fantasy as the gap between the "haves" and "have-nots" is growing greater, not smaller. Nonetheless, many Republican Mormons have adopted Skousen's beliefs as a central tenet of their religious, economic and political philosophy. It's no wonder that LDS Democrats, who widely favor public relief efforts for the destitute, are viewed with some suspicion by many Republican Church members.

If a large majority of Latter-day Saints believe the gospel is mainly conservative, and that seems to be the case, that belief appears to be having a detrimental effect on the Church missionary program as well as on the retention of current members. The perception that the Church is essentially a Republican stronghold is bound to attract like-minded people to join the Church. It also repels others. Putnam and Campbell agree that politics can play a strong role in determining one's religious preferences: "Politics can . . . shape religious choice in the sense of

---

7   W. Cleon Skousen, *The Five Thousand Year Leap*, Franklin, Tennessee: American Documents Publishing, L.L.C., 1981, pp. 87-88.

who joins, who stays, and who leaves a given faith" they wrote.[8] They also wrote that young Americans are part of an expanding number of Americans who choose not to join any church when they perceive it promotes conservative politics.[9] Is it possible that the growth of what is perceived as a strident form of conservatism in the Church is shrinking the pool of prospective converts and impacting the LDS missionary program?

Co-opting the Fourth of July

Is the gospel conservative? A high-profile venue at which Republicans attempt to link conservative politics with the gospel of Jesus Christ, the LDS Church and patriotism is the annual Independence Day Freedom Festival in Provo, Utah. It is one of the largest Fourth of July celebrations in the nation.

In 2003 and 2004, festival organizers invited the polarizing, ultraconservative commentator Sean Hannity to emcee the celebration, drawing loud criticism from those who felt Hannity's participation was tantamount to declaring the festival to be an enclave of religious Republicans. Also, in 2007, nationally known and controversial Mormon conservative radio and television talk show host Glenn Beck was the master of ceremonies for the Stadium of Fire.

The theme of the 2007 Freedom Festival was "American traditions of family, freedom, God and country." Festival director Paul Warner said event planners invited Beck because they felt that he represented the patriotic American values the Stadium of Fire was trying to promote. Warner is quoted in the media as saying, "We know Glenn Beck is conservative, but we think these [American] traditions are conservative." Warner drew criticism for implying that moderates, liberals and Democrats do not support the traditional values of family, religion

---

8   Robert D. Putnam and David E. Campbell, *American Grace: How Religion Divides and Unites Us,* New York: Simon & Schuster, 2010, p. 435.

9   Robert D. Putnam and David E. Campbell, *American Grace: How Religion Divides and Unites Us,* New York: Simon & Schuster, 2010, p. 3.

and patriotism and he politicized what should have been a celebration to unite all Americans, not just conservatives.[10]

At the 2007 festival, Beck limited his public comments to patriotic themes and did not overtly trumpet partisan views.[11] Nonetheless, because he was a widely known passionate conservative partisan and a prominent Mormon, it seems reasonable to conclude that festival organizers were content to promote what they knowingly implied were Republican values, regardless of what of he said or didn't say. Festival producers invited him back to emcee the 2008 fireworks extravaganza.

The festival's partisan environment not only promotes the GOP but has the related effect of exposing a darker side of Utah's culture where public disdain for Democrats is obvious and acceptable. Former Democratic State Senator Karen Hale recounted an experience she had while participating in the Provo festival parade while candidate for Utah lieutenant governor. As she rode on a float with gubernatorial candidate Scott Matheson, spectators booed, shouted derisive jokes and even threw things at them. One woman, who appeared to be a mother with several children around her, booed and yelled and gave them the thumbs down sign as her children looked on. "What a [bad] example [she was]," Hale said. "How unfortunate that this mom isn't seeing what she's teaching her children, that you yell and boo and show your disapproval [toward] people who don't share the same [political] beliefs as you do." [12] Democrats riding in subsequent parades have routinely been confronted by spectators who booed, held their noses and shouted jokes.

The order in which Republican and Democratic Party floats, VIP cars and candidates have been assigned to appear in the parade can also make a subtle statement, deliberate or not. It's common for the Republican contingent of politicians and floats to appear somewhere in the middle of the parade. But Democrats do not always get such

---

10   Richard Davis and Larry Brown, "Stadium of Fire Should Unite Americans," *Deseret News,* July 3, 2007, p. A14.

11   Elizabeth Stuart, "Emcee Beck will be Sticking to Patriotism—Not Politics," *Deseret News,* June 28, 2007, at http://www.deseretnews.com/article/680194709/Emcee-Beck-will-be-sticking-to-patriotism--not-politics.html?pg=all (accessed December 6, 2014).

12   Karen Hale, interviewed by author, August 23, 2011.

favorable placement. On at least one occasion, the parade car in which the Utah County Democratic officers rode was relegated to the second-to-the-last position in the long parade, when only the most diehard of spectators remained to watch. The Democrats good-naturedly quipped that Republicans were sending a subliminal message that the Democrats' political fortunes are akin to dodging miles of flattened road apples.

Conclusion

LDS Democrats and Republicans hold differing viewpoints on whether or not gospel principles are inherently conservative in nature. Many LDS Republicans believe their religious faith is synonymous with their conservative political ideology, implying that Democrats in the Church may be somewhat misguided and not quite as committed to following Church teachings as the Republicans are. Of course, Democrats disagree. Democrats say the gospel is neutral with regard to political ideology and that there are as many Democratic ideals represented in the gospel of Jesus Christ as there are Republican ones.

Mormon Republicans, overtly or subliminally, use public events, celebrities, books and other written materials and statements, and even the personal opinions of past Church authorities, to reinforce their assertion that conservative tenets are one and the same with Heavenly Father's teachings. Many Republicans in the Church also believe that their political beliefs constitute the primary basis on which a strong democracy should be built as well as the criteria with which a person's patriotism should be measured. Using the same logic, this Republican belief implies that the political principles of Democrats, including LDS Democrats, render them less patriotic, an implication that Democrats deeply resent.

Since 70 percent of U.S. Mormons are Republican or lean toward the GOP, it seems reasonable to conclude that their political and social convictions are perceived by those inside and outside the Church as being part of the official dogma of Mormonism. This bias puts LDS Democrats on the defensive and can alienate Church members and prospective converts, not only in the U.S. but abroad, who do not agree with many fundamental Republican precepts. As authors Putnam and

Campbell point out, there is a growing portion of the U.S. population, especially among the young, who are rejecting churches they identify as megaphones for Republican politics.[13]

Elder Dallin H. Oaks, in his quote at the top of this chapter, seems to agree that the gospel is not exclusively an extension of conservatism. He says, in essence, that an unchanging Heavenly Father recognizes no political dogma or party as having cornered the market on gospel living and eternal salvation. Oaks' comment sounds like an invitation for LDS Republicans to rethink their contention that their social and political values are synonymous with the teachings of the Church and recognize that LDS Democrats have at least as equal a claim to heavenly principles as they do.

---

13   Robert D. Putnam and David E. Campbell, *American Grace: How Religion Divides and Unites Us,* New York: Simon & Schuster, 2010, p. 3.

Chapter 3

Can a Democrat Be a Good Mormon?

"I distance myself from the foolish nonsense, that to be a Latter-day Saint in the United States today, requires, or even tends toward, a partisan political affiliation."[1]
— *Thomas B. Griffith, Circuit Judge on the U.S. Court of Appeals for the District of Columbia and LDS Church member*

Many LDS Democrats are asked by Republican Church members how they can be a Democrat and a good Mormon. A large number of Republicans believe the two are incompatible. That Republicans would even ask such a question often upsets and saddens Democratic Church members who are made to feel their faith is somewhat deficient because they don't affiliate with the GOP. The testimonies of many Latter-day Saints are shaken by such criticism and some withdraw from activity or even leave the Church. The presumption that membership in the Republican Party is necessary to be a good Mormon spills over into the political arena where too many Mormons assume that LDS Democratic candidates are not as fit for office as their Republican opponents, even though a great number of "Utah Democrats" are moderate, fiscally prudent, temple-recommend-carrying Latter-day Saints who faithfully perform their Church callings.

---

1   Thomas B. Griffith, "The Hard Work of Understanding the Constitution," *BYU Forum Address,* September 18, at 2012, http://byutv.org/watch/ d874d1da-9ca7-42c7-b09e-430950ba51d4/byu-forum-address-judge-thomas-b-griffith-91812 (accessed January 8, 2013).

Over 700,000 LDS Democrats in the United States Are Good Mormons

A Pew Survey in April 2015 found that 22 percent of American Mormons are Democrats or lean toward the Democratic Party.[2] At that time, there were nearly 6.5 million Latter-day Saints in the U.S.[3] According to some estimates, about half, or roughly 3.2 million (which includes both Democrats and Republicans), are active in the faith. It means that more than 700,000 *faithful, practicing* Church members in the U.S. are Democrats.

Among LDS Democrats are current and former General Authorities, general auxiliary officers, stake presidents, mission presidents, bishops, Relief Society presidents, high councilmen, and high-ranking officers of government, universities, corporations, and the armed forces. In other words, there are hundreds of thousands of LDS Democrats who are faithful Church members and devoted to the gospel and their callings. To put it in perspective, if a Latter-day Saint were to look around them in a Church meeting or in the temple, about one in five of their fellow Church goers are likely to be a Democrat. Are they less faithful than their Republican brothers and sisters?

General Authorities Speak Out

General Authorities stress that the Church is populated with Democrats who are good Mormons. Why do they go out of their way to make specific statements like that? Could it be because they are perplexed by a problematic and persistent bias toward Democrats that needs to be rebutted in public? There are many examples of such public statements, a few of which are cited below.

At a National Press Club conference in 2008, President Gordon B. Hinckley was asked, "Given the platform and positions taken by the [national] Democratic Party, can you be a good Church member and a Democrat?" President Hinckley responded, "I don't know why you

2 "A Deep Dive into Party Affiliation," *Pew Research Center,* April 7, 2015, at http://www.people-press.org/2015/04/07/a-deep-dive-into-party-affiliation/ (accessed August 3, 2015).

3 Mormon Newsroom Staff, "Facts and Statistics," *Church of Jesus Christ of Latter-day Saints,"* April 15, 2015, at http://www.mormonnewsroom.org/facts-and-statistics/country/united-states/ (accessed May 3, 2015).

couldn't. . . . We've got lots of Democrats in the Church, lots of them, and they are good people."[4]

President James E. Faust, Second Counselor in the First Presidency during President Hinckley's administration, was a lifelong Democrat. Faust said "I also support what has been said by the Brethren – that it is in the interests of the Church to have a two-party system and not to have one party that is exclusively LDS and the other party exclusively non-LDS. Both locally and nationally, the interests of the Church and its members are served when we have two good men or women running on each ticket [Democratic and Republican], and then no matter who is elected, we win."[5]

Elder Marlin K. Jensen, then a member of the Quorum of the Seventy, was directed by senior Church leaders to give an hour-long interview to the *Salt Lake Tribune* in 1998. The interview took place in the Church's worldwide headquarters in Salt Lake City and was arranged by LDS media relations director Mike Otterson. During the interview, Jensen, a Democrat, deplored the lack of political diversity among Latter-day Saints and the perception that the Republican Party is becoming "the Church party." Jensen said that too many Latter-day Saints believe, incorrectly, that the GOP enjoys the official sanction of the Church. He cautioned that the idea that a Democrat cannot be a good Mormon is wrongheaded and should be "obliterated." He added that Utah's congressional delegation should include Democrats as well as Republicans so that the interests of the state can be represented regardless of which party is in control of the White House or Congress.[6]

Hugh B. Brown, a counselor in the First Presidency under President David O. McKay, worked hard to counteract the widespread fallacy that the Church is a Republican Church. Prince and Wright write that McKay told Brown, "Since some think we are one-sided in politics…

---

4   "Transcript: National Press Club Q&A with President Gordon B. Hinckley," *Deseret News,* March 27, 2000, at http://www.deseretnews. com/article/print/155008723/Transcript-National-Press-Club-QA-with-President-Gordon-B-Hinckley.html (accessed July 5, 2011).
5   James P. Bell, *In the Strength of the Lord: The Life and Teachings of James E. Faust,* Salt Lake City: Deseret Book, 1999, p. 86.
6   Dan Harrie, "GOP Dominance Troubles Church," *The Salt Lake Tribune,* May 3, 1998, p. A1.

it might be a good thing to…let the members of the Church know that both political sides are represented in the Church."[7]

Senior Church leaders understand that not all Democrats think alike. They know faithful LDS Democrats often are independent thinkers who align with Church teachings, not with the national or state Democratic Parties when those parties' values are out of sync with Church teachings.

Mixed Signals from Lay Leaders

Despite General Authorities' statements that say, in essence, that more than 700,000 LDS Democrats in the U.S. are good Mormons, there are many lay leaders and members in the Church who resist such counsel. Lay leaders include stake presidents, who preside over a geographic area known as a stake, a body that is roughly similar to a diocese in the Catholic Church. A stake, in turn, consists of two or more wards (local congregations) which are led by lay bishops who function somewhat like priests in a Catholic parish. Bishops are responsible to help the members of their congregations weather personal challenges and improve their spiritual and temporal well-being.

Many lay leaders communicate through words and actions that they suspect that LDS Democrats may have the same leftist beliefs as the national Democratic Party (which, in my experience, is usually not true) and are, therefore, possibly out of tune with the Holy Ghost. Where do lay leaders and members get these ideas? Many probably take their lead from a few Church authorities and influential LDS writers and political philosophers like Ezra Taft Benson and W. Cleon Skousen. Others very likely misinterpret addresses or articles written by General Authorities who seem to criticize Democratic values when that is not what they were doing.

One influential source of anti-Democrat rhetoric came from Ezra Taft Benson, then President of the Quorum of the Twelve Apostles. Richard Davis, in his book *The Liberal Soul: Applying the Gospel of Jesus Christ in Politics*, paraphrases Benson as saying that one cannot be a liberal Democrat and a Latter-day Saint. Davis, a political science

---

7   Gregory E. Prince and Wm. Robert Wright, *David O. McKay and the Rise of Modern Mormonism*, Salt Lake City: University of Utah Press, 2005, p. 336.

professor at Brigham Young University and columnist for the *Deseret News*, writes that the Church issued a statement at the time to inform Church members that Benson was speaking for himself, not for the Church, when he made comments about Democrats.[8]

Church policy now forbids its General Authorities from participating in partisan politics. But lay leaders *are* permitted to engage in them, but not in a Church setting.[9] Even if the lay leaders don't express their political views while serving in their ecclesiastical roles (which some do, anyway), their views carry tremendous weight with their friends, neighbors and congregations. Since a great many Church members tend to assume that most of their lay leaders are Republicans, members often believe that GOP values are one and the same with the principles of the gospel. This belief on the part of lay leaders and members implies that a large number of LDS Democrats and their candidates are less close to God and cannot be trusted to represent the voters in public office.

Putnam and Campbell wrote about the results of interviews conducted with members of an LDS ward in Sandy, Utah. The ward members' responses underscored the challenges Mormon Democrats face within their religious culture. Liberal members described having "a big political separation" in their ward. They acknowledged that they enjoy a mutual trust and spiritual unity with their conservative brothers and sisters, but they, the Democrats, feel, nonetheless, that they are stigmatized by their liberal political beliefs. They said that political liberals in the Church are, as Putnam and Campbell wrote, "the odd ones out" in their wards and they feel constant pressure to conform to conservative political ideology. An interviewee said that "a lot of people [in the Church] are Republicans because they think that's what the leadership of the Church would like them to be." A former bishop of the ward said, "I've had people say to me that they know I'm a good person, they know that I'm a good man, they know I was the bishop,

---

8   Richard Davis, *The Liberal Soul: Applying the Gospel of Jesus Christ in Politics*, Salt Lake City: Greg Kofford Books, 2014, p. xiii.

9   Mormon Newsroom Staff, "Political Neutrality," *Church of Jesus Christ of Latter-day Saints*, at http://www.mormonnewsroom.org/official-statement/political-neutrality (accessed December 6, 2014).

but they have a hard time with me being a Democrat." He added that many liberal Mormons don't talk about their political views with fellow Church-goers because "they don't want to be branded as a person who has lower standards and lower morals."[10]

One Church lay leader revealed his disdain for LDS Democrats during a Democratic Party precinct caucus meeting in Logan, Utah. The Republican caucus was being held in the same building as the Democrats' caucus. Patricia Jones, who later became a Democratic Utah State Senator and minority leader, was participating in her party's caucus when her stake president, a Republican whom she described as an intimidating man, made a brief appearance at their door. According to Jones, "He put his head in [the door] and said, 'I don't know how any LDS person can be a Democrat and a good Mormon.'" Jones said he was serious.[11] That this senior and influential lay Church leader went out of his way to seek out Democrats in their own caucus in order to demean them, revealed an extraordinary callousness toward the feelings and self-esteem of members of his own stake.

A BYU professor related a story about a friend who was called to be a counselor in a new stake presidency. Unbeknownst to the stake president, his new counselor was a Democrat. It was during an election season when the stake president told his stake high council, "We've got to be careful that the right candidates are elected. We can't take a [Church] leadership position on that, but it's important that campaign signs appear in certain places at the right times." The new Democratic counselor turned to the president and said that his comment seemed to be pro-Republican. The stake president looked at him, and as if it should be obvious, replied "And?" The counselor revealed that he was a Democrat. The stake president couldn't hide his surprise: "You are? Oh, my goodness! I had no idea!" Another high councilman at the meeting apparently felt the need to add a second witness to this unexpected revelation by confirming the new counselor's party affiliation. "He *is* a Democrat!" he echoed. Flabbergasted, the stake president told the high

---

10   Robert D. Putnam and David E. Campbell, *American Grace: How Religion Divides and Unites Us,* New York: Simon and Schuster, 2010, pp. 366-367.

11   Patricia Jones, interviewed by author, April 24, 2013.

council, perhaps in an effort to rescue the meeting with humor, "No, he couldn't possibly be a Democrat. I saw him in the temple last week!"[12]

While many lay leaders are compliant in following the direction of the General Authorities to keep politics away from the pulpit, it happens more than many Church members might think. For instance, there was a stake president who, during a stake conference in February of 2013, gave a talk that was largely perceived in the press as a thinly veiled partisan criticism of Democrats. In it, he testified that his comments were inspired by the Holy Ghost as he chastised Americans for choosing "socialism over capitalism, entitlements over free enterprise, and redistribution [of wealth] and regulation over self-reliance." He specifically identified 2012 as the year that voters made these troubling choices, leaving no doubt that he was referring to the reelection of Democratic President Barack Obama to a second term in the White House. The stake president also paraphrased a list of talking points that national Republican leaders had used against their Democratic opponents during the campaign season.[13]

The stake president aimed much of his criticism at the government's tax-mandated redistribution of wealth from more prosperous people to the poor, particularly during the Great Recession of 2007–2012, the worst economic collapse since the Great Depression of the 1930s. He said less fortunate Church members in his stake could have done more to fortify themselves against the downturn. He reminded the stake congregation that Latter-day Saints had been warned for years to be self-sufficient and stay out of debt. He said, in essence, that if members had heeded the Church leaders' warning, they would have been less dependent on Church donations during the recession. This was undoubtedly true in some cases. But he reduced the problem to a set of statistics that pointed a finger at not only those who should have

---

12 Harold Miller, interviewed by author, May 3, 2012.
13 Peggy Fletcher Stack, "Mormon Stake President Gets Political at Church, Laments Election Results," *The Salt Lake Tribune*, March 1, 2013, at http://www.sltrib.com/sltrib/news/55876876-78/church-lds-deviss-er-political.html.csp (accessed February 25, 2013); and "President Matthew DeVisser's Talk," at http://www.scribd.com/doc/126671218/President-Matthew-DeVisser-s-Talk (accessed February 25, 2013).

been more fiscally responsible, but also those who, through no fault of their own, found themselves in dire straits during the downturn.[14]

In terms that sound like a corporate CEO reporting to his shareholders, the stake president said, "From 2008 to 2009, our stake experienced a 150 percent increase in welfare assistance to its own members. That assistance stayed about the same during 2010 and 2011. In 2012 we saw some improvement, and I am happy to report that we are now only 70 percent above our pre-2009 level of assistance."[15] While it was indeed a positive trend that fewer members were dependent on Church welfare during the years he cited, this leader chose to highlight the improvement in stark statistical terms rather than in human terms. Instead, he could have framed his remarks to show more empathy toward the struggling members of his stake. In not-so-subtle language, however, he risked embarrassing and humiliating those in the pews who had benefited from Church assistance, regardless of the reason, along with alienating many of the Democrats in attendance.

Conclusion

The bias against LDS Democrats by other Church members is palpable to those on the receiving end. It may not be obvious to Mormon Republicans, but their questioning (albeit often subtle) of the values of the Democrats among them gives the latter a sense that their faith is being evaluated. The effect it has on member unity runs contrary to the Church's mission and its ability to attract and retain members. Despite attempts by General Authorities to debunk the fallacy, many lay leaders and members persist in believing that Republican political positions and gospel values are one and the same, leading to the oft-asked question, "How can a Democrat be a good Mormon?"

---

14 Ibid.
15 Ibid.

Chapter 4

Alienation in the Church

*"I believe that if we could truly understand the Atonement of the
Lord Jesus Christ, we would realize how precious is one son or
daughter of God."*[1]
— M. Russell Ballard, Member of the Quorum of the Twelve
Apostles, Church of Jesus Christ of Latter-day Saints

Most of the time, Latter-day Saints who affiliate with the Democratic
Party believe that Republicans in the Church don't mean to deliberately question their religious faith. But not all Mormon Democrats
are able to weather what they perceive to be a questioning of their
worthiness in the gospel as well as their patriotism toward America.
It has led to the tragic alienation of many Church members in a gospel-
centered culture in which Jesus Christ has proclaimed that *every* soul
is precious in His sight.

Hurt Feelings and Lost Souls

A man in my ward, after discovering I was a Democrat, confided to one
of my neighbors that he felt I should have my temple "recommend"
(an admission card that authorizes worthy members to go into any
LDS temple to practice holy ordinances) revoked because of my party

---

1   M. Russell Ballard, "The Atonement and the Value of One Soul," *LDS
General Conference address*, April 3, 2004, at https://www.lds.org/gener-
al-conference/2004/04/the-atonement-and-the-value-of-one-soul?lang=eng
(accessed October 11, 2012).

affiliation. My detractor is a good man, but he stereotyped me based on his reflexive distrust of the national Democratic Party. What he did not understand is that not all Democrats think alike and that I don't always agree with some of the tenets of the national and state Democratic parties. Nonetheless, my fellow ward member was unable to reconcile his extreme conservative bias with my political choices.

Another example of political prejudice manifested itself in a sacrament meeting talk in my ward. The speaker gave one of the best sacrament meeting talks I had ever heard. He was genuine, insightful, funny and effective. Near the end of his talk, however, his tone and demeanor changed radically. He said he had had a rough emotional time when a presidential candidate he despised was elected. It was clear he was talking about Democratic candidate President Barack Obama. Because of the overwhelming dominance of Republicans in the Church, the speaker assumed everyone in the congregation shared his political views. He had every right to be passionate about politics and candidates, but using the pulpit to preach, or even imply, partisan politics dims the spirit and makes liberals and moderate Democrats feel defensive and alienated.

Karen Hale was a Democratic Utah State Senator when she was invited to speak at a Relief Society meeting at a ward in her senate district. The purpose of the lesson was to encourage Church members to be civically engaged in the community. The Relief Society leader who invited Senator Hale did not ask her to talk about why she was a Democrat or to make any other partisan references, which they both knew would have been inappropriate. The Senator was not going to speak until the end of the lesson so she sat quietly in the back of the room and listened. Before Hale spoke, a woman raised her hand and said, "Well you know, I think what you're saying is exactly right. It's important to get involved. And there's a great opportunity and a *need* for us to all get involved right now because there are more Democrats in our Legislature than we've seen for a long time. We've got to *do* something about it!" At that point, the class instructor said, "Thank you. Now I'd like to introduce my good friend Karen Hale who's the Democratic Senator from our district." Hale said, "You could just see this poor woman. She was only a few rows from me. You could see her shrink into her seat. You've got to hand it to her, though. She came up to me afterward and apologized."[2]

Hale said LDS Democrats have heard all the jokes in Church about being out of step and on the wrong side of the political divide. She said it's important to remind the congregation that we all come from different viewpoints and it's important to share our ideas. "There isn't a right party or a wrong party," she said. "It's okay if you're a Republican. It's okay if I'm a Democrat. We can bring a lot to the table together."[3]

Hale's concern about the political bias against Democrats she experienced in the Relief Society class was not whether or not the sister who spoke up against Democrats had the right to feel strongly about a political party and its elected officials. Of course she did. But once again, a Latter-day Saint made the naïve assumption that everyone who actively attends Church must be a Republican. A lesson about civic responsibility in a Church meeting does not require a partisan rant. It only detracts from the Spirit.

Losing Our Young

Conservatives in the Church are almost always faithful, kind and generous people. But they may not be fully aware that their political prejudice is putting a strain on member unity and the Church's attempt to retain current members and attract new converts, especially among young adults. Putnam and Campbell found that young Americans today are more tolerant and moderate-to-liberal in their social views than older Americans. They wrote that the young are more likely to reject the culture, if not the doctrine, of a rigidly conservative religious tradition where political ideology seems to have become confused with gospel principles.[4]

Many liberal LDS young adults are faltering in their identity, activity and membership in the faith. Much of it is due to their feeling that they are not valued or welcomed in the Mormon culture. It's also possible that the Church's image as a bastion of political conservatism

---

2   Karen Hale, interviewed by author, Aug 23, 2011.

3   Ibid.

4   Robert D. Putnam and David E. Campbell, *American Grace: How Religion Divides and Unites Us,* New York: Simon and Schuster, 2010, pp. 3, 434-435.

may be making it more difficult for its missionaries to attract converts among the young.

Growing up as a Mormon Democrat can have its challenges, according to Daniel Magleby, a visiting assistant political science professor at Duke University. Magleby grew up in Utah where he said his liberal political views led his fellow Mormons to question his worthiness to take the sacrament or serve in a Church calling. "If you are a liberal and a Latter-day Saint, you learn to grow thick skin," he said.[5]

But not all Latter-day Saints have a thick skin.

Dr. Harold Miller, professor of psychology at Brigham Young University, a former stake president and bishop and an LDS Democrat, confirms that there is a proven risk of losing young members from the Church because they feel unwelcome in a conservative Mormon culture. Several of his former BYU students have told him that they went inactive or left the Church because they felt alienated for having liberal views. "They have talked about feeling friendless, that there's really no one to talk to or who understands," Miller said. "Almost to a person they have said, 'I have been much happier [since leaving the Church]'"[6]

Richard Lyman Bushman related an incident that took place in his ward when he lived in Pasadena, California. In 2008, the LDS Church took a strong position in favor of Proposition 8, California's voter initiative that intended to ban same-sex marriage. Church leaders entered the political fray and publicly encouraged Latter-day Saints to work in favor of passing Proposition 8, which it did by a margin of 52 percent to 48 percent. During the battle over Proposition 8, a young woman in Bushman's ward spoke up in a Sunday School class where the subject came up. "I can understand the Church taking a [moral] stand," she said. "But why did [Church leaders] have to enter politics?" The class leader embarrassed her with a curt, insensitive response as if the reason should have been obvious to her as a matter of faith and obedience. The young woman ran to her car and sobbed. "Fortunately,

---

5 Brian Passey, "Mormon Liberals: A 'Minority within a Minority,'" *USA Today*, October 30, 2012, at http://www.usatoday.com/story/news/politics/2012/10/30/mormon-liberals-minority/1669155/ (accessed October 2, 2012).

6 Harold Miller, interviewed by author, May 3, 2012.

a very sensitive stake patriarch walked to her car and simply said, 'I want you to know, there's a place for you in this Church,'" Bushman said. "That saved her."[7]

The incident involving the young woman in Bushman's Pasadena ward should not have been about whether Church leaders were right to politicize opposition to same-sex marriage. It was about how Church members need to be sensitive and not summarily dismiss the feelings and opinions of fellow Church members who don't share their political or social views, especially when such insensitivity could be interpreted as a criticism of that person's faith.

The Thin Disguise of Humor

Humor is often used to disguise a more serious underlying prejudice toward Mormon Democrats. Members may think the joking is in good fun but many LDS Democrats don't see it that way.

"Democrats Also Welcome"

The organizers of a ward social event in Salt Lake City couldn't resist the temptation to take at dig at the Democrats in their congregation. At the bottom of the flyer they sent out to advertise the event, they printed the statement, "Democrats also welcome."[8] The comment was undoubtedly meant to be funny but its underlying spirit, even if unintended, was a reminder that Democrats can be seen as a distinct, and somewhat questionable, minority in the Church, particularly in Utah.

"Blood-sucking Democrats"

A humor writer for the *Deseret News,* the LDS Church–owned daily newspaper, wisecracked in one of his columns that he didn't like donating blood and would use any excuse to get out of it, including making a confession that he once voted for a Democrat. The columnist

---

7   Larry Alan Brown, "A Place in this Church, an Interview with Richard Lyman Bushman," *Mormon Social Science Association,* December 10, 2012, at http://www.mormonsocialscience.org/2012/12/10/a-place-in-this-church-an-interview-with-richard-lyman-bushman/ (accessed December 10, 2012).
8   Karen Hale, interviewed by author, Aug 23, 2011.

wrote, "So when I arrived [at the blood drive], I kept trying to find a way to be excused from the upcoming ordeal. I pulled two people aside at different times and in quiet, embarrassed, [but] serious tones, said, "Did you know I once voted for a Democrat?" The writer continued, "That didn't work. I will pause here to give you the opportunity to insert your own joke about people in Utah being used to being overtaxed by 'blood-sucking Democrats.'"[9]

Hard to Swallow

Dr. Thomas G. Alexander, BYU professor emeritus and former director of the Charles Redd Center for Western Studies, attended a banquet in which an LDS woman at his table told an anti-Democrat joke that he felt was inappropriate. Alexander, a self-described moderate Democrat, said, "Frankly, it is this attitude that seems to have driven politics in the Mormon community rather than the civility between people of different political persuasions."[10] Was Alexander overly sensitive? If it had been the only joke or criticism that he had ever heard, he might have brushed it off. But it is the cumulative effect of many such slights, often disguised as humor, that make Democrats so sensitive.

Liberals Pay More

George Burnett opened a juice and smoothie shop on Main Street in Vernal, Utah, a town of nearly ten thousand located 175 miles east of Salt Lake City. He called his business *I Love Drilling* where he charged liberals a dollar more for a 16-ounce drink than he charged conservatives. His two-tiered pricing depended on the honor system of customers truthfully identifying their political persuasion. While he claimed his discriminative pricing was done tongue-in-cheek, he admitted that it stemmed from his belief that liberals are to blame for government policies that stunt job growth in the extraction of oil and gas, the primary

---

9 Steve Eaton, "Lack of Sympathy Deflating after Giving 4 Gallons of Blood," *Deseret News*, June 19, 2012, p. C7.

10 Thomas G. Alexander, interviewed by author, February 1, 2012.

industry in Uintah County where Vernal is the county seat.[11] Also, it would presumably help his business in a Republican county where 62 percent of the population is Mormon.[12] Burnett's approach to discriminating against liberals, even if tongue-in-cheek, is yet another layer of overt public bias that reinforces a Mormon culture that is already strongly anti-liberal. It's a culture in which LDS children grow up believing that it's okay to make fun of Democrats.

"They Seemed So Normal!"

I attended a Utah County Democratic Party fundraising dinner during 2010, an election year. A Republican who was there made an observation that was amusing and revealing. Among the Democrats at the event were Latter-day Saints who were prominent members of the community. One had been the president of Weber State University. Two former deans of BYU's Marriott School of Business, along with the current dean, were there. Others had served as LDS bishops, stake presidents and mission presidents. Also in attendance was a much-respected former school district superintendent, numerous BYU and Utah Valley University professors and successful business people and attorneys. Another well-known Democratic attendee was Aileen H. Clyde, who served for most of the 1990s as second counselor in the General Presidency of the Church's Relief Society. Many of the Democrats were former and current candidates for public office. One Democratic candidate at the fundraiser was in a race for a seat in the Utah House of Representatives. He enjoyed the support of a number of moderate Republican donors in his district, one of whom attended the event with his wife. Afterwards, she told her husband what she thought of

---

11   Deborah Tracy, "Blending Politics and Health," *Vernal Express*, January 23, 2013, at http://www.ubmedia.biz/vernal/news/article_795cff5b-57dd-5809-b07d-800d5e7f5068.html (February 19, 2013); and Geoff Liesik, "Smoothies for Liberals $1 more at this Shop," *Deseret News,* January 19, 2013, p. B2; and Kathy Stephenson, "At Vernal Smoothie Shop, Liberals Pay More," *The Salt Lake Tribune*, January 17, 2013, at http://www.sltrib.com/sltrib/money/55642295-79/burnett-liberals-smoothie-vernal.html.csp (accessed February 19, 2013).

12   City-Data.com, at http://www.city-data.com/city/Vernal-Utah.html (accessed February 20, 2012).

the Democrats she had met at the event. "They seemed so *normal!*" she exclaimed, genuinely surprised.

Conclusion

When Church members in general experience challenges to their testimonies, the vast majority of Latter-day Saints gladly extend their full hand of fellowship to them in an effort to love and respect the one sheep out of 100 and bring him or her back into the fold. How sad and ironic it is, then, that the same Church members, who are normally so kind, generous and sensitive, should inadvertently help foster a culture in which a columnist for the *Deseret News* felt emboldened to define his more liberal fellow citizens as "blood-sucking Democrats." This bias against Democrats must change if every faithful member of the Church is to feel that his or her soul is worth just as much as anyone else's.

Part 2

Chapter 5

The Empathy Gap

"We [Republicans] talk about numbers and deficits while liberals talk about hungry children. Guess who wins that argument?"[1]
— *LaVarr Webb, Conservative columnist for the* Deseret News *and former policy deputy for Republican Utah Governor Mike Leavitt*

M ost Latter-day Saints care about the poor and are generous in donating funds and goods to them. But many Republican Church members are opposed to government safety nets for the impoverished and urge their elected officials at all levels of government, including Congress, to steeply curtail or even dismantle such programs. A great number of them believe that support for destitute citizens should come from voluntary donations, not from what they see as "forced charity" through taxation.

Why might this antipathy of so many Mormons toward public anti-poverty programs be a problem for the Church? Because it exposes it to the perception, however unfair it may be, that, despite its extensive worldwide humanitarian programs (that few outside the Church know about), Latter-day Saints might be viewed as not being as supportive of government safety nets as they should be. Of course, no Latter-day Saint wants to be falsely perceived as being unwilling to impart of their substance to help lift up the poor because it simply isn't true. But should

---

1   Frank Pignanelli and LaVarr Webb, "Education, Health Care, Poverty and Other Big Issues," *Deseret News,* January 27, 2013, p.G1.

Church members insist that such assistance should come only from private charities? After all, nowhere in the scriptures does the Savior say that governments should have no role in uplifting the downtrodden.

LaVarr Webb, in his quote at the top of the chapter, admits that many Republicans tend to default to a focus on budget costs and statistics when debating government anti-poverty policy. They display a high degree of consistency in their opposition to government safety nets for the poor. In contrast, most Democrats first consider the human costs of those who are disadvantaged. They believe government plays a critical role in alleviating poverty through tax-funded social programs. It's important to note that not all Democrats think alike about how to pay for such programs. Just about every LDS Democrat I know (including Democratic candidates for office), believe in "affordable compassion," the use of tax dollars to help the poor while remaining within a balanced budget.

The primary underlying cause of the difference between the parties and their attitudes toward helping the poor is due to what I call the "empathy gap." This chapter defines what an empathy gap is and how it determines one's attitude toward the poor and the government's role in serving them. It sets the stage for chapters 6–9. Those chapters constitute a large percentage of the book because the topic has huge implications for the temporal and spiritual well-being of the Church and its members. In those chapters, I explore common misperceptions about the poor, the causes and effects of poverty, and reasons why LDS Republicans might be well-served to reconsider their opposition to public safety nets.

Who Are the Poor?

The word "poor" in this book is generic for all those who are disadvantaged, marginalized or vulnerable and live near or below the poverty line. They include the homeless, hungry, disabled, sick, mentally ill, abused, abandoned, rejected, addicted, destitute elderly and the underemployed and unemployed.

Rarely does a single condition impact an individual, family or group, but rather a combination of them. Their status may be temporary or chronic, including families whose dependence on public or private aid is passed from generation to generation. What do the poor have in common? They are a minority of endangered Americans who rely on government or nonprofit charitable assistance to enjoy even a minimum of safety, comfort and dignity. Or, to stay alive.

What Is Empathy?

The word "empathy" is often used interchangeably with "sympathy" and "compassion." Various etymologists, philosophers, social scientists and amateur wordsmiths have expressed differing views on which of these words reflects a deeper understanding of someone else's pain. For simplicity, I've settled on the word "empathy" to generically represent the capacity of a person to vicariously experience another's feelings, whether through natural instincts, personal experience or the experiences of people close to us. In his classic poem *Song of Myself*, Walt Whitman captures the essence of empathy when he wrote, "I do not ask the wounded person how he feels, I myself become the wounded person."[2]

Within the context of this book, an empathy gap is the emotional distance that exists between one person and another who is struggling with poverty or some other disabling circumstance. For ease of discussion, I've divided empathy into three levels: average, enhanced and high. The level to which one belongs is determined by the *degree* to which he or she can identify with poor people and how much *action* they take to donate time and money to them. This is not a judgment on the goodness of people. There are circumstances that may hinder many from giving more time and money to the needy. Given the means, many would be happy to do so. But it doesn't change the fact that a person's degree of empathy, whether they're a Democrat or a Republican, depends on how much direct contact they have with the less advantaged.

An average-empathy person will almost always care about a less fortunate person and is likely to feel moved to write a check or donate food or clothing to people in their church and in their communities, directly or via charitable organizations that operate locally and throughout the world. A person at an enhanced level, in addition to doing what an average-empathy person does, is likely to devote some of their time to

---

2   Walt Whitman, *Leaves of Grass*, New York: Bantam Books, 1983, p. 54.

engage in good causes such as, for example, serving in a soup kitchen during special holidays and events. People on the high end of the empathy scale are likely to immerse themselves in sustained and direct contact with the needy, whether in their churches or communities. It might take the form of joining Big Brothers Big Sisters of America to be a positive role model for a troubled child. Or high-empathy people might volunteer to serve food in a homeless shelter on a regular basis throughout the year. Another example is they might sign up to comfort the sick and injured at a hospital on a recurring schedule. In addition to their time, high-empathy people are more likely to sacrifice a greater portion of their monetary means, including taxes to support government safety nets, to assist those who are barely able to meet even the minimal needs of day-to-day living.

Can an average-empathy person become more empathetic? Yes, by spending time visiting, face-to-face, our vulnerable citizens. This can be done safely by visiting homeless shelters, food banks, rehabilitation clinics and other controlled environments that serve the needy. We could learn their stories and feelings. We could listen to the causes of their problems and their hopes for the future. We could commit to sustained direct contact with them. And we all would be well-served to remember the humbling adage, "There but for the grace of God go I."

When It Happens to You

In my personal story in Chapter 6 (*Laying the Blame on the Poor*), I relate how I spent several years of my childhood without a father and in poverty. My firsthand experience ingrained in me a high level of empathy for children who grow up in similarly disadvantaged households. In an effort to offer some relief to and a role model for a troubled boy, I became a volunteer for the Big Brothers of America. For six years I was matched with the same youngster, from age eight to 14, whose mother was divorced, working full-time and struggling to make ends meet. Her son, I'll call him Jeff, displayed his unhappiness in a number of anti-social ways. Before I met him, his most spectacular stunt was to torch the contents of a garbage dumpster. Jeff stood next to the dumpster, fascinated by the smoke and flames, until the police and fire truck arrived. It didn't occur to him to run. He didn't think he'd done anything wrong.

After telling me the story, the Big Brothers case worker asked me if I still wanted to be matched to the boy. Of course I did, but it occurred to me that I might want to invest in some asbestos shorts.

Some of the most visible cases of increased empathy involve a number of well-known Republican politicians. In each case, they had been exposed to situations in which the experiences of loved ones or others caused the politicians to take positions that were directly counter to those of their party.

Former Republican Vice President Dick Cheney, one of the most conservative vice presidents in U.S. history, supports gay marriage. Far-right Utah Representative Mike Noel (R-Kanab) is regularly ranked in the top 25 percent of the most conservative lawmakers in Utah. Yet unlike most of his colleagues, he wants to see more state funding go toward treating substance abusers. Republican Florida Governor Rick Scott was a strident opponent of expanding Medicaid for the poor in his state. But he reversed himself and announced his support for it, angering his conservative supporters. Another high ranking Republican, U.S. Senator Rob Portman (R-Ohio), had expressed his strong opposition to gay marriage but later changed his mind and declared his support for it. Jeb Bush, former Republican governor of Florida, provoked an immediate backlash from his party because he called for compassionate immigration reform for undocumented immigrants.[3]

---

3 Stoyan Zaimov, "Dick Cheney Admits Politics Prevented Him from Supporting Gay Marriage," *The Christian Post,* January 9, 2014, at http://www.christianpost.com/news/dick-cheney-admits-politics-prevented-him-from-supporting-gay-marriage-79107/ (accessed June 9, 2014); and Ladd Brubaker, "Rally for Recovery Packs Capitol Rotunda," *Deseret News,* February 15, 2012, p. A4; and Adam R. Brown, "Ideology Scores for the Utah House of Representatives, 2013," Department of Political Science, Brigham Young University, at http://adambrown.info/p/research/utah_legislature/ideology_house, (accessed June 9, 2014); and Lizette Alvarez, "In Reversal, Florida to Take Health Law's Medicaid Expansion," *The New York Times,* February 20, 2013, at http://www.nytimes.com/2013/02/21/us/in-reversal-florida-says-it-will-expand-medicaid-program.html?_r=0 (accessed February 21, 2013); and Charles Babington, "Gay marriage: Senator's shift, GOP soul-searching," *The Deseret News,* March 15, 2013, at http://www.deseretnews.com/article/765624675/Gay-marriage-Senators-shift-GOP-soul-searching.html (accessed June 10, 2013).

Why did prominent conservative politicians adopt values that were in direct conflict with the Republican Party's social agenda and more like those held by Democrats? The difference is empathy. Cheney's daughter is gay. Noel had an alcoholic parent and a brother in a federal penitentiary on a drug charge. Governor Scott's mother had recently died after having raised five children with very little money. Portman learned that one of his sons was gay.[4] Bush's wife, Columba, is a Mexican-born Latina.[5] In each situation, their empathy gap was significantly narrowed as they emotionally identified with the circumstances of people who are close to them.

When the Funds Run Dry

Steve Olsen, a former LDS bishop, related an experience he had while running for Congress as a moderate Utah Democrat in 2006. While campaigning at the Weber County (Utah) Fair, a man approached Olsen to tell his story of how empathy turned his political ideology on its head. In Olsen's words:

"This man said he'd been a strict conservative most of his life, arguing against the government helping the less fortunate as unconstitutional do-goodism, and that families and charity must be responsible for the poor.

"Then his elderly mother became ill, eventually requiring nursing care. Before too long the cost of this care had consumed her savings and all the equity in her home. Her children were not people of much means. So under the theory of government he had espoused all his life, it was time for his mother to be tossed into the street. But of course she wasn't. In America, when the resources of the elderly are exhausted, Medicaid takes over. After the family had done all they could, We the People stepped in and took up the slack.

"After telling his story, [the man] said, 'The limited government thing sounds good in theory. But in real life, there are just too many needs out there. It would be nice if charity could do everything, but it isn't realistic. There are legitimate needs in our communities that

---

4   Ibid.
5   *Deseret News*, March 16, 2013, p.A2; and Michael J. Mishak, "Jeb Bush Remarks Expose GOP Immigration Plan," *Deseret News*, April 11, 2014, p. A7.

require the collective effort of government. I was cured of my hard-core conservatism by my experience.'"[6]

Catharsis in Finland

Harold Miller grew up as a Mormon in a very conservative home in Arizona. During his childhood, he was exposed to a relentless dosage of pro-Republican, anti-Democratic rhetoric from his ultra-conservative father. Miller adopted his father's political philosophy, as many children do, and continued to have a far-right political orientation into his late teens. Miller even considered joining the John Birch Society, decried by most Americans, including moderate Republicans, as perhaps the most extreme far-right organization in the country. He shared the common Republican concept that the poor are responsible to pull themselves out of their circumstances with few or no public assistance programs.

Miller's perspective began to change while serving an LDS mission in Finland. For the first time, he came face-to-face with people whose lives and families were decimated by alcoholism and poverty. "I felt my heart shifting," he said. He found that his close encounter with the poorest people in Finland increased his empathy for them, an experience that deeply affected him and permanently altered his view of the role of government safety nets to help those in need.[7] Eventually, he switched parties and became a Democrat as well as serving as a bishop and stake president in the LDS Church. In addition to his ecclesiastical service, he became active in politics. He lost his bid for the Utah House of Representatives but was later elected to the Provo City Council where his party affiliation was not relevant in the non-partisan race.

---

6   Steve Olsen, "Some LDS Conservatives Worship Political Dogma" *The Salt Lake Tribune,* May 14, 2011, at http://www.sltrib.com/sltrib/opinion/51713295-82/political-government-idolatry-lds.html.csp (accessed December 9, 2014).
7   Harold Miller, interviewed by author, May 3, 2012.

A Backflip on Immigration

Republican Utah State Representative Stephen Sandstrom was one of the House's most conservative hardline opponents of immigration reform. He vehemently opposed reform that would have provided undocumented immigrants an opportunity to stay in the country on guest worker visas and a possible path to eventual citizenship. He aggressively pushed for a punitive, enforcement-only approach that would have expanded police powers to arrest and deport undocumented Latinos, among other tough sanctions.

But Sandstrom did a surprising and abrupt change of heart after meeting face-to-face with a 19-year-old Latina named Sara, whose undocumented parents brought her into the U.S. at age 3. She shared with the lawmaker her personal story of how she was American in every way except her citizenship status. She told him how she graduated from high school with a high grade point average but was under constant threat of deportation and faced a bleak future with no opportunity to build her own American Dream.

Sandstrom was moved. "I put myself in her shoes and how horrible that feeling would be," he said. Her story "really pulled at my heartstrings." He shocked his far-right colleagues by reversing his stance in favor of a more moderate, balanced and compassionate approach in line with the position taken by the leaders of the LDS Church. For Sandstrom, immigration was no longer an abstract principle based on political ideology but a close-up glimpse of how legislative policy affects the lives of real people. It's another striking example of how direct and personal exposure to another's pain has the power to build empathy and change hearts.[8]

The Zip Code Effect

A strong correlation exists between income, where people live, their political affiliation and, consequently, their empathy gap with regard to the needy and government's role in helping them. Some choose to

---

8   David Montero, "Stephen Sandstrom: From Immigration Hardliner to Compassionate Conservative," *The Salt Lake Tribune*, May 7, 2012, at http:// www.sltrib.com/sltrib/politics/54025401-90/sandstrom-utah-immigration-law.html.csp (accessed September 12, 2012).

live in zip codes far from the blighted urban centers (or poor rural areas) with their impoverished neighborhoods. It stands to reason that the further the physical distance is between the well-off and the needy, the wider is the emotional gulf, or empathy gap, between them. I call this the "zip code effect."

As a rule, conservatives prefer to live further from urban centers while a significant majority of liberals are more likely to live in cities. A Pew Research Center study in 2014 established that 76 percent of those who said they were consistent conservatives preferred to live in larger homes in small or rural towns where there is more space between them. The study also found that they also favor living in close proximity to those of the same religious faith.[9] This appears to hold true especially in Utah, the stronghold of the LDS Church, where 94 percent of Utah's population lives outside the Salt Lake City metro area,[10] the most significant urban area in the state. Most Utah Democrats, on the other hand, are concentrated in the highly populated metro area.

In contrast, the Pew study reported that three-fourths of those who self-identified as consistent liberals favored living in cities where they can experience a variety of racial and ethnic groups while living in smaller, closely situated houses. They said it's important that they live in walkable communities (also minimizing their dependence on air-polluting vehicles) with convenient access to cultural attractions such as art museums and theaters. Only 23 percent of consistent conservatives felt that these factors were relevant considerations.[11] Because of their close

9   Drew Desilver, "How the Most Ideologically Polarized Americans Live Different Lives," *Pew Research Center*, June 13, 2014, at http://www.pewresearch.org/fact-tank/2014/06/13/big-houses-art-museums-and-in-laws-how-the-most-ideologically-polarized-americans-live-different-lives (accessed June 25, 2014).

10   "Salt Lake City Demographics," *Salt Lake Tourist and Visitors Center*, July 2, 2014, at http://www.saltlakecityutah.org/salt_lake_demographics.htm (accessed December 6, 2014).

11   Drew Desilver, "How the Most Ideologically Polarized Americans Live Different Lives," *Pew Research Center*, June 13, 2014, at http://www.pewresearch.org/fact-tank/2014/06/13/big-houses-art-museums-and-in-laws-how-the-most-ideologically-polarized-americans-live-different-lives (accessed June 25, 2014).

proximity and exposure to the urban poor and the charities that serve them, liberals, it would seem, might feel more empathy for the poor.

Since educational attainment so often leads to higher income, it, too, impacts where a person lives and his or her political ideology. David E. Campbell, John C. Green and J. Quin Monson, co-authors of *Seeking the Promised Land: Mormons and American Politics,* show how this linkage is more pronounced among Mormons than the general U.S. population. First, Mormons are more educated than other Americans because learning has been a priority of their faith since Mormonism's founding in 1830. Sixty-four percent of Mormons today have achieved some level of post-high school education compared to 54 percent of the non-Mormon population. Not surprisingly, the Mormons' educational advantage has translated to a higher median income than that of the general population. For example, Latter-day Saint households with incomes between $50,000 and $75,000 exceed the national median by 5 percent.[12]

Given their higher than average educational attainment and income, Mormons' connection between income and political affiliation is also stronger than in the general U.S. population. Fifty-two percent of Mormons who make less than $30,000 per year self-identify as Republicans, a rate that is twice that of the general population in that income category. At the high end of the scale, 75 percent of Mormons who earn an annual income over $150,000 are members of the GOP, a striking 33 percent higher than the national average at the same income level.[13]

Does higher income induce Mormons to favor the GOP? Does it affect their empathy toward the poor? Thomas G. Anderson, a prolific and highly respected author of books and articles on the history of Mormonism in the American West, believes it does. "As people become more wealthy, they tend to become more conservative," he said, "and they tend to think, 'well, if I can make it in this economy, then other people ought to be able to as well, and the ones who don't are lazy no-goods.'" Anderson said LDS Church members have become more

12   David E. Campbell, John C. Green and J. Quin Monson, *Seeking the Promised Land: Mormons and American Politics,* New York: Cambridge University Press, 2014, p. 20.
13   Ibid, p. 87.

prosperous since the 19th and early 20th century but have become more insulated over time, both physically and emotionally, from those who subsist below the poverty line. Anderson does not imply that prosperous Mormons lack the character or sensitivity to care about the impoverished. But he said that unless they have personal exposure to the poor, they have a hard time understanding the tremendous obstacles the disadvantaged face in their day-to-day lives. "They fail to recognize that there are people they don't know, or people they don't come in contact with, who don't get the kind of help [they] need," Anderson said.[14]

Despite the tendency of well-off people to not understand (or fully empathize with) the poor, experts on poverty have found that more prosperous people feel more empathy for the needy if they are exposed to the emotional impact of their plight. In his book, *The Liberal Soul: Applying the Gospel of Jesus Christ in Politics*, Richard Davis reinforces the notion that well-off Church members are more willing to help vulnerable people whose situation they are personally aware of rather than those whose stories they don't know. "[Wealthier people] do not lack compassion for the [impoverished] individual in front of them," he writes, "but they often fail to see that many others in similar need may not be so fortunate."[15]

Research data strongly suggest that Latter-day Saints may be more vulnerable to the zip code effect and a wider empathy gap than the U.S. population at large. Putnam and Campbell provide evidence that the correlation is real. They refer to data from the Faith Matters Survey of 2006 which disclosed that less than 42 percent of Mormons believed that government safety nets should be the primary caregivers for the poor. It ranked Latter-day Saints as the least supportive of public welfare programs compared to all other religions measured in the survey. Even Evangelical Protestants were more supportive, with 60 percent preferring government as the main provider of aid to the less fortunate.[16]

---

14   Thomas G. Alexander, interviewed by author, February 1, 2012.

15   Richard Davis, *The Liberal Soul: Applying the Gospel of Jesus Christ in Politics,* Draper, Utah: Greg Kofford Books, 2014, p. 73.

16   Robert D. Putnam and David E. Campbell, *American Grace: How Religion Divides and Unites Us,* New York: Simon and Schuster, 2010, p. 257.

Overall, Putnam and Campbell found that antipathy toward government aid to the destitute was strongest among people of faith and, particularly, Latter-day Saints. "By and large, religious America has offered little support for public action to redress growing class inequities," they wrote.[17] Six years after the Faith Matters Survey, the Peculiar People Survey of 2012 revealed a startling trend. It discovered that the percentage of Mormons who said government can't afford to help the poor had risen from 42 percent in 2006 to more than three-fourths in 2012.[18]

Republicans might argue that their opposition to tax-funded welfare programs does not mean they lack empathy for the poor, but that it means they strongly believe that private charities can do a much better job providing them the basics of life. However, I make the case in Chapter 8 (*Sharing Our Wealth*) and Chapter 9 (*Myths about Charities*) that the problem of poverty is more immense (and growing quickly) than most people realize or acknowledge, and charities are not as well run or effective as is generally thought. I believe it will become obvious in those chapters that government anti-poverty programs are irreplaceable in meeting the moral imperative that all Americans provide for the least among us.

Conclusion

Mormons are known for their concern for those who are less fortunate. But here in the U.S. they are often far removed from poor people and unaware of the degree of their plight. No one can fully appreciate the depth and urgency of another's needs unless they walk in their shoes and feel a high level of empathy for them, either through firsthand or vicarious experience. Empathy is a potent force for good. It has the power to reduce ethnic, racial, and political conflict. It can magnify one's generosity of spirit to reach across economic classes and serve as a lifeline to the downtrodden and rejected. It opens our eyes to the

---

17   Ibid, p. 258.
18   David E. Campbell, John C. Green and J. Quin Monson, *Seeking the Promised Land: Mormons and American Politics,* New York: Cambridge University Press, 2014, p. 104.

immensity of the problem of poverty in this country and how charities, important as they are, cannot alone begin to put more than a small dent in the overall problem. In the following chapters, my objective is to shed light on the crucial role empathy plays in our perception of the needy, how we can avoid unfairly judging the poor, why the poor are getting poorer, what we need to do to help them, and why the need for government anti-poverty intervention cannot be overstated.

Chapter 6

Laying the Blame
on the Poor

*"Whenever you feel like criticizing any one… just remember that all
the people in this world haven't had the advantages that you've had."*[1]
— F. Scott Fitzgerald, American novelist

Latter-day Saints hold dear the scriptures that inspire us not to judge
or disrespect the downtrodden or show favoritism for the rich over
the poor. In the Epistle of James, chapter 2, verses 2–3 in the King James
Bible, the Savior clearly warns us not to look down on the poor. In that
scripture we read, "For if there come unto your assembly a man with
a gold ring, in goodly apparel, and there come in also a poor man in
vile raiment; And ye have respect [favoritism] to him that weareth
the gay clothing, and say unto him, Sit thou here in a good place; and
say to the poor, Stand thou there, or sit here under my footstool." Also,
according to James 2:8–9, those who are well-off but despise the poor
and do not love their neighbors as themselves, will be guilty of com-
mitting sin and are condemned for breaking the law of God.

The Book of Mormon serves as a second witness to the Bible that
those with ample material means are condemned if they withhold their
wealth from the poor. In Mosiah 4:23, King Benjamin preaches the
gospel of Jesus Christ to his people: "I say unto you, wo be unto that

---

1   F. Scott Fitzgerald, *The Great Gatsby*, New York: Scribner, 2004, p. 1.

man [who does not share his wealth with the poor], for his substance will perish with him . . . and if ye judge the man who putteth up his petition to you for your substance that he perish not, and condemn him, how much more just will be your condemnation for withholding your substance, which doth not belong to you but to God, to whom also your life belongeth."

Is it wise of LDS Republicans to oppose government subsidies that help the needy have access to healthcare, rent subsidies, food, job training and other essentials? Can Latter-day Saints, regardless of political persuasion, afford to judge whether a poor person is deserving of their assistance or not? Does the Lord discriminate between the downtrodden and least among us who bring poverty on themselves from those who do not? Does He say it is alright to permit the transfer of our wealth to the needy only through voluntary charity but not through public programs?

A Pew/*USA Today* 2014 survey found that a majority of Republicans believe the poor bring poverty on themselves by making bad choices and should find a way to work their way out of it with little or no government intervention.[2] Democrats, on the other hand, generally believe much poverty is the result of circumstances beyond the control of the poor and should have government assistance extended to them. Who is right? How would we know? Are there decisive, objective statistics that would settle the issue? If we erred on the side of generosity, would it, as conservatives fear, reward reckless behavior and incentivize the poor to remain dependent on government welfare? Or, as Democrats insist, should more prosperous Americans err on the side of government intervention because the poor, almost a third of whom are single mothers with kids,[3] must have their basic needs met before they can hope to escape their disadvantaged condition? Who has

---

2   "Most See Inequality Growing, but Partisans Differ over Solutions," *Pew Research Center,* January 23, 2014, at http://www.people-press.org/files/legacy-pdf/1-23-14%20Poverty_Inequality%20Release.pdf (accessed March 9, 2015).

3   Carmen DeNavas-Walt, Bernadette D. Proctor, Jessica C. Smith, "Income, Poverty, and Health Insurance," *U.S. Census Bureau,* September 2013, pp.13, 15, 17-19, at http://www.census.gov/prod/2013pubs/p60-245.pdf (accessed March 9, 2015).

the experience, knowledge and the right to judge? In this chapter, I offer suggestions that may increase our understanding of and empathy for those living in destitution and the often insurmountable barriers they face.

Do Bad Choices Cause Poverty?

In a *Deseret News* article, Rachel Sheffield , an analyst with the Heritage Foundation, a conservative public policy think tank based in Washington, DC, is quoted as saying, "Poverty is caused by the choices people make: things like using drugs, abusing alcohol, dropping out of school and having children outside of marriage."[4] Another conservative think tank, the New York City-based Manhattan Institute for Policy Research, posted online an article by Steven Malanga that appeared in the *Chicago Sun-Times*. In the article, entitled "The Truth about Poverty: Bad Choices, Not a Bad Economy, are to Blame," Malanga echoes the Republican line that poverty is due to irresponsible decisions, not from a lack of available jobs (a claim I debunk in Chapter 7, *What Jobs?!*). He claims that impoverished adults who choose to work make an adequate income to meet their needs. "It's not that the adults who head families in poverty don't earn enough; they don't work enough," he writes.[5]

In a *CBS News* article in 2012, Republican vice presidential candidate Rep. Paul Ryan (R-Wisconsin), known as his party's chief "budget hawk," proposes slashing social safety nets to help balance the nation's budget. Ryan acknowledges that there are extreme exceptions, those who cannot help themselves and deserve government assistance. But he accuses the rest of the poor of deliberately shunning work and dodging self-sufficiency, suggesting that they find poverty a more desirable lifestyle than improving their lives by working. He is quoted as saying that unless tax-funded safety nets are cut, they will continue

---

4   Mercedes White, "Experts Disagree on How, Why U.S. Lost War on Poverty," *Deseret News*, January 19, 2014, p. A4.
5   Steven Malanga, "The Truth about Poverty: Bad choices, not a Bad Economy, are to Blame," *Chicago Sun-Times*, February 4, 2007, re-posted by the *Manhattan Institute for Policy Research*, at http://www.manhattan-institute.org/html/_chicsuntimes-the_truth_about_poverty.htm (accessed January 26, 2014).

to provide a "hammock, which lulls able-bodied people into lives of complacency and dependency."[6] In other words, Ryan restates a basic tenant of Republican ideology, that most welfare recipients are lazy and unwilling to do their part to lift themselves out of poverty.

Donald Trump was president-elect of the United States in December 2016 when he selected Dr. Ben Carson, a black far-right conservative, to serve as Secretary of Housing and Urban Development. HUD's mission is to subsidize low-income families so they can afford to buy homes in safe neighborhoods. The nomination of Carson, who had never led any government organization (especially one as large and complex as HUD), deeply alarmed advocates of low-income housing. Much of their worry stems from a quote attributed to Carson in an article in the *New York Times* in which reporter Sheryl Gay Stolberg wrote, "Mr. Carson once told a television interviewer that he had risen above his circumstances by realizing that 'poverty is really more of a choice than anything else,' by which he apparently meant that people should be able to escape poverty through hard work."[7] One would think that Carson, who rose from poverty in Detroit to become a world-renowned neurosurgeon, would have more empathy for the impoverished people he grew up with. Occasionally, though, there are exceptions, like Carson, who show disdain for those who remain trapped in poverty or, as he seems to argue, *choose* to remain trapped because of their bad choices and a lack of initiative. It appears that people like Carson believe that, because *he* made good (with what most people would agree is a genius level intelligence), everyone else should be able to do the same, regardless of their innate intelligence and circumstances. Perhaps one lesson to be learned from Carson's life is that, regardless of a child's socioeconomic status, many have the intelligence to improve their lot in life, but only if given the right opportunity.

6   Rebecca Kaplan, "On Day of Damage Control, Ryan Promises Better Social Safety Net," *CBS News,* September 18, 2012, at http://www.cbsnews. com/news/on-day-of-damage-control-ryan-promises-better-social-safety-net/ (accessed April 16, 2014).
7   Sheryl Gay Stolberg, "Critics Worry Over How Ben Carson, Lacking Expertise in Public Housing, Will Lead It," *The New York Times,* December 5, 2016, at http://www.nytimes.com/2016/12/05/us/trump-ben-carson-hud-critics.html (accessed December 12, 2016).

Bruised in Buffalo: A Personal Story

How many people are in poverty due to bad choices? My experience as a child may serve as a useful insight. My father abandoned my younger sister, my mother and me in the mid-1950s when I was seven years old. He was an alcoholic who couldn't hold down a job. He didn't pay alimony or child support. My mother went back to work as a full-time secretary in Buffalo, New York and became a member of what we refer to today as the "working poor." She took the bus because we could not afford a car. We lived in a creaky, worn-out apartment. We didn't have health insurance. When my sister and I caught the measles, a highly contagious and sometimes fatal respiratory virus, we didn't have the money to go to the doctor. We didn't go to restaurants or movies or have new clothes.

For a while, we tried to make it on our own. But the financial burden became too much and we were forced to move into a cramped apartment with my aunt and uncle and their children where my sister and I slept on the living room floor and my mother on the couch. Government safety nets such as food stamps, Medicaid and housing subsidies were not available until the 1960s, relegating the poor of our era to fend for ourselves. Would my mother still have chosen to work if she had had government benefits? Probably, because even if a safety net had existed at the time, her meager salary would not have covered all of our basic needs such as rent, health insurance and nutritious food, the same tough tradeoffs the poor of today have to make. And if we had not had family close by who were willing and able to take us in for a time—a situation not available to many poor families—where would we have gone? Did we become poor because we made bad choices? No, we became poor because my father made bad choices.

The Historical Roots of Poverty

It's all too easy to assume that nearly all impoverished people are responsible for their lot in life by making bad choices. But if we take a closer look at the historical development of certain racial and ethnic cultures in the U.S., we may find that their reflexive responses to America's modern social and economic systems are deeply, often subconsciously, influenced by their historical roots. That's not to say that one's racial history irrevocably consigns him or her to a life of poverty. There are exceptions, like Ben Carson, that prove otherwise. Even so, I believe it's useful to explore the historical roots of certain major racial and ethnic groups to rebut the false notion that impoverished citizens, especially minorities, deserve to be stereotyped as having brought their problems upon themselves. Instead, we may find they are held down by the ingrained limitations and low expectations they have inherited from their ancestors after centuries of painful conditioning and that these limitations are reinforced by the realities of their present circumstances.

Since before the founding of the nation, non-white minorities have been marginalized and fenced off from what they unsurprisingly perceive to be a hostile mainstream American culture. They have congregated for mutual support in impoverished, tightly knit, insular subcultures where they cling to their cultural identities, values and native languages. It's not surprising that living in such isolated environments inhibits assimilation into the nation's economy, which, in turn, makes it extremely difficult for poor minorities to gain access to quality education and employment opportunities. Do poor minority people choose to live in such places? Do they remain there because they see a life of welfare as a "hammock," as Paul Ryan asserts, preferable to working their way into mainstream America?

A Tale of Three Minorities

There are three minorities in the U.S. — American Indians, Black Americans, and Mexican Americans — who have the highest percentage of their members living in destitution and who depend on public assistance for the basic necessities of life. As such, I have chosen their American histories for the closest examination. According to the U.S. Census Bureau and Centers for Disease Control and Prevention (citing U.S. Census Bureau figures for 2013), 27 percent of 5.2 million American Indians, including Alaska natives, are poor (1.4 million people).[8] Also among the ranks of the impoverished are Black

---

8 CDC Staff, "American Native and Alaska Native Populations," *Centers for Disease Control and Prevention*, at http://www.cdc.gov/minorityhealth/populations/REMP/aian.html (accessed May 16, 2014); and Suzanne Macartney,

Americans whose 41.7 million people suffer a poverty rate of 25.8 percent (10.8 million people).[9] And of the 33.7 million Mexican Americans in the nation, 27 percent rely on government anti-poverty programs to survive (9.1 million people).[10] Together, they make up more than 45 percent of the 47 million Americans who live below the poverty line.[11] Given their huge impact on the welfare system, I have chosen to examine their cultural roots to shed light on how their experiences prior to and throughout U.S. history are directly related to their current place in the nation's welfare system.

American Indians

American Indian culture was essentially frozen in time after they were forcibly removed from their ancestral lands in the eastern U.S. and other regions, many of which were lush with dense forests, plentiful rivers and abundant game. They were forced to live in desolate, isolated reservations located in remote regions in the West. U.S. military forces under the command of Andrew Jackson, who would later become the seventh president of the United States, initiated the large scale separation of American Indians from their lands in 1814. The mass confiscation was legalized by the "Indian Removal Act," passed

---

Alemayehu Bishaw, and Kayla Fontenot, "Poverty Rates for Selected Detailed Race and Hispanic Groups by State and Place," *U.S. Census Bureau,* February, 2013, at http://www.census.gov/prod/2013pubs/acsbr11-17.pdf (accessed May 16, 2014)

9   CDC Staff, "Black or African American Populations," *Centers for Disease Control and Prevention,* at http://www.cdc.gov/minorityhealth/populations/REMP/black.html (accessed May 16, 2014); and Suzanne Macartney, Alemayehu Bishaw, and Kayla Fontenot, "Poverty Rates for Selected Detailed Race and Hispanic Groups by State and Place," *U.S. Census Bureau,* February, 2013, at http://www.census.gov/prod/2013pubs/acsbr11-17.pdf (accessed May 16, 2014).

10   Ana Gonzalez-Barrera, "A Demographic Portrait of Mexican-Origin Hispanics in the United States," *Pew Research Center,* May 1, 2013, at http://www.pewhispanic.org/2013/05/01/a-demographic-portrait-of-mexican-origin-hispanics-in-the-united-states/ (accessed May 16, 2014).

11   Carmen DeNavas-Walt, Bernadette D. Proctor, Jessica C. Smith, "Income, Poverty, and Health Insurance," *U.S. Census Bureau,* September 2013, pp.13, 15, 17-19, at http://www.census.gov/prod/2013pubs/p60-245.pdf (accessed February 11, 2015).

by Congress in 1830, and justified under the doctrine of "Manifest Destiny," the belief that the United States was destined to expand westward across the continent. White settlers were now legally permitted to drive tribes from their traditional hunting grounds and claim the land for themselves.[12]

The unrelenting encroachment by settlers and military garrisons in the ancient territories of the eastern and plains Indians led to the violent clash of two irreconcilably opposed cultures, open warfare and atrocities on both sides. Eventually, the superior technology and firepower of army weaponry took a tremendous toll. By 1875, the last remnant of American Indian resistance was finally crushed. Their conquest was hastened when they lost a vital source of food and clothing, the buffalo, when the beasts were nearly exterminated. Between 1868 and 1881, white hunters killed an estimated 31 million for their lucrative hides.[13]

The American Indians were herded onto reservations where there was little game, and tribes which had, for centuries, been nomadic hunters, had to take up subsistence farming, a change for which they were ill-prepared. The federal government promised annuities, tools and food. But corrupt federal agents at the Office of Indian Affairs rarely paid the annuities, the tools were shoddily made and the food, when it came, was inadequate and of poor quality. American Indians who faced starvation had to kill their horses and mules for food.[14] It broke the once-proud and self-reliant Indians and made them utterly dependent on white men for their meager existence, a condition that still exists today for many of their race.

The alienation of American Indians from mainstream society continues unabated. More than one-fourth of them are dependent on government programs. In an article in *Forbes,* John Koppisch wrote that those who live on the country's 310 Indian reservations are among those who

---

12   "Indian Removal," *Public Broadcasting System,* at http://www.pbs.org/wgbh/aia/part4/4p2959.htmly (accessed August 15, 2012).
13   S.C. Gwynne, *Empire of the Summer Moon,* New York: Scribner, 2010, pp. 258-262, 285.
14   Ibid, pp. 233,262, 288.

languish in the bottom one percent of the U.S. economy.[15] Long distances from decent schools, jobs and medical facilities, rampant alcoholism and drug abuse, high birthrates among single women, poor health and absentee fathers continue to plague life on the reservations. American Indians have inherited a culture of defeat and welfare dependency, rooted in early American history, which has left them a legacy of isolation, low expectations and failure. And yet, American Indians are stereotyped, along with other impoverished racial minorities, as being lazy, irresponsible and the victims of their own bad choices. Even today, when someone is described as going "off the reservation," it's a derogatory term that describes a person who is accused of defying the will of a superior authority or ignoring the powerful mores of a culture.

Black Americans

Nearly 11 million Black Americans live below the poverty line. Their tradition of intergenerational poverty has its roots in the era of slavery. The first black slaves were shipped in chains to America in 1619 to work in the tobacco fields of Jamestown, Virginia, a year before the Pilgrims in the Mayflower landed at Plymouth Rock, Massachusetts. For the next 246 years, until the end of the American Civil War in 1865, slave owners suppressed slaves in a vicious system in which slaves were made completely dependent on the welfare of their owners. They were not taught to read or write for fear that educated slaves might foment rebellion. The so-called "marriages" of slaves were not considered legal but were used to "breed" new generations to work the plantations. Owners readily split up slave families by selling or trading away adults and children in business transactions, corrupting the concept of family ties or commitments.[16]

The law of the land relegated slaves to the status of property in the South until Congress, in 1865, passed the 13th Amendment to the

---

15   John Koppisch, "Why are Indian Reservations so Poor? A Look at the Bottom 1%," *Forbes.com,* December 13, 2011, at http://www.forbes.com/sites/johnkoppisch/2011/12/13/why-are-indian-reservations-so-poor-a-look-at-the-bottom-1/print/ (accessed May 14, 2014).

16   History.com staff, "Slavery in America," at *History.com,* http://www.history.com/topics/black-history/slavery (accessed May 12, 2014).

Constitution which abolished slavery. But the amendment did very little to change hearts and minds. The embedded culture of racism and segregation that plagued the South also contaminated major northern cities such as Boston, New York and Chicago where businessmen invested in Southern plantations to profit from low-cost, slave-produced raw materials. Rampant, hostile bigotry prevailed throughout the post-war Reconstruction period (1865-1877) and continued unabated until the Civil Rights Movement, with its mass protests, civil disobedience and legal battles of the 1960s.[17]

It took nearly a century after the enactment of the Thirteenth Amendment before President Lyndon B. Johnson and Congress passed the Civil Rights Act of 1964. At best, it provided a tenuous legal basis for the redress of wrongs. In reality, it encountered intense resistance that obstructed its enforcement for many years. Even so, the law meant Black Americans had taken a historic step forward, at least on paper, to set the stage for gaining their elusive rights envisioned in the Declaration of Independence.

Entrenched social attitudes, fueled by centuries of racial hatred and mistrust, do not change quickly or easily. For three and a half centuries, Black Americans were looked upon and despised as sub-humans. Only in the last 50 years have they been able to fitfully pry from American society an improved degree of access to mainstream social, educational, political and economic opportunities. An increasing number have risen into the middle class or higher and have become self-sufficient through education and political activism. And they are teaching their children to do the same. But is it rational to expect Black Americans, in the span of a single lifetime (as measured by us "baby boomers"), to say all is forgiven, that they are now completely healed of the painful legacy passed down by their enslaved ancestors? There are still millions more who may need, for some time, the empathy of all Americans as well as government assistance until they can achieve equitable access to education and jobs. In writing chapters 7 (*What Jobs?!*) and 8 (*Sharing Our Wealth*), I found discouraging evidence that shows that the ability of poor minorities to get the necessary educational and

---

17   Ibid.

employment opportunities are slipping further away, not growing closer.

There are those who argue Black Americans can no longer use their long history of oppression as an excuse for being on the public welfare rolls. Many may believe the recent influx of foreign-born blacks renders the claim moot. But the increased immigration of blacks from outside the U.S. has not made much difference. As of 2007, the portion of Black Americans who can trace their blood lines to human bondage, stood at 92 percent.[18] As a result, those descended from slaves remain an overwhelming majority for which the legacy of slavery continues to be a raw and enduring scar.

Mexican Americans

There are nearly 34 million Mexican Americans in the U.S. Over 11 million of them are immigrants born in Mexico and additional 22.3 million who were born in the U.S.[19] Twenty-seven percent, more than nine million people, live below the poverty line.[20] As with American Indians and Black Americans, an examination of their cultural history will help explain why they represent a disproportionately high percentage of the impoverished class today.

The origin of Mexican Americans can be traced to the Spanish conquest of the Aztecs in the early 1500s. For the next 300 years, most of the native population in Mexico was forced into slavery. It wasn't until 1829, twenty years after Mexico won its freedom from Spain, that the last slaves were freed. Today, 75 percent of Mexico's

---

18   Mary Mederios Kent, "Immigration and America's Black Population," *Population Bulletin*, December 2007, at http://www.prb.org/pdf07/62.4immigration.pdf (accessed May 15, 2014).
19   Ana Gonzalez-Barrera and Mark Hugo Lopez, "A Demographic Portrait of Mexican-Origin Hispanics in the United States, *Pew Research Center*, May 1, 2013, at http://www.pewhispanic.org/2013/05/01/a-demographic-portrait-of-mexican-origin-hispanics-in-the-united-states/ (accessed January 30, 2015).
20   Suzanne Macartney, Alemayehu Bishaw, and Kayla Fontenot, "Poverty Rates for Selected Detailed Race and Hispanic Groups by State and Place," *U.S. Census Bureau*, February, 2013, at http://www.census.gov/prod/2013pubs/acsbr11-17.pdf (accessed May 16, 2014).

population, including those who immigrate to the U.S., can claim at least one ancestor who was a slave.[21]

Mexicans began to migrate to what is now the American Southwest during Spanish rule and continued after Mexico took control of the territory. Their early settlements make them the second-oldest culture in the U.S., after American Indians.[22]

After the U.S. victory in the Mexican War of 1846-1848, Mexico surrendered its extensive land holdings in the American Southwest. For the first time, Mexicans living in the territory became known as Mexican Americans. In the Treaty of Guadalupe-Hidalgo of 1848, the U.S. promised to protect their rights, including being able to retain ownership of large tracts of land. It wasn't long, however, before the government and white settlers violated the treaty, overwhelmed them and, through exploitation and violence, forced them off their lands. Once again, the doctrine of Manifest Destiny was invoked to justify the abrogation of civil rights, the illegal seizure of property and the subjugation of the two oldest races who had occupied and worked the land for centuries. Like the American Indians, Mexican Americans were reduced to a sub-class, a status that has overshadowed many of them to this day.[23]

An examination of the cultural heritage of Mexican Americans in the 1800s is not adequate, of itself, to explain their status as an impoverished group today. In addition to their early history, there are three major influences that led to their transformation into the nation's fastest-growing minority with one of the highest poverty rates: an ongoing influx of first-generation immigrants, a high fertility rate and low educational attainment.

First-generation Mexican emigres have been entering the U.S. in multiple waves since the early 1900s, ebbing and flowing with the availability of work in the American economy and national immigration policy. Typically, they are unable to speak English well and lack the skills for

---

21   Shep Lenchek, "Slavery in Mexico," *Mexconnect*, January 1, 2011, at http://www.mexconnect.com/articles/666-slavery-in-mexico (accessed January 26, 2014).

22   R.A.Guisepi, ed., "The Story of Hispanics in the Americas," *International World History Project,* updated January 1, 2001, at http://history-world.org/hispanics.htm\ (accessed June 30, 2014).

23   Ibid.

all but the most menial jobs. They suffer from high unemployment, ethnic isolation and a subsistence-level existence. Second, third, and fourth generations, on the other hand, are fluent in English. More of them are able to assimilate into the mainstream economy than their parents. But even as the younger generations struggle to dig their families out of the economic basement, their hard-fought gains as an ethnic group are offset by the ongoing arrival of more first-generation Mexicans who have to start the cycle all over again. It's one reason they remain, decade after decade, at the bottom of the economic ladder.[24]

Another contributor to Mexican American poverty is their high fertility rate. As recently as 2010, 90 percent of first-generation Mexican Americans were Catholic,[25] a religion that discourages birth control and promotes large families (not unlike generations of Mormons). Also, incoming Mexicans, on average, are younger than the white majority and other ethnic groups and are in their prime child-bearing years.[26] An impoverished family with more mouths to feed finds it difficult to maintain a subsistence life much less get ahead.

Not surprisingly, researchers have found that a low level of educational achievement is the leading cause of low income and poor assimilation into the mainstream economy for poor Mexican Americans. Even subsequent generations of U.S.–born children, despite being fluent in English, fall below the national average of educational achievement. A study compiled by the University of California at Los Angeles looked at 40 years of data and concluded that "institutional barriers, persistent discrimination [and] punitive immigration policies . . . have made integration more difficult for Mexican Americans." The researchers found that the younger generations are willing to adopt American values, but they are left behind by a public, mostly inner-city,

---

24 Letisia Marquez, "Mexican American Integration Slow, Education Stalled, Study Finds," *UCLA Newsroom*, March 20, 2008, at http://newsroom.ucla.edu/releases/ucla-study-of-four-generations-46372 (accessed May 24, 2014).

25 Ibid.

26 Paul Taylor, et al, "The Mexican-American Boom: Births Overtake Immigration," *Pew Hispanic Center*, July 14, 2011, at http://www.pewhispanic.org/files/reports/144.pdf (accessed August 5, 2015).

school system, which is chronically underfunded—a common theme of all underachieving poor minorities.[27]

We Reap What We Sow

It may be controversial for me to assert that nearly half of those who live below the poverty line are there largely because of their cultural roots in early American history. Critics will argue that this point of view perpetuates a victim mentality and a self-fulfilling excuse for remaining dependent on taxpayers. They reason that minorities have had adequate time since the founding of the Republic to shed the influences of the past. That argument rings hollow. The minorities' dependence on public assistance today is, at least in large part, almost certainly, a powerful inheritance from the past. It is the bitter fruit of centuries of conquest, exploitation, and the trampling of their God-given rights, violently executed by white Americans, propped up by the government and enforced by cruel slave owners and the U.S. Army. As long as disdain for poor minorities continues to be a belief of many Americans, and as long as Republicans maintain that the destitute are victims of their own bad choices, the longer it will take for the poor to become self-sufficient and contributing members of society.

Decision-making Under the Pall of Poverty

The argument that many poor people decline into or remain in poverty because of their own choices does not hold up, according to a study published in the journal *Science* and reported in the *Deseret News*. In the study, the authors found that the cause-and-effect relationship is often the opposite, that it is the acute stress of poverty itself that causes bad decision making. Their research established that the cognitive ability of poor people is low because of their chronic struggle with money, hunger, fatigue and poor health. Impaired brain development contributes to their poverty, trapping them in a downward spiral of underemployment or unemployment that renders them unable to

---

27　Letisia Marquez, "Mexican American Integration Slow, Education Stalled, Study Finds," *UCLA Newsroom,* March 20, 2008, at http://newsroom.ucla.edu/releases/ucla-study-of-four-generations-46372 (accessed May 24, 2014).

afford healthy food which often results in a higher risk of obesity and heart disease. Nearly one-third of poor Americans have been diagnosed with depression.[28] In turn, depression makes them less able to engage in long term, positive interpersonal relationships, especially single moms whose mood disorders and the burden of children may be seen as too much baggage for prospective suitors.[29]

Additional studies recognize that poverty leads to impaired brain development and erratic judgment. According to an article by Lane Anderson in the *Deseret News* entitled "Research Finds Being Poor Can Hurt Brains," researchers at the University of Virginia discovered that while some poverty is caused by the genetic inheritance of a low IQ, it is a stressful home environment, by far, that is the major cause of lower brain function. The study concludes that high IQ children born into severe poverty are less likely to escape the cycle of poverty because their native intelligence is suppressed by their situations.[30]

At the University of Pennsylvania, a research team compared the cognitive function levels of both rich and poor youngsters. According to their analysis, the amount of mental and physical stimulation in a child's environment is a key factor in determining their ability to make decisions. The authors report that children from privileged households enjoy a much higher level of stimulation, often with parental involvement, such as travel, reading, discussions and athletic opportunities. In contrast, poor kids suffer from a low level of stimulation in their environment which translates to lower brain function. However, some experts have included that poor children are not irrevocably condemned to a life of low achievement. Research by the Boston Children's Hospital posits that negative environmental influences on young minds can be reversed if they are taken out of poverty and placed in a positive environment, allowing them to catch up with their more prosperous peers.[31]

---

28   Lane Anderson, "Research Finds Being Poor can Hurt Brains," *Deseret News*, July7, 2014, p. A1.
29   Devon Merling, "Research Finds Poverty May Lead to Bad Decision-Making," *Deseret News*, October 19, 2013, p. A1.
30   Lane Anderson, "Research Finds Being Poor can Hurt Brains," *Deseret News*, July7, 2014, p. A1.
31   Ibid.

Barriers to Self-sufficiency

There are anti-poverty programs, private and public, which claim that it is their mission to motivate the poor to become self-sufficient. But there are those who argue that not all poor people should be allowed to take advantage of the programs. Some say there should be a process for weeding out applicants if they are not deemed worthy to participate in the programs.

Paul C. Godfrey, associate academic director at the Melvin J. Ballard Center for Economic Reliance at LDS Church–owned Brigham Young University, asserted that every program for the poor should have an admissions "filtering process." The filtering is necessary, he argued, to deny participation to low income people who do not appear motivated to do their part to be helped. Godfrey praised a program in Salt Lake City whose director applied such a litmus test. The director said his organization refused to provide rides or child care for prospective participants because, the director said, "If they can't get over that hurdle, then they won't be able to do the rest of the things in the program."[32] However, I believe the director's philosophy is counterproductive because he screens out the very people who could benefit the most from his program. By not serving those who are so poor that they can't find their own transportation and child care, program leaders deny them the opportunity to become self-sufficient and learn to how to afford such basics on their own. To deny them that opportunity is akin to a pastor telling a sinner to stay away from his church until he has stopped sinning.

Charities (at least some of them) are not the only organizations to erect barriers that make it more difficult for the disadvantaged to gain self-sufficiency. State government often does the same, especially for critical anti-poverty programs such as education and health care. For example, a Utah State Senator sponsored a bill in the 2015 legislative session with the well-intended objective of enabling poor people to receive the education they need to attain self-sufficiency for themselves and their kids. The bill proposed a tax reimbursement of $1,500 per

---

32   Lane Anderson, "BYU Professor Suggests 5 Ways to End Poverty," *Deseret News*, April 10, 2014, p. A1.

year for low-income families to use for education. The catch? To qualify, parents must already have a job. But the working poor almost always lack the time, transportation or money for the child care required to allow them or their children to take advantage of the benefit. Also, applicants' annual income must be no higher than 150 percent of the federal poverty level to qualify for the funds.[33] For a family of four in 2015, the 150 percent threshold amounted to $36,375 per year, or just under $9,100 for each member.[34] With income that low, it is likely a parent would be more motivated to put food on the table and pay the rent rather than trying to find the time and energy to pursue education for themselves or their children.

As long as private charities and government continue to erect barriers to self-sufficiency to those who most need it, the cycle of intergenerational poverty is here to stay.

Conclusion

Do the poor bring poverty upon themselves because they've made bad decisions? Sweeping, negative stereotypes of entire minorities are perpetuated mainly by those whose life's experiences and inherited economic benefits make them the least qualified to understand or empathize with the people they criticize. They cannot understand the pangs of chronic hunger if they've never missed a meal. Lawmakers in Congress and state legislatures, most of whom enjoy a life of relative affluence and good health, should not deem themselves justified in assigning low budget priorities to children's health insurance, homelessness, mental illness and preschool education for poor children. If we haven't walked in the shoes of the vulnerable, it would be wise not to judge them.

LDS Apostle Jeffrey R. Holland urges Church members not to withhold their means from the needy and broken-hearted by making the

---

33   Marjorie Cortez, "Bill would Help Fund Education for Families Experiencing Poverty," *Deseret News*, February 26, 2015, p. B1.
34   "Annual Update of the HHS Poverty Guidelines," *Federal Register: Health and Human Services Department*, January 22, 2015, at https://www. federalregister.gov/articles/2015/01/22/2015-01120/annual-update-of-the-hhs-poverty-guidelines (accessed August 6, 2015).

mistaken assumption the poor bring their dire circumstances on themselves. At the Church's November 2014 General Conference, Holland delivered an address entitled "Are We Not All Beggars?" In it, he admonished members not to withhold their generosity to the poor "because we see the poor as having brought their misery upon themselves. Perhaps some *have* created their own difficulties but don't the rest of us do exactly the same thing?" said Holland."[35]

---

35   Jeffrey R. Holland, "Are We Not All Beggars?" *Ensign*, November 2014, p. 41.

Chapter 7

What Jobs?!

"Together we will create an America that is open, so every citizen has access to the American Dream; an America that is educated, so every child has the keys to realize that dream; and an America that is united in our diversity and our shared American values that are larger than race or party."[1]

— *George W. Bush,*
43rd President of the United States

In his victory speech of December 13, 2000, President-elect George W. Bush, a Republican who popularized the phrase "compassionate conservative," expressed a vision in which *every* citizen has access to the promise of the American Dream. It was not a guarantee that everyone would achieve it. But it was a call for every American, *together*, to contribute to providing the tools necessary for every American to have an opportunity to share in the nation's prosperity if they are willing to work. This raises a pressing question: *What* jobs are Republicans talking about?" Are there in fact enough lower-skilled jobs available for less advantaged people to fill?

In this chapter my objective is to counter the myth that there are enough jobs available that pay well enough to keep lower-skilled workers — the "working poor" — off public assistance. I offer insights into the economic forces that have frustrated their attempts to work themselves off the welfare rolls. Finally, it's my aim to offer conservatives

---

1   CNN.com Staff, "George W. Bush Delivers Victory Speech, Reaches Out to Democrats," *CNN.com*, December 13, 2000, at http://www.cnn.com/TRANSCRIPTS/0012/13/bn.23.html (accessed August 11, 2015).

a glance into the real world of diminishing lower-skilled employment opportunities so they may avoid an ideological trap that could put not only Mormon Republicans at odds with gospel principles, but anyone else who accuses the poor of being lazy for not finding the jobs that Republicans wrongly seem to think exist in abundance.

The Paycheck Exodus

The "paycheck exodus" is not just a phenomenon that refers to the disappearance of lower-skilled jobs (that once paid middle-class salaries) due to automation, foreign competition and other economic forces. It also refers to an increasing number of jobs that still may be available but pay so little that their annual salaries often fall below the 2016 federal poverty level of $24,300. In fact, an article in *WashingtonsBlog* cites Social Security Administration data that reported that nearly 40 percent of all American workers made less than $20,000 in 2014. It also said that more than 50 percent of all American workers earned less than $30,000 that year, a mere $5,700 above the poverty line.[2] It's a trend that's getting worse every year despite the fact that unemployment in the U.S. declined from 9.8 percent in January 2010 to 4.9 percent in January 2016.[3] The upshot is that the most vulnerable in our midst, even those who were fortunate enough to find jobs, continue to struggle despite the surge of new jobs that have been created from 2010–2016.

Since the early 1950s, better-paying entry-level manufacturing positions in the U.S. have plummeted from 30 percent of the economy to less than 10 percent. Meanwhile, openings in the low-paying services sector (e.g., retail, hospitality, travel), with few or no benefits, have jumped from under 50 percent of the economy to nearly 70 percent in the same

---

2   Michael Snyder, "Goodbye Middle Class: 51 percent of All American Workers Make Less Than 30,000 Dollars a Year," *WashingtonsBlog,* October 21, 2015, at http://www.washingtonsblog.com/2015/10/goodbye-middle-class-51-percent-of-all-american-workers-make-less-than-30000-dollars-a-year.html (accessed December 13, 2016).

3   "Data bases, Tables & Calculators by Subject," *Bureau of Labor Statistics,* November 15, 2016, at http://data.bls.gov/timeseries/LNS14000000 (accessed December 13, 2016).

period.[4] This radical turnabout is due in large part to evolving business practices at large U.S. firms. To remain competitive in an increasingly interlocked world economy, corporations have taken advantage of improved manufacturing methods, low-cost foreign labor, loopholes in a lax tax code and transportation and communication technology to rake in record sales and profits. The firms' behavior is aimed at minimizing costs, a natural competitive requirement for any business. But their behavior also helps explain why so many low-skilled jobs have gone away in the U.S., debunking the fantasy of so many conservatives that there are plenty of jobs available for the poor to lift themselves out of their impoverished conditions. In the rest of this chapter, I delve more deeply into the causes and effects of job loss and its impact on Americans on the lower rungs of the nation's economic ladder.

Technology and Automation

Innovation in manufacturing and administrative technology is inevitable and necessary. It enables the use of human and material resources in a more efficient way to produce lower cost products and services. In turn, it makes products more accessible to more customers and generally raises their standard of living. But it does not help the disadvantaged, whose standard of living is not improving but is, in fact, losing ground.

Rapid technological advances have enabled employers to produce more with fewer workers. Corporations are replacing humans with robotic tools to increase productivity and quality. Entire classes of jobs have been eliminated. For example, many service functions such as hotel reservations and airline ticketing have been replaced by online computer applications. The Boston Consulting Group predicts that cheaper, better industrial robots will be adopted by companies at a faster rate over the next 10 years. By 2025, robots will have replaced

---

4 "The Onrushing Wave," *The Economist,* January 14, 2014, at http://www.economist.com/news/briefing/21594264-previous-technological-innovation-has-always-delivered-more-long-run-employment-not-less (accessed November 18, 2014).

over 23 percent of the jobs that lower-skilled factory workers had previously filled, the group says.[5]

In previous eras, when new technology displaced certain types of jobs, it often created new industries with new job opportunities that exceeded the number that were lost. But it doesn't appear to hold true in recent years, especially for those with less education. New jobs that are created through automation often require more education and training than previous ones, advantages that are out of reach for most of the poor, especially as funding for training and education for lower-skilled Americans has been drying up.

Offshoring

Not all jobs are lost due to automation. Over the last 40 years, American companies have transferred millions of production, administrative and engineering jobs to foreign countries to take advantage of low labor costs in the emerging economies of India, China, and other countries. This practice of "offshoring" has decimated, and in some cases nearly destroyed, entire industries in the U.S. A large number of the American victims of this trend had been earning middle-class salaries without the need for formal education. They were able to advance by virtue of on-the-job training and hard work. Not anymore.

An increasing share of the record profits garnered from offshoring has gone to a growing elite class of American executives and shareholders. But they're not the only ones who have grown rich from the system. Much of the wealth has gone to foreign offshore business owners who have become the new financial and political elites of their societies. According to an article in the *Boston Review*, the offshore business owners keep their costs down by using exploitive labor practices that include "child labor, hazardous working conditions, excessive hours

---

5   Paul Wiseman, "Robots Replacing Human Factory Workers at Faster Pace," *abcNews*, February 10, 2015, at http://abcnews.go.com/Business/wireStory/robots-replacing-human-factory-workers-faster-pace-28849962 (accessed February 23, 2015).

and poor wages."[6] The subsequent human costs endured by foreign workers are high, sometimes tragic, so consumers can enjoy paying lower prices for the products produced by offshore foreign companies. They are the human costs that, in the U.S., labor unions and lawmakers have struggled for over a century to eliminate but which U.S. companies consider too expensive to provide to American workers.

U.S. companies are aware of such exploitation. Yet they have systematically neglected to monitor and compel improvements in working conditions at their foreign suppliers. The first revelations of these conditions, very common in countries with the largest number of offshored jobs, were made public over 20 years ago but a large number of U.S. companies still have not adequately incentivized their suppliers to make meaningful changes.[7]

Why are U.S. companies reluctant to demand that their offshore partners improve working conditions? Because it would cut into the U.S companies' profits. The incidents detailed below are only two of many such tragedies that illustrate some of the extreme human costs of offshoring.

An article in the *New York Times* said that in April 2013, more than 1,130 people died when a factory collapsed in a pile of rubble at the Rana Plaza in Bangladesh, a nation that has one of the world's largest garment-export industries, second only to China. The disaster was blamed on owners who had added four floors on top of four existing ones. The upper levels were shoddily constructed without the legal permits do to so. The entire building had been built on a substandard foundation. Despite the appearance of visible cracks in the building, production workers were ordered to go to work the next day, even though shops and a bank branch on the lower floors had been evacuated. The director of a labor rights organization said, "The price pressures these [big corporate] buyers put on factories undermines any

---

6   Richard M. Locke, "Can Global Brands Create Just Supply Chains?" *The Boston Review*, May 21, 2013, at http://www.bostonreview.net/forum/can-global-brands-create-just-supply-chains-richard-locke (accessed November 3, 2014).

7   Ibid.

prospect that factories will undertake the costly repairs and renovations that are necessary to make these buildings safe."[8]

Another tragedy struck the Tazreen Fashions factory in Bangladesh. According to an article in the *New York Times*, a fire swept through the factory's eight stories and claimed the lives of 112 apparel workers and severely burned 200 more. When a fire alarm sounded, the workers (who had been laboring to fill an urgent order from a foreign company) were told to ignore what their bosses may have thought was a false alarm and told to go back to work. The *Times* reported that windows covered by iron grilles blocked possible escape routes and "Some of the managers closed collapsible gates to block workers from running down the staircases." The article also revealed that the company had not been certified to be in compliance with fire safety laws.[9]

Bangladesh is not the only developing country where foreign workers have been exploited by U.S. companies. According to an article in the *Boston Review*, the giant athletic footwear retailer Nike was found in the early 1990s to be profiting from "underpaid workers in Indonesia, child labor in Cambodia and Pakistan and poor working conditions in China and Vietnam." As the result of tremendous public backlash, the article said Nike poured "millions of dollars into improving working conditions at its [foreign] supplier factories." Nike's efforts did raise

8 Julfikar Ali Manik and Jim Yardley, "Building Collapse in Bangladesh Leaves Scores Dead," *The New York Times,* April 24, 2013, at http://www.nytimes.com/2013/04/25/world/asia/bangladesh-building-collapse.html?pagewanted=all (accessed November 3, 2014); and Julfikar Ali Manik and Ellen Barry, "Months After Deadly Fire, Owners of Bangladesh Factory Surrender to Court," *The New York Times,* February 9, 2014, at http://www.nytimes.com/2014/02/10/world/asia/owners-of-bangladesh-factory-surrender-in-deadly-fire.html, (accessed November 3, 2014).
9 Julfikar Ali Manik and Ellen Barry, "Months After Deadly Fire, Owners of Bangladesh Factory Surrender to Court," *The New York Times,* February 9, 2014, at http://www.nytimes.com/2014/02/10/world/asia/owners-of-bangladesh-factory-surrender-in-deadly-fire.html (accessed November 3, 2014).

the standards at some of its foreign suppliers, but, many years later, many still fail to comply with Nike's requirements.[10]

The *Boston Review* article went on to say the garment industry is not the only business sector engaged in labor exploitation in developing countries. Raw materials for electronic components built mostly in the Far East for American corporations come from mines in Asia and Africa where workers are exposed to hazardous conditions.[11]

It's easy to understand why U.S businesses offshore the manufacture of their products. In order to satisfy consumer demand for low-cost items, they use the practice to compete with foreign companies that do the same. However, if Americans would be willing to spend a bit more for products with labels that said "made in the U.S.A," lower-skilled jobs would become more cost effective to produce products in America. Jobs would return to the U.S., employing workers who would pay taxes and reduce the need for costly taxpayer-supported anti-poverty safety nets.

Corporate Welfare: Milking the System

Corporate America's culture of exploitation is not limited to the off-shoring of jobs. They have found lucrative ways, at the expense of American taxpayers and workers, to pad profit margins. Many call it "corporate welfare," a government-assisted environment in which big business reaps windfall profits by avoiding trillions of dollars in federal taxes, dollars that could go to public or private programs to educate and train low-skilled workers to compete for employment in a changing workplace.

It is not a new trend. For decades, corporate tax breaks have shifted a growing portion of the nation's total tax burden onto the shoulders of everyday Americans. In the 1950s, at the same time manufacturing jobs started their downward slide as a percentage of the workforce, private citizens paid 60 percent of the nation's taxes while companies

---

10   Richard M. Locke, "Can Global Brands Create Just Supply Chains?" *The Boston Review,* May 21, 2013, at http://www.bostonreview.net/forum/can-global-brands-create-just-supply-chains-richard-locke (accessed November 3, 2014).
11   Ibid.

covered the remaining 40 percent. Since then, the ratio has shifted markedly until, by 2012, Americans paid 82 percent with the corporations' contribution having shrunk to 18 percent.[12]

There are many ways in which corporate welfare is made possible. Among them, three examples are worthy of mention. One is what some tax experts call the "tax-incentive civil war" between cities and states to lure companies to move to or expand in their locales. Another is tax free bonds. The third is an enormous tax dodge called "inversion" which is buried in a tangled federal tax code with hundreds of loopholes and policy shortfalls that are all-too-often defended by the companies' friends in Congress. The loopholes incentivize huge U.S. corporations to engage in legal but questionable tactics to maximize their profits.

The Tax-Incentive Civil War

An estimated $50 billion per year is being lost in taxes as cities and states battle each other to see who can offer the steepest tax reduction incentives to coax businesses to move to, expand or stay in their current locales. The breaks are offered with the belief that new, well-paying jobs will come into the state, spur economic growth and expand the tax base. However, evidence indicates that tax breaks not only fail to expand the local economy, but are likely to end up costing more in the form of costly new public services, including education and infrastructure, to support companies and their employees. This is especially true if a company increases the local population by hiring out-of-state workers to fill positions that the local workforce is not qualified to do (which is a huge and growing problem in Utah and in many other states). Any shortfall in tax revenue would have to be made up by increased taxes or reduced public services. Worse, numerous studies agree that 9 out of 10 companies would have made the same relocation or expansion decisions without the tax breaks.[13] Even if new jobs *were* created, it's

---

12 Rick Newman, "Here's Who Pays the Bills for Apple's Tax Avoidance," *The Exchange*, May 21, 2013, at http://finance.yahoo.com/blogs/the-exchange/pays-bill-apple-tax-avoidance-183327111.html (accessed November 5, 2014).
13 "Tax Incentives: Costly for States, Drag on the Nation," *Institute on Taxation and Economic Policy*, April 14, 2013, at http://itep.org/itep_reports/2013/08/tax-incentives-costly-for-states-drag-on-the-nation.php#.VNPnMZ3F-So (accessed February 5, 2014).

unlikely that many of the poor would have the education or training to fill them.

Tax-Exempt Municipal Bonds

Another enabler of corporate welfare is tax-exempt municipal bonds which are issued by corporations to borrow money to build facilities, buy equipment, etc. This type of bond is referred to as a tax-exempt "private equity bond." Unlike taxable bonds, the private equity bonds allow corporations to avoid paying billions of dollars in taxes every year.

Municipal bonds were originally intended to help city and state governments meet their needs for infrastructure improvement, buildings for education and other long term investments to benefit the public. But their usage has expanded into the private sector, resulting in the loss of enormous sums of federal, state and local tax revenue including, in some cases, local property taxes. Ostensibly, these tax breaks would make it possible for the benefitting companies to expand their businesses and grow the local economy. But there are no guarantees that such an expansion in the number of new jobs and capacity would take place or produce enough added tax revenue to make up for the breaks given to the companies.[14]

An analysis by the *New York Times* found that a wide variety of businesses have benefited from tax-exempt bonds. They included $650 million to build the Bank of America Tower in Lower Manhattan, $2.6 billion to Chevron to expand a factory in Pascagoula, Mississippi at the same time it was raking in a profit of $26 billion in 2013 alone, and $250 million to renovate an aluminum plant in Iowa. The analysis also reported that "once-forbidden projects like stadiums, hotels and golf courses" were taking advantage of the bonds.[15]

There are hundreds of similar accounts which amount to taxpayer subsidies for private enterprises. While the total monetary impact of the bonds on taxpayers might be small compared to the overall loss

---

14   Mary Williams Walsh and Louise Story, "A Stealthy Tax Subsidy for Business Faces New Scrutiny," *The New York Times,* March 4, 2013, at http://www.nytimes.com/2013/03/05/business/qualified-private-activity-bonds-come-under-new-scrutiny.html (accessed January 4, 2017).
15   Ibid.

of corporate tax revenue due to tax loopholes, it is yet another glaring example of how government tax policy fosters an environment in which corporations have come to expect such entitlements.

Inversions

An inversion is when a U.S. multinational corporation reincorporates and moves its headquarters to another country with lower tax rates, even if most of its operations remain in the U.S. where they use public services paid for by American taxpayers. The pace of inversions has quickened in recent years. Between 1983 and 2003, 29 companies utilized the strategy. From 2004–2013, 47 did.[16] While inversions are legal per the tangled, outdated federal tax code, many politicians and American companies that don't have an international presence accuse the tax-dodging multinationals of being unpatriotic and gaining an unfair advantage over their U.S.-based competitors.

Through inversion, multinationals reap staggering amounts of money by using tax loopholes that enable them to park profits from foreign sales (which generally exceed their U.S. sales, especially in the technology, raw mineral extraction and energy production sectors) in foreign countries with low tax rates. In 2013, Bloomberg reviewed the securities filings from 307 U.S.-based companies and reported that the accumulated profits they have sheltered abroad totaled $1.95 *trillion*, up nearly 12 percent in one year.[17]

Not Paying Back

Critics of corporate welfare argue that American companies are not paying back their fair share to the country in which they got their start. Monumental taxpayer investments were essential to incubate and nurture the companies. Government policies have sustained a robust free-market environment in which they were able to hone their

---

16   Paul Wiseman and Stan Choe, "High Dollar Dents U.S. Company Earnings," *Deseret News,* January 17, 2015, p. A8.

17   Richard Rubin, "Cash Abroad Rises $206 billion as Apple to IBM Avoid Taxes," *Bloomberg,* March 12, 2014, at http://www.bloomberg.com/news/2014-03-12/cash-abroad-rises-206-billion-as-apple-to-ibm-avoid-tax.html (accessed November 11, 2014).

competitive edge so that they could create and penetrate markets worldwide. They've benefited from a society stabilized by constitutional protections and the rule of law, which in turn, is financed by a far-reaching public justice system. Except in rare cases, in wartime or when corporate bailouts are necessary to preserve hundreds of thousands of jobs, government will not seize private companies, unlike in countries run by dictators. A powerful military protects the freedoms with which the business sector can thrive. (American armed forces also expend great sums to help protect many of the tax-sheltering countries to which the multinationals have run.) Other tax-supported essentials include a modern transportation system, government labs and think tanks that develop and spin off technology to the private sector (for example, the Internet), a supply of talented workers from public schools and universities, police and fire protection, quality-of-life enhancing entertainment venues like sports stadiums and concert halls, and other federal, state and local services that have provided a stable, supportive environment.

It's natural to speculate how a reformed tax code with competitive corporate tax rates could help the government collect billions of dollars more in tax revenue. One possible use for the additional money would be for the government to sponsor scholarships for disadvantaged students to get training from vocational schools in an era in which state and federal funds for such training have undergone significant cuts. Or corporations could reinvest in America by digging into their windfall profits to directly provide training and jobs to many of those they have displaced through automation, offshoring and corporate welfare.

One proven type of on-the-job training used to lift up workers is the apprenticeship, a centuries-old way for youth of humble means to learn a trade and pay their own way in society. But U.S. business lags far behind other countries in offering apprenticeships. Per 1,000 employees, Australian companies fund 400 apprenticeships; Germany provides 390, Canada 300, and the United Kingdom 20. U.S. corporations sponsor just six,[18] one more way in which U.S. corporations have

---

18   Eric Schulzke, "College is Not for Everyone," *Deseret News,* February 24, 2015, p. A1.

compiled an abysmal record of denying employment opportunities for the poor.

One thing is clear. Until Congressional Democrats and Republicans find the will to compromise on genuine tax reform and farsighted, socially responsible priorities, it will be business as usual with private citizens shouldering an ever-increasing share of the nation's tax burden, including welfare for the jobless, while American companies flee to friendlier tax havens and take their profits with them.

The Soaring Costs of College

The soaring costs of higher education as well as significant cuts in government aid in the form of grants and scholarships have ruined the dreams of low-to -middle class Americans who crave to attend college and gain the knowledge and skills that would make them competitive for better jobs. Bloomberg reported that the cost of obtaining a college degree has increased 12-fold since the late 1970s, an astonishing 1,120 percent, or four-times faster than the consumer price index. The article quoted Iowa's Democratic Senator Tom Harkin, then-Chairman of the Senate Health, Education, Labor and Pensions Committee: "For millions of young people, rising college costs are putting the American dream on hold, or out of reach."[19]

The meteoric rise of college tuition and fees is attributed to a number of reasons, including the bloating of university administrative staffs, the subsidization of intercollegiate athletics, the "amenity wars" in which colleges build luxury dorms with one-person rooms and private bathrooms, among other perks, in a frenzied competition to attract students. Also, competition for top research talent has driven up faculty salaries. Professors are pressured to "publish or perish," requiring additional faculty to teach classes

Throughout the U.S., state support for higher education has declined 30 percent, in real dollars (adjusted for inflation), from 1987 to 2012. The reduction of government funds, along with the burgeoning expenses

---

19   Michelle Jamrisko and Ilan Kolet "Cost of College Degree in U.S. Soars 12-Fold: Chart of the Day," *Bloomberg.com,* Aug 15, 2012, at http://www.bloomberg.com/news/2012-08-15/cost-of-college-degree-in-u-s-soars-12-fold-chart-of-the-day.html (accessed July 19, 2014).

of running a university, has hiked tuition and fees and forced students to take out excessive loans which total over $1 *trillion* nationally.[20] The poor are the least able to qualify for such loans or pay them back.

Utah allocates the lowest amount of state financial aid per higher education student in the nation, according to Richard Kendell, education advisor for two education-related initiatives, Education First and Prosperity 2020. The initiatives are backed by the Salt Lake Chamber of Commerce and the Utah business community.[21] The business sector launched the initiatives in an attempt to influence the Utah Legislature to earmark significantly more resources toward incentivizing more students, especially lower-income students, to complete college or vocational certification training. The leaders of the two initiatives cite the state's growing inability to provide enough qualified residents to fill the potential job openings projected for the state in the next several years. Conservative columnist LaVarr Webb said Utah legislators "are failing in the most important area of all—education. The biggest crisis facing Utah is a poorly educated workforce."[22]

Why is this such a problem in Utah? Since its founding, the LDS Church and its members have revered the pursuit of education as a God-given priority. So why does the Utah Legislature chronically underfund higher education in direct contradiction of this value? Perhaps Mormons are electing legislators who don't truly represent them.

Trade Training Under Fire

Vocational training leading to associate degrees or certification in the trades has historically been an effective, less expensive vehicle for ambitious low-income students to escape poverty and make a better living. But federal appropriations for vocational training have been drastically cut over the past 14 years. Funding for career technical education was lower in fiscal year 2014 ($1.1 billion) than in 2000 ($1.2 billion).

---

20   Douglas Belkin, "How to Get College Tuition Under Control," *The Wall Street Journal*, October 8, 2013, at http://online.wsj.com/news/articles/SB10 001424127887324549004579068992834736138 (accessed July 24, 2014).

21   Richard Kendall, "Prosperity Achieved Through Education is Involving Business," *Deseret News*, November 23, 2014, p. G2.

22   Frank Pignanelli and LaVarr Webb, "2015 Legislative Review: 'Zion Curtain, Taxes and More," *Deseret News*, November 23, 2014, p. G1.

Inflation during that period has reduced the value of a dollar by more than 38 percent. In other words, funding for career technical education, in real dollars, has declined nearly 40 percent from 2000–2014. In 2012 alone, the federal Department of Education cut its spending for vocational education by more than 20 percent.[23]

Democrats are trying to mitigate the problem. In March of 2015, Democratic President Barack Obama announced that his administration was coordinating a $100 million effort, called TechHire, for industry to train and hire disadvantaged Americans so they can become qualified for much better paying jobs in the technology sector. Those who lack education and are poorly skilled would be trained to fill understaffed positions in disciplines such as software development, network administration and cybersecurity. In an industry that is sorely lacking in qualified workers and increasingly challenged to compete in a growing global market, it would be a boon for companies, poor workers, and taxpayers alike. Obama announced at the time that more than 300 companies and 21 cities, states and rural areas around the nation had signed up to participate in TechHire and jointly compete for government-sponsored grants in cooperation with training schools and local governments. Money for the program would come from participating corporations and funds from existing programs. "These tech jobs pay 50 percent more than the average private sector wage, which means they are a ticket to the middle class," Obama said.[24]

Two years later (by the end of 2016), the TechHire program had grown to over 70 communities and, according to the White House's blog, "Nearly 4,000 people had been placed into jobs paying well above

---

23 "Federal Appropriations for Career Technical Education (CTE): Fiscal Years 2000–2014 ," *National Association of State Directors of Career Technical Education Consortium,* at http://careertech.org/sites/default/files/Carl%20D.%20Perkins%20Act%20Funding%202000-14%20NASDCTEc.pdf (accessed November 9, 2014); and "Inflation Calculator: 2000-2014," *U.S. Inflation Calculator,* at http://www.usinflationcalculator.com/ (accessed November 10, 2014); and Bruce Watson, "Why College Might Not be the Best Choice for Your Education Dollar," *Daily Finance,* August 9, 2012, at http://www.dailyfinance.com/2012/08/09/college-vs-vocational-education-better-wages-less-debt/ (accessed November 9, 2014).
24 Jim Kuhnhenn of the Associated Press, "Obama Calls for Boost in High-tech Training," *Deseret News,* March 10, 2015, p. A3.

the average private sector median wage." Also, the time it takes for participants to become qualified for employment in entry-level tech jobs takes only months in "immersive and on-the-job training" as opposed to formal education programs that can take years to complete. Given that there are an estimated 600,000 unfilled technology jobs in the U.S. today, the TechHire model is expected to provide hundreds of thousands of lower-skilled workers the opportunity to lift themselves into self-sufficiency and pay tax dollars rather than to live off them.[25]

But the election of Republican Donald Trump to the presidency in 2016 means that Republicans control the White House, Senate and House of Representatives. It remains to be seen whether or not they will support TechHire. Given their track record of reducing benefits for the poor, along with Trump's promise to eliminate the Department of Education (which administers TechHire) it would appear that Republican support for this proven program could easily evaporate in an era of meat-axe cost cutting.

The Working Poor

Despite the formidable hurdles described earlier in this chapter, many Republicans maintain that very few of the poor want jobs or are actively looking for work. Statistics tell a different story. Data from the U.S. Bureau of Labor Statistics shows that, in 2013, 23 percent of those below the poverty line nationwide (10.4 million of the more than 46 million in poverty), met the government's definition of "working poor," which is a person who has a full-time or part-time job or has been actively looking for employment for at least six months of the year.[26] The percentage was corroborated by the Rescue Mission of Salt Lake [City], Utah, which reported that an average of 25 percent of the homeless guests

---

25   Ryan Burke, "What's Next for TechHire," *whitehouse.gov/blog*, December 2, 2016, at https://www.whitehouse.gov/blog/2016/12/02/whats-next-techhire (accessed January 2, 2017).

26   Brad Plummer, "Here's Why 10.4 Million American Workers are Still in Poverty, *The Washington Post*, April 12, 2013, at http://www.washington-post.com/blogs/wonkblog/wp/2013/04/12/heres-why-10-4-million-amer-ican-workers-are-still-in-poverty/(accessed November 10, 2014).

who stay in their emergency shelter are employed, but their wages are too low to afford housing.[27]

The actual number of working poor is higher, probably much higher, than 25 percent, when factoring in those who failed to meet the definition of working poor because they held temporary jobs that lasted less than six months or were laid off within a half-year of being hired. The poor are usually the last hired and first fired during corporate layoffs or economic downturns. Also, many have resumes with gaps in their employment history, a common shortfall among the poor that is used by prospective employers to eliminate candidates. Others were too unhealthy to work or became discouraged and quit searching. A great number of the poor (perhaps millions) who didn't seek or find jobs were single mothers, many of whom undoubtedly chose to supervise their children rather than see them drop out of school, get into drugs, join gangs or get pregnant out of wedlock. Or they didn't have the means to pay for child care or transportation or have the requisite experience or training to qualify for even the lowest-paying jobs. Also, steep cuts in state and federal aid for education and training have made it extremely unlikely that less fortunate Americans could qualify for jobs or advance themselves in the workplace.

In Utah, two-thirds of the working poor do not have health insurance. The rest are medically unable to work.[28] When they become sick, diseased or injured in an accident, and if they make too much to qualify for Medicaid, they must dig into their rock-bottom wages for medical aid for themselves and their children, or forgo it altogether. While there are many generous healthcare professionals who donate their time to the poor, they cannot possibly cover all the needs of the destitute, even if they have jobs.

---

27   Rescue Mission of Salt Lake Staff, "Helping the Working Poor Find Employment and Jesus," *Rescuer: the Monthly Newsletter of the Rescue Mission of Salt Lake,* April 2015, p. 4.
28   Wendy Leonard, "Herbert Unveils His Version of Medicaid Expansion," *Deseret News,* December 5, 2014, p. A1.

Conclusion

Many Republicans are reluctant to acknowledge there are powerful market forces that have denied employment opportunities for lower-skilled Americans. Some market forces, such as technological advances and changing consumer tastes, represent the natural evolution of business in a capitalistic economy. But questionable practices by big business (often abetted and motivated by a mishmash of a federal tax code, political bickering, incompetence and successful special-interest lobbying), also play an outsized role in contributing to the growth of an impoverished class. Runaway increases in the cost of education and dwindling government funds for vocational training, along with a dearth of apprenticeship opportunities in private industry, have ravaged the aspirations of disadvantaged would-be students who want a chance to compete in the workplace and make better lives for themselves and their children.

The widening economic and social chasm between prosperous Americans and impoverished people has shrunk the middle class and driven millions below the poverty line. It makes a mockery of the American Dream, the ideal that trumpets that prosperity may be shared by anyone who is willing to seek training and work hard, especially those who weren't born into privilege. Robert J. Samuelson, a nationally syndicated columnist for the *Washington Post*, writes, "The great middle class fear today is that the connection between personal aspirations and societal opportunities is breaking down."[29]

If the trend continues, and today's market forces, congressional gridlock, and a growing empathy gap suggest it will, the welfare cost of providing the basics of life to the poor will rise, as will the animosity between Republicans, a great number of whom favor cutting the poors' benefits, and Democrats, who believe the government has a moral obligation to help them.

---

29 Robert J. Samuelson, "In 2015, Repairing Middle Class will Help Restore American Dream," *Deseret News*, December 30, 2014, p. A9.

Chapter 8

Sharing Our Wealth

"I speak here of difficult societal needs that go well beyond the members of the [LDS] Church."[1]
— Jeffrey R. Holland, Member of the Quorum of the Twelve Apostles, Church of Jesus Christ of Latter-day Saints

M ormons gladly give tithes and offerings to the Church and other charities to help build the kingdom of God and support the disadvantaged and vulnerable, not only in the U.S. but abroad. LDS Charities helps relieve suffering caused by natural disasters such as earthquakes, tsunamis, hurricanes, fires, and flooding—not just for Mormons, but for non-members as well. In partnership with the Red Cross, the Red Crescent (Muslim relief organization), and other charities and governments, the Church provides sanitation kits, food, clean water, temporary shelter and medical supplies, among other critical needs. But is this level of support enough to address the basic needs of the extremely disadvantaged in the U.S.? Should Mormons do more?

The Immensity of the Problem
The early 1900s was an era in which the gap between the rich and poor was extensive and growing. Putnam and Campbell relate how a Salvation Army leader at the time observed that private philanthropy fell

---

1 Jeffrey R. Holland, "Are We Not All Beggars?" *Ensign*, November 2014, p. 41.

well short of meeting the needs of the poor. They quoted the leader as saying, "To right the social wrong by charity [alone] is like bailing the oceans with a thimble."[2]

A century later, things have not changed much. Numerous practicing and academic anti-poverty experts confirm that the need for assistance for the destitute far outstrips the capacity of churches and private charities to meet it. They have shot holes in the conservative dogma that private donations can cover the existing scope of poverty, especially with the substantial cuts in government programs being clamored for by Republicans in Congress.

A reporter for *philly.com,* the online publication of the *Philadelphia Inquirer,* interviewed several anti-poverty experts. In the article, Elizabeth Boris, Director of the Center on Nonprofits and Philanthropy at the Urban Institute, was quoted as saying, "There's a myth [about] charity out there. Anyone who thinks that private charity will make up for lowered government budgets is whistling Dixie." Boris' observation was echoed by Kathy Saile, Director of the Office of Domestic Social Development for the U.S. Conference of Catholic Bishops. "Americans are very generous but people don't appreciate the scope of poverty in the United States," she said. "The amount of hunger reduction by the federal government dwarfs what charities in the faith community are doing."[3]

Following World War II, Americans who had been trapped in poverty found themselves with a golden opportunity. An expanding American industrial sector was hungry to fill tens of millions of well-paying jobs with eager workers. The new prosperity gave rise to a strong middle class which, in turn, became the engine that drove the unprecedented growth of the nation's economy. It also narrowed the economic gap between the haves and have-nots. For the first time, regular people were optimistic they could participate in the American Dream, a life

---

2   Robert D. Putnam and David E. Campbell, *American Grace: How Religion Divides and Unites Us,* New York: Simon & Schuster, 2010, p. 258.
3   Alfred Lubrano, "Charity Can't Fill Holes in Aid to Poor," *philly.com,* May 2, 2013, at http://articles.philly.com/2013-05-02/news/38960249_1_charity-hunger-special-supplemental-nutrition-program (accessed April, 13, 2013).

where everyone had a chance to better themselves through opportunity and hard work.

But after more than half a century of prosperity, the nation is again seeing a widening of the economic gap with the rich becoming richer, the middle class shrinking, and more Americans sliding into poverty.[4] With less middle class money to pump into the economy, it's just a matter of time before the economy contracts. The trend is feeding a vicious cycle of job loss, an increasing number of Americans in need of assistance and reduced government revenues with which to help them.

Living Below the Poverty Line

It's important to understand how the "poverty line" reveals the extent to which the ranks of the poor are growing in America. In 2016, a family of four was considered to be living at the federal poverty level if they had an annual income of $24,300,[5] which amounts to $6,075 per person. To put it in perspective, the cost of one season ticket to the Utah Jazz professional basketball team sold for up to $7,260 for the 2016–2017 season.[6] The U.S. Census Bureau estimates there are close to 47 million impoverished people, or 15 percent of the total U.S. population. Of that number, 16 million children under age 18 make up one-third of the nation's poor. Single mothers, who shoulder the brunt of the burdens of poverty, represent nearly one of every three single-adult family households who live below the poverty threshold.[7]

4   "America's Shrinking Middle Class: A Close Look at Changes Within Metropolitan Areas," *Pew Research Center,* May 11, 2016, at http://www.pewsocialtrends.org/2016/05/11/americas-shrinking-middle-class-a-close-look-at-changes-within-metropolitan-areas/ (accessed November 19, 2016)

5   "Poverty Guidelines," *U.S, Department of Health and Human Services,* January 25, 2016, at https://aspe.hhs.gov/poverty-guidelines (accessed December 29, 2016).

6   "Season Membership," *44 United,* at http://go.lhmse.com/jazzseason-ticketsn (accessed December 29, 2016).

7   Carmen DeNavas-Walt, Bernadette D. Proctor, Jessica C. Smith, "Income, Poverty, and Health Insurance," *U.S. Census Bureau,* September 2013, pp.13, 15, 17-19, at http://www.census.gov/prod/2013pubs/p60-245.pdf (accessed February 11, 2015).

An additional 15 million people are defined as struggling in "near-poverty" with an annual family income between 100 and 125 percent of their poverty threshold.[8] For a family of four, 125 percent comes to $30,375, or $7,594 per person. All told, there are 62 million people in poverty and near-poverty in the U.S., approximately the entire population of the United Kingdom.[9]

The "Deep Poor"

The "deep poor" are those whose annual income is less than 50 percent of the government's poverty threshold. Their percentage of the impoverished population has, since 1975, jumped from 3.7 percent to 6.6 percent. Today, they number nearly 20 million people, an increase of 42 percent since the start of the Great Recession in 2007.[10]

What Counts as Income?

It's a little-known fact that the annual income earned from employment is not the only income used to determine whether a person or family falls below the poverty line. Their annual income also includes cash benefits from government anti-poverty programs. According to the U.S. Census Bureau, cash benefits include educational assistance, child support, unemployment compensation, workers' compensation, Social Security, Supplemental Security Income, veterans' payments, survivor benefits, pension or retirement income and other forms of public assistance.[11] If government benefits for the poor are cut, as Republicans in Congress plan to do, many more millions of low-income people

---

8   Charles Hokayem and Misty L. Heggeness, "Living in Near Poverty in the United States: 1966–2012," U.S. Census Bureau, May 2014, at https://www.census.gov/prod/2014pubs/p60-248.pdf (accessed February 14, 2015).
9   "Countries of the World," Worldatlas, at http://worldatlas.com/aatlas/populations/ctypopls.htm (accessed February 14, 2015).
10   Neil Shah, "U.S. Poverty Rate Stabilizes – For Some," The Wall Street Journal, October 11, 2013, at http://online.wsj.com/news/articles/SB10001424052702304500404579127603306039292 (accessed July 18, 2014).
11   "How the Census Bureau Measures Poverty," United States Census Bureau, at https://www.census.gov/hhes/www/poverty/about/overview/measure.html (accessed February 2, 2015).

will fall below the poverty line and swell the ranks of the poor and deep poor.

Tithes and Taxes: How the LDS Church and Governments Pool Resources

There's a strong belief among many conservative Mormons that they should share their wealth only with charitable donations to the Church (through tithes and offerings) and nonprofit agencies but not through "forced charity" to government anti-poverty programs. However, unknown to many Church members, Church leaders recognize that there are those needy for whom Church and other private resources are not enough and must be used in combination with government tax-funded welfare programs, directly or indirectly, to offer a greater level of anti-poverty assistance.

For example, LDS Humanitarian Services and LDS Charities donated $1.5 million in March 2014 to kick off the fundraising effort to build the Lantern House, a facility in Ogden, Utah that would provide a soup kitchen and temporary housing for homeless families. The facility was a project of the St. Anne's Homeless Shelter whose mission is to help residents become self-sufficient and find stable private housing. In addition to voluntary contributions, major funding came from the State of Utah. Also, the city of Ogden donated the land for the new facility.[12] St. Anne's also relied on federal TANF (Temporary Assistance for Needy Families) funds[13] authorized by the American Recovery and Reinvestment Act (ARRA) of 2009, passed by the Democratic majority in Congress and signed into law by President Barack Obama.

---

12   Marie Michel, "New Homeless Shelter Breaks Ground in Ogden," *Intermountain Catholic,* May 2, 2014, at http://www.icatholic.org/article/new-homeless-shelter-breaks-ground-in-ogden-8386673 (accessed May 10, 2014).
13   Cathy McKitrick, "Down to the Wire for Ogden Homeless Shelter Funding," *Standard-Examiner,* February 27, 2014, at http://go.standard.net/Local/2014/02/26/Down-to-the-wire-for-Ogden-homeless-shelter-funding.html (accessed May 11, 2014).

The Church donated $1.8 million in March of 2015 to the American Red Cross, which also receives funding from local, state and federal governments.[14]

In January 2013, the Church announced it was offering a $200,000 challenge grant to help fund an expansion of Salt Lake City's Detoxification Center, a now-completed project that has opened up dozens of new beds for the treatment of those who struggle with alcohol and drug addictions. The center is run by the Utah unit of Volunteers of America with whom the Church has an ongoing partnership. According to Zach Bale, Vice President of External Affairs, about half of the funding for the Center came from tax-supported public funds and half from the LDS Church and other community sources. In addition to the cost of the expansion, the annual operating budget of Utah's unit, which keeps the facility open, receives 95 percent of its support from government funds.[15]

Another sizable Church donation of $341,000 was designated to improve and expand a transitional housing center in Provo, Utah. The Food and Care Coalition operates the facility and partners with outside organizations to provide mental health and dental services as well as temporary housing. As with the Lantern House, it aims to help residents transition to private outside housing and utilizes state and federal funds from the Pamela Atkinson Homeless Trust Fund, Community Development Block Grant, Emergency Shelter Grant and the Federal Emergency Management Agency (FEMA).[16]

Several years ago the Church donated $250,000 to support construction of a residential facility to provide permanent housing for patients with severe chronic mental illness. The donation was made to mental health care provider Valley Mental Health, which served

14   Jason Swensen, "LDS Donate $1.8 Million to American Red Cross," *Deseret News*, March 13, 2015, p. B1.
15   Zach Bale, telephone interview with author, August 27, 2014.
16   Genelle Pugmire, "LDS Church Donates $341,000 to Provo Homeless Shelter," *Daily Herald*, November 9, 2010, at http://www.heraldextra.com/news/local/central/provo/lds-church-donates-to-provo-homeless-shelter/article_e07ceb5d-35bd-5849-a88f-9b2e6baa2d13.html (accessed August 28, 2014).

its clients with annual funding from state and county governments.[17] Since residents can only afford to live there if they receive federal Medicaid funds, the Church's donation, along with tax dollars, helped meet the needs of a vulnerable segment of the population.

The Church also sponsors Mormon Helping Hands, an organization that taps local volunteers in areas in the U.S. and around the world. According to the Church's News Room, they "partner with government and nonprofit organizations" in projects that range from natural disaster relief to community beautification efforts that often benefit the poor.[18] In many cases, the tens of thousands of volunteer hours donated by Mormon Hands saves millions of government dollars that taxpayers would have otherwise had to spend on the same projects.

The examples above are only a sampling of the many causes to which the LDS Church has made significant monetary and volunteer contributions to augment public government funds. While Church leaders emphasize the use of voluntary charity to incentivize self-sufficiency and alleviate as much human suffering as possible, they also realize that it must be combined with tax-financed safety nets to address the growing problem of poverty. It would seem to be a good reason for Latter-day Saints to support public welfare safety nets.

The Worthy and Unworthy

As I explained in Chapter 6 (*Laying the Blame on the Poor*), influential Republicans believe most of the poor have brought their troubles upon themselves by making bad choices. *Forbes* reported the results of a study that found that charitable donors who define themselves as having a moral social conscience are empathetic *only* toward those who they judged to be the "worthy" poor, those who they assumed were *not* responsible for their own plight. Consequently, consultants have advised nonprofits to change their marketing approach to assure

---

17   Church News, "Donation to Aid Mental Health Facility," *The Church of Jesus Christ of Latter-day Saints,* June 25, 1994, at http://www.ldschurch-newsarchive.com/articles/25131/Donation-to-aid-mental-health-facility. html, (accessed July 28, 2014).

18   Mormon Newsroom, "Mormon Helping Hands," *The Church of Jesus Christ of Latter-day Saints,* at http://www.mormonnewsroom.org/article/helping-hands (accessed July 28, 2014).

prospective donors that the recipients of their dollars will go only to the so-called worthy poor.[19]

However, it's unclear how nonprofits and their donors can judge who is worthy and who is not. There do not seem to be any uniform criteria for getting inside the heads and hearts of poor people, or to be familiar enough with their personal histories to be able to make the distinction. Is it right or moral to arbitrarily withhold our wealth from the poor on the unfounded premise that some are worthy and some are not? What would Jesus Christ do?

The Poor Give More

Even in the U.S., the wealthiest nation in the world, the combined efforts of private charities and government welfare programs fall far short of meeting the basic living needs of the vulnerable. One would think that people with higher incomes would be willing to sacrifice a greater share of their wealth to the less fortunate, including support for government safety net programs. But such is not the case. It is instructive to note that the poor have been found to give a higher percentage of their meager assets to their fellow poor than those who are better off.

A survey by McClatchy Newspapers found that the poor give at more than twice the rate to their fellow poor than high income people do, by a margin of 4.3 percent to 2.1 percent.[20] Researchers at the University of California at Berkeley and the University of Toronto conducted several experiments to see if they could replicate the McClatchy findings. They confirmed that poor participants in the experiments were more generous than their wealthier counterparts. They also found that higher-class participants would donate at the same rate as the poor, as long as they were exposed to the suffering of others in a highly emotional context (such as viewing well-publicized disasters like earthquakes, tsunamis, or starving children in war-torn nations), experiences that

19   Tom Watson, "What Makes People Generous: Charity, Empathy and Storytelling," *Forbes,* June 14, 2014, at http://www.forbes.com/sites/tomwatson/2014/06/30/what-makes-people-generous-charity-empathy-and-story-telling/ (accessed August 22, 2014).
20   Michael de Groote, "Studies Try to Find Why Poorer People Are More Charitable than the Wealthy, *Deseret News,* May 26, 2012, p. A1.

boost feelings of empathy. The researchers concluded that, in general, "lower class individuals proved to be more generous, compassionate, trusting and helpful compared with their upper class counterparts."[21]

In an article in *FoxBusiness*, Kate Rogers writes that multiple sources corroborated both the McClatchy and Berkeley study results. She referred to an article by Ken Stern in *The Atlantic* entitled "With Charity for All: Why Charities are Failing and a Better Way to Give." Citing Stern, Rogers wrote, "In 2011, Americans with earnings in the top 20% of income levels contributed, on average, 1.3% of their income to charity. Those at the bottom 20% donated 3.2% of their cash to charity — more than double of what their more-wealthy counterparts donated."[22]

The *FoxBusiness* article reported a similar finding by Ken Berger, CEO of the Charity Navigator, an organization that evaluates private, non-profit charities. Berger said data compiled by Charity Navigator indicates the rich give about 3 percent of their income to charity compared to between 4 and 5 percent by low-income people. Middle class donors give the least of all, at two-and-a-half percent. But the percentages don't tell the whole story. Berger said most charitable contributions made by the rich, about two-thirds, don't go to impoverished people, but to the arts, healthcare research institutions, and elite universities such as Yale, which has an endowed fund of over $19 billion, and other universities where most students come from wealthy families.[23]

Why do the poor give a greater share of their money to their fellow poor than those who are better off? Empathy. Pamela Atkinson is a well-known, highly respected advocate for the homeless in Salt Lake City. "[Poor people] know that even a small amount of giving can make

---

21 Paul K. Piff, et al., "Having Less, Giving More: the Influence of Social Class on Pro-social Behavior," *Journal of Personality and Social Society*, Vol. 99 (5), November 2010, at http://socrates.berkeley.edu/~keltner/publications/piff.2010.pdf (accessed May 22, 2013).

22 Kate Rogers, "Poor, Middle Class and Rich: Who Gives and Who Doesn't?" *FoxBusiness*, April 24, 2013, at http://www.foxbusiness.com/personal-finance/2013/04/24/poor-middle-class-and-rich-who-gives-and-who-doesnt/ (accessed August 4, 2014); and Ginia Bellafante, "Bulk of Charitable Giving Not Earmarked for the Poor," *The New York Times*, September 8, 2012, at http://www.nytimes.com/2012/09/09/nyregion/bulk-of-charitable-giving-not-earmarked-for-poor.html?_r=0 (accessed May 2, 2013).

23 Ibid.

a huge difference," she said. "They know it is going to make a differ-ence because they have experienced the difference themselves."[24]

Why is it important for all Latter-day Saints to know that the poor give more to their fellow poor than prosperous Americans do? Because, by virtue of their higher average income and spiritual responsibility to succor the destitute, it is hoped that their awareness of this fact would influence them to dig deeper into their pockets to give more to pri-vate charities as well as support government anti-poverty programs, despite the fact that they already tithe to the Church.

The Widow's Mite

If one looks at absolute dollar amounts instead of percentage of income, the wealthy donate a hefty three-fourths of the total income that goes to nonprofits. But it's the *percentage* of one's total assets contributed to charity that is the most telling indicator of a person's priorities and the degree of empathy he or she has for the poor. The biblical story of the widow's mite underscores this principle. In Mark 12:41–44, Jesus Christ demonstrates the clear gospel measure of charity: "And Jesus sat over against the treasury, and beheld how the people cast money into the treasury: and many that were rich cast in much. And there came a certain poor widow, and she threw in two mites, which make a farthing. And he called *unto him* his disciples, and saith unto them, Verily I say unto you, That this poor widow hath cast more in, than all they which have cast into the treasury: For all *they* did cast in of their of their abundance; but she of her want did cast in all that she had, even all her living." The widow's example reinforces the gospel principle that we should give as much of our means as we can to help those in need, especially those of us who are blessed with greater means. In line with this, wouldn't it be reasonable, as a sign of our faith, to expect people of good will to support public assistance for the poor rather than tear down such programs? Unless Americans are prepared to voluntarily donate enough money to replace the loss of state and federal assistance, and then some, we will surely find ourselves at odds with this basic Christian principle.

---

24   Michael de Groote, "Studies Try to Find Why Poorer People Are More Charitable than the Wealthy, *Deseret News,* May 26, 2012, p. A1.

Conclusion

Private charities, as crucial as they are in the fight against poverty, can supply only a fraction of the resources needed to lift the economic and social burdens from the backs of an immense and growing population of the poor. Therefore, public agencies are also essential to help provide the most basic of services to the most vulnerable among us. Yet many Republican representatives in federal and state governments, along with some Latter-day Saints and other conservatives, are bent on cutting public safety nets for the vast majority of those who languish below the poverty line. Democrats, on the other hand, are determined to give low-income people the benefit of the doubt without judging how they became destitute. Democrats see how the promise of the American Dream is fading quickly for those who are being driven out of the middle class by stagnant wages, declining employment, unaffordable education and the reduction of public assistance. If the more blessed among us shirk our moral obligation to give relief to our fellow men, women and children, we make a mockery of the widow and her mite.

Chapter 9

Myths about Charities

"[The] great enemy of the truth is very often not the lie – deliberate, contrived, and dishonest – but the myth – persistent, persuasive, and unrealistic."[1]

*John F. Kennedy, 35th President
of the United States*

Latter-day Saints risk being perceived as not being as compassionate toward the poor, especially the non-Mormon poor, as they purport to be. Many Mormons staunchly oppose government anti-poverty safety nets and believe that private charities, if adequately funded, could meet the needs of the downtrodden in the U.S. It's true that private charities are an essential component in the quest to help relieve the burdens of the poor. Most charities deserve all the contributions and volunteer time they can get. According to prevailing public opinion, mostly among conservatives, they are also believed to be more trustworthy, competent and efficient than government agencies at delivering much-needed services to the destitute. It will surprise most Americans, then, that close analysis of the nonprofit sector reveals that an extraordinary number of charities are not as forthright, trustworthy or efficient as Americans believe them to be.

---

1   John F. Kennedy Presidential Library and Museum Staff, "Commencement Address at Yale University, June 11, 1962," *John F. Kennedy Presidential Library and Museum,* at http://www.jfklibrary.org/Asset-Viewer/Archives/JFKWHA-104.aspx (accessed February 11, 2015).

Competition for donor dollars compels charities to underreport their costs and artificially make their overhead seem lower. They can't retain talented leaders and routinely suffer from bare-bones, inefficient staffing and infrastructure, shortcomings that force them to scale down their missions. Trustworthy? Most are. But fraud and waste are much higher in the nonprofit sector than the general public knows. And that is only the data that is reported, the tip of the iceberg. It's the purpose of this chapter to dispel the myths about charities and demonstrate how government safety net programs are generally better equipped to help the needy than the private sector, and, in many cases, may even be more cost-effective in doing so.

A Clash of Ideals

An ongoing dispute between conservatives and liberals is over which anti-poverty organizations are most effective at providing basic needs and educational opportunities for the poor — nonprofit charities or government programs. Conservative Republicans believe that charities that compete for donations in a free market system will be, through the weeding out process, more qualified and motivated to serve the nation's poor than, as they attest, wasteful and inefficient government programs. They argue that every tax dollar the government takes out of their pocket for public safety nets is a dollar they could have given to a nonprofit or spent to boost the economy (ostensibly to trickle down to the poor in the form of job opportunities). Liberals and moderate progressives, on the other hand, support the supplemental role of nonprofits but believe that robust government programs are also needed if America is to meet even a fraction of the need.

The Overhead Illusion

Before donors will contribute to a charity, they want to know which organizations will make the best use of their dollars. But they unwittingly damage the health of the charities they scrutinize by the near-exclusive use of a single criterion by which to make their assessment: overhead. Donors mistakenly believe that charities with the lowest overhead are invariably the best managers of their money.[2] Of course, keeping overhead as low as is *reasonably* possible is an important management skill. But the practice of using overhead alone to determine a charity's strength is one of the most hotly debated issues today among nonprofit experts. One group defends it. But a growing body of professionals argue that a charity should also be measured by its performance (also called its "cost-effectiveness") – its ability to spend just enough to meet its goals.[3]

What Is Overhead?

Overhead is expressed as a percentage of each dollar a charity spends on "front office" operating costs (often called "indirect costs"). If a charity says 25 cents of each dollar goes to overhead, it means the remaining 75 percent goes directly to its program activities in the field, which is explained in more detail below. Overhead consists of three types of front office expenditures: administration, fundraising and long-term investment.[4]

Administration includes management staff salaries and health insurance, office space and utilities, functions such as accounting, finance, public relations and legal concerns, the cost of liability and fire insurance, and compliance with reporting requirements such as tax forms, annual reports and audit results, among other centralized services.[5]

Fundraising keeps the flow of contributions coming in to keep a charity's doors open. It pays for the cultivation of donors, the salaries

---

2 Don Howard and Ann Goggins Gregory, "Don't Compromise 'Good Overhead' (Even in Tough Times)," *The Bridgespan Group,* October 28, 2008, at http://www.bridgespan.org/getattachment/17087e35-4d4d-4f79-a157-3b2b10bfc99a/Don-t-Compromise-Good-Overhead-%28Even-in-Tough-Time.aspx (accessed September 3, 2014).

3 "The Overhead Myth," *GuideStar,* June 21, 2013, at http://overheadmyth.com./faqs/ (accessed August 24, 2014).

4 William Bedsworth, Ann Goggins Gregory and Don Howard, "Nonprofit Overhead Costs: Breaking the Vicious Cycle of Misleading Reporting, Unrealistic Expectations, and the Pressure to Conform," *The Bridgespan Group,* April 1, 2008, at http://www.bridgespan.org/getdoc/c19b42a6-50c0-457e-89e3-6750309f277e/Nonprofit-Overhead-Costs-Break-the-Vicious-Cycle.aspx#.VAphffldWSp (accessed September 3, 2014).

5 Ibid.

and benefits of staff members and the materials for marketing and postage. It also pays for the cost of writing grant requests and applications to foundations, governments and individuals, and all other related expenses.[6]

Long-term investment makes possible the purchase of computers, materials and training (also called infrastructure) required to optimize a charity's current and anticipated needs in order to strengthen and expand its impact in the community. Investments are the least-funded of all the overhead components and the first to be cut in the effort to keep costs low.[7] In a widely quoted article in *The Stanford Social Innovation Review* entitled "The Nonprofit Starvation Cycle," the authors refer to the chronic underfunding of investments as a downward spiral, which they call the "starvation cycle," in which infrastructure improvements are perpetually underfunded, crippling both the charities' current performance and long-term vision.[8]

Overhead costs are not to be confused with *program costs*, often called "direct costs," which are not counted as overhead but are separately budgeted items used to put benefits directly into the hands of the intended recipients. They pay for hot meals, purchase and repair of vehicles (wheel chair accessible vans, etc.), utilities for homeless shelters, soup kitchens, drug rehab centers, facility maintenance, management of the receipt and disbursement of food, clothing, etc., and the compensation of personnel who recruit and manage volunteers.[9]

Cost-effectiveness

A growing number of experts in the nonprofit sector say donors should evaluate a charity by its overall performance, or cost-effectiveness, not just overhead. Cost-effectiveness is commonly referred to as getting the most "bang for the buck," with *bang* being how well a charity meets its mission and *buck* representing how much the organization spends

6   Ibid.

7   Ibid.

8   Ann Coggins Gregory and Don Howard, "The Nonprofit Starvation Cycle," *Stanford Social Innovation Review,* Fall 2009, at http://www.ssireview.org/articles/entry/the_nonprofit_starvation_cycle/ (accessed September 15, 2014)

9   "The Overhead Myth," *GuideStar,* June 21, 2013, at http://overheadmyth.com./faqs/ (accessed August 24, 2014).

to achieve it. An organization is cost-effective when it delivers an excellent, timely service while spending *no more than necessary* in terms of time and money. But becoming cost-effective will almost always increase overhead because it requires an optimal (not minimal) level of investment in management experience and capability, fundraising and improved infrastructure to keep the charity from falling behind in its ability to serve its poor recipients. Some nonprofits are good at one end of the cost-effectiveness equation but not at the other. For example, an organization might claim an extremely low overhead (cost) but do a poor job of delivering services to the poor (effectiveness). Conversely, it can do a wonderful job providing benefits to the needy but spends more money than necessary to do so. Neither of these cases is desirable. The best managed charity is one that achieves both optimal cost and effectiveness.

The Depth of Deception

As I mentioned above, charities routinely manipulate and underreport their overhead numbers to make themselves look good and more competitive for funders' dollars. The Bridgespan Group, a consultant to nonprofits, turned to a 2004 study by the Urban Institute's Center on Nonprofits and Philanthropy and the Center on Philanthropy at Indiana University to highlight the prevalence of irregular reporting. Researchers combed through the tax reports of 220,000 nonprofits and found "widespread reporting that defies plausibility." One in eight claimed to have spent no funds on management or administration. More than a third said they had not incurred any fundraising costs, an omission that allowed them to claim an overhead of 10 percent or lower. The expense of applying for foundation and government grants, an administrative task that requires significant staff hours, was underreported by over three-fourths of the charities.[10]

---

10   William Bedsworth, Ann Goggins Gregory and Don Howard, "Nonprofit Overhead Costs: Breaking the Vicious Cycle of Misleading Reporting, Unrealistic Expectations, and the Pressure to Conform," *The Bridgespan Group*, April 1, 2008, at http://www.bridgespan.org/getdoc/c19b42a6-50c0-457e-89e3-6750309f277e/Nonprofit-Overhead-Costs-Break-the-Vicious-Cycle. aspx#.VAphffldWSp (accessed September 3, 2014).

Deceptive reporting practices almost always go unchallenged by the Internal Revenue Service. Vague rules and definitions and loopholes on Form 990 along with the IRS's limited capacity to audit the forms has spawned a culture in which charities have a lot of wiggle room to make their own interpretations of what constitutes overhead without fear of running afoul of the law. Only organizations that are actually found to have deliberately failed to file the form run the risk of prosecution. In 2000, a survey by *The Chronicle of Philanthropy* found that "a majority of nonprofits said their accountants advised them to report zero in the fundraising section of (IRS) form 990."[11]

Estimates of Actual Charity Overhead Costs

A quick survey I conducted of the literature of a number of well-known charities found they claimed an average overhead of about 25 percent. For example, the March of Dimes quoted 24.4 percent. The Special Olympics said it spends 27.3 percent. The national office of the ALS Association reported 26.8 percent. The Muscular Dystrophy Association's rate was 24.2 percent. Yet a Bridgespan Group analysis found that a charity's reported overhead would increase by an estimated 5 to 20 percent if it reflected its actual investment requirements.[12] I've taken the average reported rate of 25 percent and added a compromise figure of 10 percent to account for what the real costs of investing would be if it was done realistically. I estimate, then, that a truthful average overhead rate over a range of charities would be about 35 percent if they were adequately funding their total operations. It should be noted that many charities report their overhead rates as being in the single digits, but such claims would appear to be in the extreme minority or deliberate exaggerations, unless the charities are very small and depend on part-

---

11   Ann Coggins Gregory and Don Howard, "The Nonprofit Starvation Cycle," *Stanford Social Innovation Review*, Fall 2009, at http://www.ssireview.org/articles/entry/the_nonprofit_starvation_cycle/ (accessed September 15, 2014).

12   William Bedsworth, Ann Goggins Gregory and Don Howard, "Nonprofit Overhead Costs: Breaking the Vicious Cycle of Misleading Reporting, Unrealistic Expectations, and the Pressure to Conform," *The Bridgespan Group*, April 1, 2008, at http://www.bridgespan.org/getdoc/c19b42a6-50c0-457e-89e3-6750309f277e/Nonprofit-Overhead-Costs-Break-the-Vicious-Cycle.aspx#.VAphffldWSp (accessed September 3, 2014).

time volunteers, as opposed to the salaried full-time staffs for the larger charities, to run the operations.

The Unintended Consequences of Underfunding Charities

As charities report deceptively low overhead numbers to attract prospective donors, they undermine their already-strained capacity to serve the needy. The practice inflates expectations, underfunds charity operations and creates a host of unintended consequences that threaten their missions and, in many cases, their viability. It also contradicts the belief of so many Republicans that charities are better equipped to address the scourge of poverty than government.

Erosion of Productivity

An example of how donor-forced underreporting of overhead erodes charities' productivity is they cannot be as productive as they need to be without updated computer systems. In order to increase their cost-effectiveness and long-term viability, nonprofits must have the funds to make the transition from antiquated and time-intensive manual processes to computerized ones. For those who already have computer networks in place, the great majority urgently need to upgrade or replace old, hand-me-down and mismatched hardware and software that are, in technology terms, several generations old. Updated computers with better designs will be much less likely to break down as often as the old ones, protecting valuable data from being lost. New computers will have higher storage capacity to retain and retrieve more data. New versions of software will not run on the older computers, denying users the advantages of cutting-edge, productivity-enhancing features. Updated systems will increase the accuracy, timeliness and transparency of tasks involving accounting and financial controls, donor list development, budget tracking, tax forms, grant requests, facility capacity usage, inventory, and performance metrics in the field. However, new technology is only as good as the people who use it. Staff training is also crucial to ensure maximum efficiency is realized with the updated equipment.[13]

Decimated Management Staffs and the Office Space Squeeze

With the charities' overhead budgets being squeezed, they are often forced to leave one or more executive management positions unfilled. It leaves less-experienced managers to wrestle with the higher responsibilities such as profit and loss analyses, budget projections, donor cultivation, public relations and strategic planning for capital projects, among other things. Also, budget cuts often force one or more charities to share office space, resulting in cramped and less efficient operations.[14]

The Intern Exodus

Charities historically have hired interns who are eager to serve the vulnerable among us and pursue careers in social work. They are viewed as the next generation of managers who will lead nonprofits in the years ahead. Charities would like to offer compensation, even if nominal, to attract interns, many of whom live on a shoestring. But shrinking budgets have caused charities to offer mostly unpaid internships, discouraging more and more prospective trainees and sending them searching for better opportunities. One prospective nonprofit intern saw her peers in different fields making more money and questioned whether a career in charitable work was worth it. Another said she had been "priced out" of her first (nonprofit) career choice.[15]

Volunteer Burnout

Charities depend heavily on volunteers who become discouraged when they see staffs are being cut and the charity's ability to fulfill its mission is compromised. Many volunteers, most of whom are passionate

---

13   "Getting What We Pay For: Low Overhead Limits Nonprofit Effectiveness," *Center on Nonprofits and Philanthropy, Urban Institute Center on Philanthropy, Indiana University,* August 2004, at http://webarchive.urban. org/UploadedPDF/311044_NOCP_3.pdf (accessed September 3, 2014).
14   Ibid.
15   Amy McDonald, "Nonprofit Internships: Can You Afford to Work for Free?" *Deseret News,* September 5, 2014, p. A5.

about helping their cause, receive less training and lose their sense of satisfaction and leave. It's not uncommon for those who remain to attempt to take on a greater workload. However, they are also at risk of burning out and leaving.[16]

Fraud, Waste and Abuse

Another myth about charities is that they are more honest, trustworthy, frugal and careful stewards of their donors' money than government programs. Despite the admirable job that many charities do as stewards of other people's money, the facts show that the nonprofit world has a major fraud, waste and abuse problem of its own.

From 2008 to 2012, the *Washington Post* did an analysis of nonprofit disclosure forms submitted by charities to the federal government. The purpose was to determine how much money the nonprofits lost from embezzlement and other unauthorized means. The losses, referred to as "diversion-of-funds" in nonprofit jargon, amounted to hundreds of millions of dollars. The analysis found that more than 1,000 nonprofits had had significant unapproved shortfalls in the previous year. The deficit due to embezzlement by a senior executive at one nonprofit alone tallied $3.4 million. An examination of ten of the largest nonprofits revealed that their losses "potentially totaled more than half a billion dollars." In 2009 alone, 285 diversion-of-funds totaled $170 million.[17]

The reported losses are just the tip of the iceberg. An estimated half of the organizations did not report the full amounts they lost. They weren't required to report unless the diverted amount totaled $250,000 or more or exceeded 5 percent of their annual income. Out of fear of ruining their reputations and alienating donors, many nonprofits

---

16   John Barrymore, "How Volunteer Burnout Works," *Howstuffworks.com*, April 28, 2009, at http://money.howstuffworks.com/economics/volunteer/ information/volunteer-burnout.htm (accessed September 9, 2014).

17   Joe Stephens and Mary Pat Faherty, "Inside the Hidden World of Thefts, Scams and Phantom Purchases at the Nation's Nonprofits," *The Washington Post*, October 26, 2013, at http://www.washingtonpost.com/investigations/ inside-the-hidden-world-of-thefts-scams-and-phantom-purchases-at-the-na-tions-nonprofits/2013/10/26/825a82ca-0c26-11e3-9941-6711ed662e71_story. html (accessed September 18, 2014).

don't prosecute wrongdoers in order to keep the case from becoming part of the public record. Another reason the total losses are higher than reported is not all charities are required to register with the federal government and report their financial status. Unlike the 1.6 million nonprofits that are registered, an additional 700,000, such as churches and smaller organizations, are exempt from having to submit reports.[18]

To put the nonprofit fraud problem in perspective, the *Post* reported that Marquet International, a Boston-based firm that conducts an annual analysis of white-collar fraud, discovered that "nonprofits and religious organizations accounted for one-sixth of all major embezzlements, second only to the financial services industry."[19] Clearly, the nonprofit sector, including anti-poverty charities, suffers from its own fraud, waste and abuse problem and cannot guarantee that a donor's contributions are better used than his or her taxes for government programs.

Is Government Better?

Government anti-poverty agencies, like charities, incur financial losses from fraud, inefficiencies, and the errant issuance of benefits. Some 80 federal programs that provide cash, food, housing, medical care and social services are administered by different agencies with overlapping missions, poor coordination, inconsistent means-testing and fragmented delivery systems. Efforts to reform the system have met resistance due to bureaucratic inertia and a lack of resolve by lawmakers. Despite these problems, government agencies offer a number of important advantages that the nonprofit sector cannot match.

Is it possible to make a thorough apples-to-apples comparison between the cost-effectiveness of government anti-poverty programs and charities? The short answer is no. There are a number of differences in the way government and charities define overhead and performance. Yet the numbers give rise to a provocative question: Is it possible that some of the government's largest low-income assistance programs deliver more services more efficiently than charities? A look at the

18   Ibid.
19   Ibid.

reported overhead rates for a number of large public anti-poverty programs provides intriguing food for thought and invites further research.

Many government programs, despite their inefficiencies, have a tremendous economy-of-scale advantage. Their overhead costs are pegged by some sources as being less, sometimes much less, than my estimated overhead rate of 35 percent for private nonprofits, if adjusted for their real investment needs. A study by the Center on Budget and Policy Priorities evaluated the administration costs of nine large programs, including Medicaid (the largest) and the food stamp program, now known as SNAP—Supplemental Nutrition and Assistance Program. It found that the average government administration costs across the programs, as a percentage of the cost of claims processed (which I compare to a charity's indirect expenses), ranged from 1 to 8 percent.[20]

For example, the *combined* federal and state administrative costs for Medicaid totaled 4.6 percent.[21] The Kaiser Health News, an editorially independent publication of the politically neutral Kaiser Family Foundation, wrote that Medicaid's administration costs were less than 7 percent.[22] The American Academy of Family Physicians issued a paper in which it said Medicaid's administrative costs ranged 4 to 6 percent of claims paid, which ranked it "among the lowest of any healthcare payer in the country."[23]

20   Robert Greenstein, "Romney's Charge that Most Federal Low-Income Spending Goes for Overhead and Bureaucrats is False for Major Low-Income Programs, More than 90 percent Goes to Beneficiaries," *Center on Budget and Policy Priorities*," January 23, 2012, at http://www.cbpp.org/cms/?-fa=view&id=3655 (accessed September 13, 2013).

21   Ibid.

22   Phil Galewitz, "Medicaid, True or False?" *Kaiser Health News,* July 1, 2009, at http://www.kaiserhealthnews.org/stories/2009/july/01/medicaid-true-or-false.aspx (accessed September 13, 2013).

23   Tim M. Henderson, "Medicaid Topics, State-by-State Comparisons Administrative Costs," *American Academy of Family Physicians,* December 2005, at http://www.aafp.org/dam/AAFP/documents/advocacy/coverage/medicaid/ES-MedicaidAdministrativeCosts-121305.pdf (accessed September 13, 2013).

The Advantages of Government Safety Nets

Several criteria demonstrate how government assistance programs have built-in advantages over the private sector. Several examples are provided below.

Means Testing

A major difference that affects the overhead of charities and government is means-testing, the administrative cost of determining a person's eligibility to receive welfare benefits. Government programs devote a significant percentage of their anti-poverty program overhead budget to reduce fraud, waste and abuse by determining who is eligible for assistance, whose eligibility should be recertified at prescribed intervals and who no longer meets the criteria for aid. On the other hand, poverty-focused charities, with some exceptions, don't means-test at all, preferring to serve all who come to them for assistance without presuming to know who deserves help and who doesn't.

Adequate Office Space

Another factor that makes it difficult to make a comparison between charities and government overhead is the cost of leasing office space. Some government programs include "building lease management" in their overhead to ensure, for the most part, that they have enough space (sometimes barely) to function as expected. Similarly, many charities pay for office space while others use donated offices and, in some cases, share the space and cost with other charities. The sharing option among charities is almost always the result of inadequate funding and often creates such cramped conditions that they are unable to function in a cost-effective way.

Continuity and Resilience of Service

During downturns in economic cycles, unemployment goes up along with the number of poor who need safety net services. At the same time, nonprofits undergo painful cutbacks in their revenue streams, especially by corporate funders who cut donations as they realize lower profits. The fickleness of donors (even in the best of times) interjects a high degree of uncertainty with regard to charities' budgets, rendering them unable to plan resources or react to the increased demand for their services during a tough economy. In comparison, government social programs are more insulated from economic cycles. Their beneficiaries are able to count on a consistent flow of assistance, unless Congress cuts benefits.

Low Management Turnover

Turnover is the rate at which managers leave an organization. One advantage of government safety nets is the presence of a professional, experienced management team, ostensibly with a relatively low turnover due to competitive salary, benefits and retirement programs. While critics decry such employees as an "entrenched bureaucracy," supporters appreciate them as a consistent, reliable cog in a system where their ability to navigate a myriad of laws, rules and regulations (albeit in need of simplification) is essential. Smaller charity budgets, on the other hand, lead to higher management turnover.

Geographical Reach

The governments' massive benefit distribution pipeline has a geographical reach that even the largest of charities cannot match. With a few exceptions, such as national organizations like the Salvation Army, charities are local or regional in nature and can only serve people located close to their facilities. Government programs, on the other hand, extend to every corner of the nation and are better positioned to help the needy where they live, including in less-populated areas where most charities cannot afford to operate.

Savings through Fiscal Clout

The sheer size of government agencies enables them to negotiate steep discounts for medical procedures, drugs, IT equipment and thousands of other commodities, discounts that charities can't get. The net result is that government agencies save billions of dollars each year.

Dampening the Ripple Effect

The Republican belief that dismantling government anti-poverty programs would save taxpayer money is false. By significantly slashing or eliminating such programs, the expensive social costs of a fast-growing class of downtrodden people trapped in poverty would have a powerful ripple effect throughout society. Even *with* the government programs, the social cost is stunning. A study by the *Center for American Progress* reported that childhood poverty today already costs taxpayers half a trillion dollars per year.[24] Rather than bolstering the already inadequate educational and job prospects for the vulnerable, the costs of poor health, gang membership, a rapid acceleration of crime and an overwhelmed criminal justice and penal system would soar.

Conclusion

There's an ingrained myth that private charities are superior to government programs in delivering services to the poor. But, as we have seen, there is a compelling body of evidence that says this isn't true. While charities are a tremendous, indispensable asset in the fight against poverty, their resources are much too meager and dependent upon uncertain private donations to provide a reliable flow of aid to those in need. Only the government, with its vast resources, is capable of providing the aid necessary to provide the basics of life to so many millions of the needy, especially during economic downturns when the need is greatest. It's also important to note that thousands of charities would go out of business if their volunteer donations were not augmented by government grants provided by public anti-poverty programs.

Whether or not we are guided by faith in a higher power, regardless of our political ideology or affiliation, our challenge is to ask ourselves if we are sharing enough of our blessings with a rapidly growing family of our destitute fellow men, women and children who hurt for the lack of them. Latter-day Saints, given their well-known opposition to public safety nets, need to be aware of the risk of being perceived by the public at large as being less sensitive to the poor than they should be.

---

24   Editorial staff, "In Our Opinion: Fighting Poverty is More than a Clear Moral Imperative; it is Also an Economic Necessity," *Deseret News,* October 27, 2012, at http://www.deseretnews.com/article/765613897/Fighting-poverty-is-more-than-a-clear-moral-imperative-it-is-also-an-economic-necessity.html?pg=all (accessed October 2, 2013).

Part 3

Chapter 10

Lean and Mean Republican Government

"I think government can't be compassionate."[1]

— Becky Lockhart, The late Republican Speaker
of the Utah House of Representatives
and LDS Church member

Political power held by Latter-day Saint Republicans can be felt in states where their numbers are significant enough to give them an influential voice in determining the makeup of their state legislatures and congressional delegations. This is true in Arizona, Idaho, Wyoming, Nevada and Utah. It's also true in other states where no party has more than a thin majority, where even a small but unified bloc of voters can tip the scales in a close election. Of course, Utah is where Latter-day Saints affiliated with the GOP have the greatest sway, given their sheer numbers as a percentage of the state population. Utah is where LDS Republican ideology is amplified to so great an extent that it inundates its political institutions at all levels of government. So, while Utah's political environment is the focus of this chapter, the lessons learned from its long-term domination by the Republican Party provides useful insights as to how that domination has a significant effect on the Church and its members in the U.S. and internationally.

---

1   Becky Lockhart, interviewed by author, August 15, 2013.

Republicans are widely (and in many individual cases, unfairly) characterized as lacking empathy for the poor, that they put cost ahead of the depth of the needs of the disadvantaged when prioritizing resources. Even prominent LDS Utah Republicans acknowledge there is a perception that their party does not care enough for poor citizens. The late Becky Lockhart, then-Speaker of the Utah House of Representatives, conceded that "there's this belief that somehow Republicans, or conservatives, hate poor people and don't want to help poor people." She countered that "*even* conservatives" [italics added] believe government safety nets are appropriate in cases where people cannot help themselves."[2] Does this stance by Lockhart and the most vocal members of the overpowering Republican majority in Utah's Legislature, some eighty percent of whom are Mormons, cast the Church in a bad light? (In Chapter 12, *The Church Gets Blamed*, examples of how "blame-by-association" tarnishes the Church's reputation and its ability to perform its mission are addressed.)

Lockhart gave an example of what she believed constituted an case of Republican generosity toward the disadvantaged. She cited how Utah Republican lawmakers joined Democrats in voting for funds to support a preschool program for autistic children. The first reason she gave for the passing the bill was that it would save taxpayers' money in the long run. "These kids are going to grow up whether they have early therapy or not," Lockhart said. "And they're going to burden public education." She said it would be a better investment for the state to send an autistic child to a preschool program where he or she would cost only $10 per month (Lockhart used made-up numbers for the sake of simplicity), as opposed to waiting until the child reaches Kindergarten when the cost could be more like $30 per month. The Speaker added that her ideological philosophy as a conservative Republican was to minimize government's cost and role in providing such support. "So it's a conservative thing to do. It's also compassionate" she said. But she quickly corrected herself: "Maybe I shouldn't have said 'compassion' because I think government can't be compassionate."[3]

---

2   Ibid.
3   Ibid.

Many LDS Democrats would agree with Lockhart's view that the cost of public safety nets should be an important consideration when making policy for the treatment of the poor and disadvantaged. But they believe that it's the government's responsibility to engage in "affordable compassion," that government should *first* consider the magnitude of the plight of the poor, and, secondly, rationally prioritize funds to commit an appropriate share of a balanced state budget to meet their needs.

The Best-managed State?

Governor Gary Herbert and Republicans in the Utah Senate and House of Representatives have done many good things for the people of Utah, especially in terms of fostering a business-friendly environment. And they trumpet Utah as the "best-managed state" in the nation, according to *Forbes,* a pro-business publication. They credit their conservative fiscal policies for leading the state out of the eighteen-month Great Recession of December 2007–June 2009, with a robust economic recovery and an unemployment rate that dropped from 8.4 percent to 3.6 percent between 2009 and 2014, adding nearly 90,000 jobs. (As of 2016 the state's unemployment rate stood at 3.1 percent). The governor said the state's strong economy is "the rising tide that lifts all boats."[4] But are the poor in the same boat? Can the state really claim the mantle of "best-managed" when a growing number of disadvantaged Utahns are falling below the poverty line?

The Growth of Poverty in Utah

Despite the state's improving employment picture, it appears that relatively few of the new jobs are being filled by poor people. In fact, poverty has increased at the same time that better-off Utahns are gaining employment. The Department of Workforce Services reports that the number of people living in poverty has "risen steadily" since 2000. The U.S. Census Bureau reports that between 2000 and 2012 Utah's poverty rate increased 4.1 percent compared to the national average of 3.7 percent. It ranks Utah in the bottom one-third of all states with

---

4   Gary Herbert, "Executing Fundamentals for a Better Bottom Line," *Deseret News,* April 13, 2014, p.G2.

major poverty problems.[5] Utah's Department of Welfare Services estimates there are over 380,000 Utahns living in poverty, or 13.6 percent of the population. It says that more than 16 percent of the state's children under 18, or almost 137,000, live below the poverty line.[6] Does this sound like something the best-managed state would allow to happen?

Public Education: A Shaky Prospect for the Poor

Education is the key to future success for the less fortunate. It is one of the most powerful tools for minorities, low-income and special needs students to successfully integrate into mainstream society and become self-sufficient. But for decades, Utah's Republican lawmakers have .not devoted adequate resources to K-12 public education, leaving behind disadvantaged minority students who need additional help to keep up with their wealthier peers. The Utah State Board of Education issued a news release in November 2016 that shows that the rate of Utah Hispanics who graduate from high school is 13 percent below that of white students. Blacks lag behind whites by 14 percent and American Indians suffer a 17 percent deficit compared to white Utahns.[7] Board of Education data says the gaps are slowly closing but without a substantial increase in funding by the Legislature, these small gains are at significant risk of being reversed.

Today, Utah is mired at the bottom of the 50 states and the District of Columbia in terms of per-pupil spending.[8] Utah's teachers' morale is low. They are often scapegoated for poor school results. They suf-

---

5   Bishaw, Alemayehu, "Poverty: 2000 to 2012," *U.S. Census Bureau,* September 2013, p. 5 (table 2), at https://www.census.gov/prod/2013pubs/acsbr12-01.pdf (accessed October 15, 2014).

6   "Utah's Second Annual Report on Intergenerational Poverty, Welfare Dependency, and the Use of Public Assistance, *Utah Department of Welfare Services,* 2013, at https://jobs.utah.gov/edo/intergenerational/igp13.pdf (accessed October 16, 2014).

7   Mark Peterson, "Utah's High School Graduation Rate Rises to 85 percent in 2016," *Utah Board of Education,* November 22, 2016, at http://schools.utah.gov/main/INFORMATION/Online-Newsroom/DOCS/2016/November22.aspx (accessed January 3, 2017).

8   Benjamin Wood, "We're Num*ber 51: Utah Last Again for Per-Student Spending,"*The Salt lake Tribune, June 2, 2015, at http://www.sltrib.com/news/2579711-155/were-no-51-utah-last-again (accessed January 3, 2017).

fer burnout from large class sizes, a shrinking number of teachers' aides and too few counselors which results in a lack of much needed one-on-one attention for those who need it the most.

Also, Utah's teachers have among the lowest starting salaries in the nation. In an article in the *Deseret News,* the National Education Association indicates that "Utah was ranked 36th in 2012 in the nation for its starting salary of $33,081." In 2016, the situation was not much better with teachers' salaries starting at $35,768,[9] less than 150 percent of the 2016 federal poverty level, or about $8,900 per person per year for a family of four.

Teacher turnover in Utah has also reached crisis levels. The Utah State Office of Education reports that fully one-third of first-year teachers drop out of the profession and opt not to go on to a second year. The dropout rate is even higher for teachers who quit within five years — 42 percent — at a time when more than 10,000 students are being added to Utah's public school system each year.[10]

Many bright but disadvantaged students suffer from low graduation rates and are unable to qualify for higher paying jobs. It perpetuates a downward cycle in which Utah is graduating an inadequate pool of qualified workers and the well-documented inability of corporations to fill existing and future job openings in the state. A study by Georgetown researchers predicts that, by 2018, 66 percent of the jobs in Utah will require employees to have training or education beyond high school.[11] A shortage of qualified workers threatens to discourage corporations from adding jobs to the state's economy. It's likely to cause a downward spiral in which state income tax receipts go down while an increasing number of uneducated, underemployed, unemployed and needy Utahns put a strain on dwindling social welfare budgets.

For the state to be able to provide enough qualified people to fill the projected number of high quality job openings, the education system

---

9 Morgan Jacobsen, "Utah's Teacher Problem," *Deseret News,* June 10, 2016, p. A1.

10 Ibid.

11 Jasen Lee, "State Should Invest in Education to Meet Job Growth, Analysts Say," *Deseret News,* February 15, 2011, at http://www.deseretnews. com/article/705366765/State-should-invest-in-education-to-meet-job-growth-analyst-says.html (accessed January 29, 2013).

will have to tap the too-often unrealized potential of its minority students. According to Education First, a Salt Lake City–based education advocacy group that claims some 50,000 members, the diversity of Utah's population is growing more quickly than in most other regions. The group projects that by 2050, nearly one-third of Utah's population will consist of racial and ethnic minorities.[12]

While it's convenient to put all the blame on the Legislature for grossly shortchanging the K-12 education system, the culpability also lays with Utah's taxpayers who have historically balked at raising taxes to support the schools. They'll have an opportunity to change this. Senior leaders in Utah's business community have formed an organization called Our Schools Now to put an initiative on the ballot in 2018 to give the public a chance to vote to increase their state property taxes from 5 percent to 5.875 percent. If approved, it would raise an estimated $744 million per year to improve Utah's schools, universities and colleges. Zions Bank President and CEO Scott Anderson, co-chair of Our Schools Now, said the state's economy can't be expected to grow unless Utah taxpayers approve the ballot initiative.[13] If the initiative fails, Utah's public school system will continue to suffer from its ignominious reputation as one of the worst-supported education systems in the nation, with its teachers and students (particularly minorities) bearing the brunt of it.

How can Utah's leaders say they preside over the best-managed state when the state's public education system has declined to such a great extent?

The State Employee Pension Fund Fiasco

At the same time Utah's Republican lawmakers are crowing over the state's supposed ranking as the best-managed state by *Forbes*, they've been mishandling the state's public employees' pension fund known as the Utah Retirement System (URS). Lawmakers have resorted to making up for their shortsightedness by raiding over $200 million in tax dollars

---

12 Benjamin Wood, "Report Shows Utah Schools Improving," *Deseret News,* August 8, 2013, p.A1.

13 Ben Lockhart, "Business Leaders Push Tax Hike for Schools," *Deseret News,* November 30, 2016, p. B1.

that should have gone to education and diverting them to the pension fund to keep it from defaulting on its promises to public employees. Utah State Auditor John Dougall issued a report in December 2016 in which he criticized the Legislature for not making the tough budgetary choices to stave off the pension crisis.[14]

It isn't the first time Dougall has warned state lawmakers that they're underfunding the $23 billion pension fund and threatening the benefits of Utah's 40,000 retired and more than 80,000 active employees. As early as 2013, he alerted the Legislature that their prolonged lack of action to plug the gap between their promises to public employees and the pension's solvency was rapidly making the problem worse.[15]

According to a *Deseret News* article, Dougall, a former Republican member of Utah State House of Representatives, said in his 2016 report, "[Underfunding the pension] is just one example of the painful consequences of the temptation of previous generations to mortgage their children's future by spending money [lawmakers] did not have." He said if the $204 million that had been diverted to the pension had been spent instead on education it could have raised teachers' salaries by about 14 percent or provided for other critical improvements. Certainly, a major cause of the legislators' lack of accountability is the fact that "Utah is the only Western state that allows its retirement system to conduct business behind closed doors," wrote a reporter for the *Deseret News*.[16]

The poor management of the public pension fund and sequent diversion of tax dollars from a deteriorating education system is hardly a hallmark of a well managed state, much less the best-managed state.

Preschools Starved of Funds

Preschool (also called "Pre-K," for pre-Kindergarten) education is an important tool and indicator of future success in education, especially

---

14   Dennis Romboy, "Report: Public Education Lost $204M, Diverted to Pensions," *Deseret News*, December 14, 2016, p. B1

15   Dennis Romboy, "Audit Questions Long-term Viability of State Pension Fund," *Deseret News*, February 26, 2013, at http://debtdiagnosis.com/wp-content/uploads/2013/03/Audit-questions-long-term-viability-of-state-pension-fund-_-Deseret-News-1.pdf (accessed December 17, 2016).

16   Dennis Romboy, "Report: Public Education Lost $204M, Diverted to Pensions," *Deseret News*, December 14, 2016, p. B1.

for the one out of six young Utah children who live in low income households. But Utah legislators have long been lukewarm, at best, toward such programs and have provided minimal funding, mostly for half-hearted pilots. Both the Sutherland Institute and Eagle Forum, two powerful conservative lobbying organizations that have substantial influence over legislative policy in Utah, have come out against spending public funds for preschools.

One such program is Head Start, a time-tested and widely used federal program that provides food and clothing for at-risk kids and teaches them learning and social skills as well as nutritional and health education. For example, a major eight-year study of 44,000 preschool-aged students (including 19,000 low-income Head Start kids) by researchers at the University of Michigan found that a significantly higher percentage of obese Head Start students, after one year, were able to achieve normal weight compared to other groups.[17]

Yet Utah is one of only seven states that does not provide any funding to supplement federal dollars for the 50-year old program. Despite increasing demands and expenses for its services, the Legislature's unwillingness to support Head Start has resulted in a waiting list of some 800 vulnerable children at one Salt Lake County Head Start provider alone.[18]

When children are not offered an early introduction to learning and social skills, studies show they have a high risk of falling into intergenerational poverty, addiction, crime, teen pregnancy and domestic abuse. In addition to fulfilling a moral imperative, the state would be dollars ahead if it helped educate its poor to gain jobs and pay income taxes rather than living off them.

Low Priority for Mental Illness and Addiction

A state should not claim it is the "best-managed" until it makes the compassionate treatment of the mentally ill and those addicted to drugs and alcohol a higher funding priority. According to the 2014 Annual Report

---

17   Lindsey Tanner, "Obese Kids May Slim Down with Head Start," *Associated Press via Deseret News*, January 12, 2015, p. A3.

18   Amy Choate-Nielsen, "The War on Poverty: Why It's Still Being Waged 50 Years After it Began," *Deseret News*, January 19, 2014, p.A1.

of Utah's Division of Substance Abuse and Mental Health, only slightly more than 19 percent of adults and children suffering from substance abuse and mental illness received the treatment they needed.[19] It still left 81 percent untreated. Without therapy, their symptoms almost always get worse and often lead to arrest and imprisonment for preventable drug and other offenses. This lack of therapy denies the mentally ill and the addicted a reasonable chance to receive education and gainful employment. Not only that, by incarcerating people who could otherwise avoid prison with appropriate therapy, taxpayers are burdened with a heavy cost since it costs the state nearly $30,000 per year to house a single prisoner.[20] .

Utah State Prison: "The Largest Mental Health Institution in the State"

The Utah State Prison has been called the largest and the most inept behavioral health institution in the state. Steven Gehrke, then-spokesman for the Utah Department of Corrections, said close to 40 percent of the total inmate population — then at 6,991 — are known to suffer from a mental illness. "Prisons aren't designed to cater to the mentally ill," Gehrke said.[21] Correctional officers are not trained to handle the inmates. There is a severe shortage of clinicians and therapists and a lack of beds in its psychiatric wing. And the response to mentally impaired prisoners who are difficult to handle is often to put them in solitary confinement, where their condition is almost sure to worsen, where, in some cases, it has led to suicide.[22]

---

19   2014 Annual Report, *Utah State Tax Commission, January 2015,* pp. 17–18, at http://dsamh.utah.gov/pdf/Annual%20Reports/2014%20Annual%20 Report%20Final%20Web%201_22_15.pdf (accessed April 14, 2015).

20   Kelsey Warner, "These States Have the Highest Cost Per Prisoner," *thetimesnews,com,* May 3, 2016, at http://www.thetimesnews.com/ news/20160503/state-by-state-how-much-does-it-cost-to-keep-someone-in-prison (accessed March 10, 2017).

21   Wendy Leonard, "Study: Jails Becoming Nation's New Asylums," *Deseret News,* April 11, 2014, p. A1.

22   Katie McKellar, "Advocates Urge Criminal Justice Reforms," *Deseret News,* March 10, 2015, p. A1.

Many mentally ill offenders are arrested because they self-medicate with and become addicted to drugs and alcohol, leading to substance abuse-related crimes. Historically, they have been remanded to prison because state laws defined such offenses, even non-violent ones, as felonies instead of less-punitive misdemeanors. In recognition of this long-standing problem, the 2015 Utah Legislature, to their credit, passed a "criminal justice reform" law to downgrade some substance abuse-related violations to misdemeanors with a provision that substance abusers receive appropriate treatment.[23] Lawmakers appropriated $14 million from the general fund for rehabilitation services[24] with the objective of reducing a high rate of recidivism (estimated to be 46 percent)[25] and disrupting the "revolving door" cycle that sees repeat offenders return to prison, in many cases multiple times.

But will $14 million per year be enough to achieve the reduced imprisonment rates envisioned by the Legislature? Many would call it inadequate, especially since it's estimated that the savings realized by reducing the prison population would be more than $500 million over 20 years[26] Given the tremendous expected return on investment (ROI being an overriding criterion for GOP lawmakers), it would be much more likely to succeed if legislators would invest more in the program. This is especially true during the critical start-up phase when experts and support personnel are hired and related resources are purchased. It's a complex process during which entire program goes through early growing pains before it becomes efficient and effective and starts producing the hoped for outcomes.

---

23   Katie McKellar, "Herbert Signs Bills for Education Funding, Criminal Justice Reform," *Deseret News,* March 31, 2015, http://www.deseretnews. com/article/865625470/Herbert-signs-bills-for-education-funding-criminal-justice-reform.html?pg=all (accessed April 6, 2015).
24   Michael Kennedy, Utah State Representative (R-Alpine), email exchange with author, March 24, 2015.
25   Lisa Riley Roche, "Expert: Reforms Can Control Prison Costs," *Deseret News,* January 16, 2015, p. A1.
26   Lisa Riley Roche, "Bill Would Make 'Epic Shift' in Crime Cases," *Deseret News,* February 19, 2015, p. A1, and Adam Gelb (related expert), "Utah's 2015 Criminal Justice Reforms," Pew Charitable Trusts, June 18, 2015, at http://www.pewtrusts.org/en/research-and-analysis/issue-briefs/2015/06/utahs-2015-criminal-justice-reforms (accessed January 4, 2017).

There are many other questions related to funding for the treatment program. Will $14 million be enough pay for the additional probation and parole supervision resources called for by the bill's sponsors? How well will it meet the needs of an expanded mental health court system that has been chronically underfunded? Rehabilitation programs must be augmented by effective community-based efforts to provide training and employment for those that need them, particularly the high percentage that are poor. Will the funding achieve that? Since it's most likely to take several years for the rehabilitation program to take root and show discernable results, will lawmakers have the patience to let it mature or will they declare it a failure after a year or two and shut it down? The Legislature has taken a step in the right direction but it remains to be seen if the uncertainty surrounding the availability of funding and other resources can be resolved.

The Needy: More than Just a Healthcare Budget Item

The less fortunate are much more than just a dollarized line item on the Utah State budget. They are real people suffering real pain. They depend on the empathy of elected officials to help relieve their suffering. Their plights often lead to escalated medical crises and financial ruin which makes them even more dependent on government programs to survive. A large part of the problem in Utah is that the Utah State Legislature has repeatedly chosen not to accept federal Medicaid dollars to expand Medicaid funds or liberalize eligibility requirements so that many of the poor in crisis go unserved.

The following stories tell how unfortunate Utahns urgently need but have not received adequate government-supported healthcare. They are but a few of the thousands of such stories in Utah.

Elyza Carrillo

Three-year-old Elyza Carrillo spends much of her life with a feeding tube in her stomach. She was born with a hole in her heart. Children with this condition typically don't eat enough because they can't develop the suction ability to ingest adequate amounts of food. The tube shunts liquid nourishment into her body. She has never tasted nutritional foods much less birthday cake, ice cream or popcorn.

Her father, Eric Carrillo, works as a technical services contractor for the Utah Council of the Blind in Salt Lake City. Legally blind himself, Carrillo can't drive himself to work, relying on his wife Patrice to drive. Patrice also goes door-to-door selling handmade crafts to supplement their income. Medicaid doesn't pay enough to cover all of Elyza's medical expenses so her parents have to pay the difference out of their combined meager earnings of about $2,000 per month, which hovers at just about the federal poverty level.

Their dream is to take Elyza to the St. Joseph's Hospital Center for Pediatric Feeding and Swallowing in Patterson, New Jersey for a four-month stay in search of a cure. Medicaid would pay for a part of Elyza's treatment but the Carrillos would have to pay out of pocket for their travel and lodging. It's beyond their ability to pay.

Patrice feels the emotional strain of trying to provide as normal a life as possible for her daughter. In an article in the *Deseret News,* she is quoted as saying, "It makes me feel like I have failed as a mom when my daughter is struggling, or ends up in the hospital."[27]

The Carrillos are already on the ragged edge of being able to afford their daughter's daily treatment. If the Utah Legislature doesn't expand (or even cuts) Medicaid benefits or liberalize eligibility requirements for people like the Carrillos, it would threaten Elysa's already tenuous grip on daily life. It would, in all probability, end her parent's quest to find a cure to transform their child's life. Providing greater accessibility to Medicaid for people like the Carrillos in the long run would almost certainly save taxpayer dollars that now go to support her daily care.

Ben Williams

One out of every four Americans, according to the Centers for Disease Control, fall into economic hardships because of crushing medical bills. Ben Williams is one of them. An article in the *Deseret News* described how he couldn't afford surgery or medication to relieve years of escalating pain as the result of an injury to his back when he was a child. MRIs show that nerves are being pinched by the pressure of his bones grinding on each other, severing nerves and causing his legs

---

27 Wendy Leonard, "Helping Elyza Eat," *Deseret News,* March 26, 2012, p.A1.

to occasionally go out from under him. It kept him from holding on to steady employment, which made him unable to pay his medical bills. The article also revealed that Williams didn't earn enough to enroll in the Affordable Care Act but he also didn't qualify for Medicaid. But if Utah lawmakers would expand Medicaid, he would have a much greater chance of getting the care that he needs to hold more steady employment and pay taxes.[28]

Katie Hilton

By the time Katie Hilton was two years old, she was diagnosed with cerebral palsy as well as a debilitating stomach condition after her adoptive parents brought her to their home in Orem, Utah from an orphanage in India. Katie is also deaf and required around-the-clock tending. Her parents, Heidi and Sterling Hilton, applied to the state's Medicaid-funded Division of Services for People with Disabilities (DSPD) for financial assistance to provide respite care for their daughter. That's when a caregiver comes into the home for a few hours and watches over a disabled person. This gives family members time to run errands and engage in other activities outside the home. But the Hiltons were put on a long waiting list.[29] A check of the DSPD website revealed that the agency served approximately 5,000 people but had a waiting list of nearly 1,900 applicants. They were told to expect to wait over five years before they could get help.[30]

There are thousands of similar stories throughout the state. Health care analysts estimate that some 60,000 Utahns don't receive adequate medical coverage, leaving them increasingly vulnerable to worsening sickness, disabilities and mounting debt.[31]

---

28 Nkoyo Iyamba, "Study: Medical bills force economic hardships for 1 in 4 Americans," *Deseret News,* February 2, 2014, p. B4.

29 Angie Welling, "Waiting List," *Deseret News,* May 19, 2007, p. A1.

30 "Utah Medicaid Waiver, Disability Services and Waivers," *Division of Services for People with Disabilities n.d.*, http://medicaidwaiver.org/state/utah.html (accessed December 31, 2014).

31 Nkoyo Iyamba, "Study: Medical bills force economic hardships for 1 in 4 Americans," *Deseret News,* February 2, 2014, p.B4; Lois M. Collins, "Broken by the System," *Deseret News,* October 19, 2009, p.A1.

The lack of availability of federal and state Medicaid funds is only bound to get worse. As President-elect in November 2016, Donald Trump chose Tom Price, a far-right Republican Congressman from Georgia, to be Secretary of Health and Human Services, a massive government department with responsibility for Medicaid, Medicare and many other large social programs. Price has a long record in the U.S. House of Representatives of advocating sharp cuts to federal Medicaid funding[32]and can expect a Republican-controlled Congress to support him. Such an action will certainly result in innumerable more stories of extreme hardship throughout Utah and the country, stories such as those of Elyza Carrillo, Ben Williams and Katie Hilton. It makes it even more imperative for Utah, as well as for the rest of the nation, to make up for the anticipated reduction of federal dollars for those who need it most.

Conclusion

Republicans in the Utah Legislature and Congress are generally characterized by many in the country as being less sensitive to the plight of the poor than Democrats. Have Republicans earned the reputation? Very few would suggest that most conservatives are without some degree of empathy. But their record shows that many consider vulnerable citizens to be a budget line item first, and second, human beings with personal crises that need taxpayer intervention. Ironically, Republicans are walking into a fiscal trap in which their short-term frugality on social programs, such as health care, education, job training and crime prevention, will significantly increase welfare costs over time. Already, Utah lawmakers are faced with a situation where they will have to decide if they're going to provide more financial support for a growing population of the disadvantaged in a state that already has a weak record of serving them. It's hardly a record that would support the claims of Utah's government leaders that the state is the best-managed in the nation.

---

32   Tracy Seipel, "Could Trump's Pick for Health Care Czar Upend Obamacare, Medicaid and Medicare?" *The Mercury News,* November 29, 2016, at http://www.mercurynews.com/2016/11/29/nomination-of-hhs-secretary-tom-price-concerns-california-healthcare-experts/ (accessed December 2, 2016).

Chapter 11

The Perils of Unchallenged Power

"I'm not convinced that a state would be better off with all Republicans. As a matter of fact, I've been in [Utah] . . . for the last three years. It's not a good thing."[1]

— Mitt Romney, Then-candidate for Governor of Massachusetts and LDS Church member

In 2002, Mitt Romney won his race for the governorship of Massachusetts. To win in that predominantly Democratic state, he had to position himself as a moderate Republican. His quote above was in reference to the three years he lived in Utah while leading the Salt Lake Olympic Organizing Committee that hosted the 2002 Winter Olympic Games. He was almost certainly pointing to the alarming weaknesses in the state's democratic process that spring from a deeply rooted one-party rule.

As in Chapter 10 (*Lean and Mean Republican Government*), the example most useful in demonstrating the ills caused by long term one-party rule can be found in the state of Utah. Even when LDS Democrats and their candidates for public office are faithful members in good standing in the Church, there is an irrational belief by a great number of Latter-day Saints that Democrats are disdainful of (and, in some cases, even hostile to) LDS church views and interests. This tendency to cast

---

1 Michael Luo, "Democrats Release Romney Video," *The New York Times*, July 12, 2007, at http://thecaucus.blogs.nytimes.com/2007/07/12/democrats-release-romney-video/?_r=0 (accessed September 12, 2013).

an uninformed blanket of disapproval, or at least doubt, over all who wear the Democratic label, results in the unhealthy overrepresentation of one party over another. This imbalance leads to a multitude of weaknesses that undercut the democratic process. They include uncompetitive elections, unprecedented voter apathy, the blackout of transparency and debate while crafting important legislation, and an almost universal absence of officeholders' accountability to their constituents, among other troubling symptoms.

The situation poses a perplexing question: Do Mormons truly believe in promoting healthy governance or have they settled into a comfortable acceptance of a seemingly unending domination of Utah politics by LDS Republicans? Does such a virtually unchallenged dominion encourage LDS Republican officeholders to engage in extreme behavior that embarrasses the Church? Do the repercussions extend beyond Utah to endanger the ability of the Church to present a uniformly positive image to the rest of the world?

This chapter offers numerous, compelling examples of how unchallenged power has led to the demise of a true two-party system in Utah and has unplugged the checks and balances that were meant to prevent the concentration of too much power in too few hands.

Dead End at Stanford

Many years ago, I had a humorous experience that provides an apt analogy for what happens when you don't know what you're doing, something you'd like to keep hidden from others but can't. After attending a college football game at Stanford University in Palo Alto, California, I got into my car to exit the campus. I couldn't remember exactly which turns to make to get to the freeway and I had lost sight of the cars in front of me that I could have followed. But I quickly gained confidence that I was going the right way because a long line of cars formed behind me. I trusted my intuition, made a couple of turns, and was heartened to see that the line continued to follow me, further assuring me I was going in the right direction. After a few minutes, though, I drove down a stretch of road that dead-ended in a dense grove of trees. Sheepishly, I made a U-turn and, hunched over my steering wheel, endured the glare of a dozen or more irritated drivers as they passed by me going in the opposite direction on their way to the dead end. Judging by the contorted expressions on their faces, they must have been thinking, or maybe even shouting, what an ignorant dolt I was for leading them in the wrong direction. I got defensive, glared back as best I could, and mumbled that they got what they deserved for being stupid enough to follow me in the first place.

While my mistake at Stanford was innocent and unintended, it was, much to my discomfort, performed in the open, transparent and available for everyone to pass judgment on it. The same cannot be said of the far-right Utah legislative leaders who often knowingly mislead not only the people of Utah, but the lawmakers in their own party who trustingly (or are intimidated to) follow them. In a state where voters routinely elect, decade after decade, a domineering supermajority of Republicans, the democratic process becomes distorted, resulting in behavior and bills that are too often not in the best interests of the people. In other words, much of the people's business, often its most important business, is conducted in the shadows.

The Ned and Claralyn Hill Story: A Cautionary Tale

Claralyn Hill is a Provo attorney who ran for the Utah House of Representatives in 2008 as a moderate Democrat. During her campaign, she emphasized the need for ethics reform in the state Legislature. She's married to Ned Hill, a moderate Republican who served for 10 years as the highly respected dean of Brigham Young University's Marriott School of Business.

Ned Hill was a finalist to fill the position of president of Utah Valley University, a fast-growing institution in Orem, Utah. The Utah System of Higher Education's Board of Regents is the body responsible for selecting university presidents. The Board's regulations specifically require that the names of candidates be kept confidential, especially from legislators, to ensure appointments are based on qualifications, not political patronage.

So Ned Hill was greatly dismayed to receive a phone call from a member of the Board who grossly violated the confidentiality policy. In a conversation with me, the Hills related how the caller warned him that his candidacy would be at risk unless Claralyn, who had already lost the election to incumbent Republican Representative Chris Herrod, apologized to the local Republican legislative delegation for allegedly questioning their ethics. (Claralyn Hill had not targeted any specific lawmakers during her campaign for better ethics, but had kept it general in nature.) Ned Hill said he then received a second call, this time directly from a Utah County Republican legislator who demanded that Claralyn not only apologize, but that she must do so in person. Once again, the caller implied that Hill's candidacy for the UVU position would suffer if he didn't comply. The Hills refused. Rather than become ensnared in a dishonest and politically tainted selection process, Ned Hill withdrew his candidacy for what would have been, if he had been selected, the crowning achievement of a long and distinguished career.[2]

The Hills knew who the callers were but declined to divulge their names. But an internal investigation by the Board of Regents quickly led to the resignation of Board member Joel Wright when it found that Wright, a political appointee from Utah County, was involved in pressuring the Hills to cave in to Republican demands to apologize.[3] The lawmaker who had made the second call had, like all of his fellow Utah County Republicans, been easily reelected.

Any reasonable person can't help but recognize the sad irony that Claralyn Hill, who championed ethics reform, was, along with her husband, the victim of heavy-handed and unethical intimidation tactics. This shameful and inexcusable behavior of a Utah County Republican legislator and a member of the Board of Regents is symptomatic of a deeper disease eroding Utah's democracy. When the overwhelming dominance of a political party goes unchallenged for too long, party loyalists feel free to act with impunity with the knowledge that the election in nearly every legislative district in Utah is a guaranteed victory for any Republican, regardless of their unethical behavior. Until Utah voters start selecting candidates based on their qualifications and character instead of a party label, this disgraceful abuse of power will continue.

---

2   Ned Hill and Claralyn Hill, interviewed by author, January 20, 2009.
3   Wendy Leonard, "Brent Brown Joins Board of Regents," *Deseret News*, March 6, 2009, p. B2.

The "Scary Session"

Another abuse of power by the Republican supermajority was revealed by a member of their own party. Immediately following the 2013 Utah State legislative session, moderate Republican representative Kraig Powell (R-Heber City) acknowledged in an op-ed in the *Deseret News* that his own party engaged in "scary" behavior. He wrote that his party's leadership delayed votes on a great majority of legislative bills until the last week of the annual session. It resulted in a rushed process in which inadequate time was allowed for lawmakers to study the bills or allow for ample public debate before sending bills to the House and Senate for a vote.

Powell wrote that there are, essentially, two phases of each annual session. He called them the "simple session" and the "scary session." The simple session consisted of the first six weeks of the seven-week session when 60 to 70 percent of all bills were passed. During this phase, bills went through the normal vetting and refining process of multiple committee hearings, public comment, debates, media analysis and floor votes. But the scary session took place during the last six or seven *days* of the session when upwards of 200 bills, many of which Powell described as "the most significant and far-reaching bills," were passed. After the sixth week, when the scary session began, committee hearings were rarely held, were hastily scheduled, and the media and general public were given almost no time to study and comment on the impact of the bills.

Powell concluded that bills that are crammed through the scary session "result in bad policy, unintended consequences and hidden favors for special interest groups . . . and [is] a subversion of the democratic process."[4]

The scary session phenomenon was not limited to the 2013 session. Political writers Lee Davidson and Bob Bernick, Jr., reporting on the 2010 legislative session, wrote that of the total of 478 bills that were passed, 45 percent were made into law during the last four days.[5] The

---

4   Kraig Powell, "Now it's Time for the 'Scary Session,'", *Deseret News*, March 13, 2013, p. A12.

5   Lee Davidson and Bob Bernick, Jr., "Republicans Surge Past Demos in Laws," *Deseret News*, April 2, 2010, p. B1.

same thing took place in the 2014 session. One lawmaker said it was like "drinking water from a fire hose" because about one-third of the 800 bills that were proposed were voted on in the last three days.[6]

Clearly, the GOP's unchallenged freedom to rush important legislation into law without public awareness or input casts a shadow over the democratic process. It would not be possible for them to do that if there were a healthy two-party system of checks and balances in the Legislature.

Gutting GRAMA

Another example of Republican lawmakers' attempts to shroud the public's business behind a curtain of secrecy was a bill they hurried to pass in 2011 to decimate the state's existing Government Access and Management Act (GRAMA). Because the GRAMA dispute is an excellent example of majority party overreach, it's treated in substantial detail in this chapter.

The original GRAMA law was enacted in 1991 to protect the citizens' right to access government records with the exception of private correspondence between lawmakers and their constituents. The alleged primary reason for changing the law in 2011 was to address new technology and how it dramatically altered the way Utah's Legislators communicate.[7] Several other motives, however, some stated and others unstated, are believed to have given special impetus to the bill.

Opponents of the amended law, led by the media, said it went too far, too fast. Known as HB477, it largely exempted the legislative branch from having to reveal any records it deemed confidential. The bill's sponsors stripped away practically all of the public's right to access electronic communications, including voice messages, emails, texts, instant messaging and online chats created by legislators in the conducting of public business.[8] Critics warned that the overhauled GRAMA law

---

6 Madeline Brown, "Lawmakers Say They Made Strides This Session but Need to Look to the Future," *Deseret News*, March 18, 2014, p. B8.
7 "Herbert's Welcome Influence," *Deseret News*, March 8, 2011, p. A14.
8 Paul Koepp, "House Oks Limits on Accessing Records." *Deseret News*, March 4, 2011, p. A1.

would also deny public access to police records such as arrest reports, dashboard video recordings and the outcomes of investigations.[9]

GRAMA and Increased Republican Dominance

Republican lawmakers rushed to enact the new GRAMA law so that it would take effect just in time to remove what had historically been public access to the Legislature's once-a-decade redrawing of all of the state's electoral districts. The process, also known as "gerrymandering," is based on an update of decennial census population figures. It gives the majority party in every state legislature in the U.S. the opportunity to achieve political advantage by creating "safe" districts for their candidates. Utah Republican legislators planned to use the new GRAMA law to restrict public access to their gerrymandering process so they could avoid the kind of negative national publicity they endured in a scathing 2001 article in the conservative-leaning *Wall Street Journal*. The article says Utah's redistricting machinations were "a scam" and one of the worst in the nation. They wrote that it was an obvious ploy to "produce effective disenfranchisement" of many of its voters. "The sad truth is that incumbents and party hacks are using this year's gerrymanders to fix next year's elections in advance," the article concluded.[10] The new GRAMA law would make the "scam" more extreme than ever.

Prohibitive Costs

In addition to denying public access to most important documents, lawmakers planned to use the new law to discourage public scrutiny of the few remaining records they *could* access by imposing prohibitive hikes to the cost of having copies made. The new rate, $200 per hour or more for an attorney to review each request, had the practical effect of eliminating all but the most well-funded of requestors.[11]

9   Pat Reavy, "New Law May Cut Access to Police Records," *Deseret News*, March 12, 2011, p. A1.

10   "The Gerrymander Scandal," *The Wall Street Journal*, November 7, 2001, http://online.wsj.com/articles/SB1005097828258686800 (accessed October 16, 2014).

11   Paul Koepp, "Senate votes to restrict access," *Deseret News*, March 5, 2011, p.A1.

Removal of Intent Language

To rub salt in the wound, the Legislature removed "intent language" from the proposed new GRAMA that had been a part of the original GRAMA, language that had guaranteed that citizens would be given open access to public documents, with limited exceptions. The old version had put the burden of proof on the state to explain why it should deny a public request. But in the new law, Republican lawmakers reversed the intent and put the burden of proof on the public, who would be required to produce a "preponderance of evidence" to demonstrate why they should be allowed access. Intent language is critical because it provides guidance to the courts, including the Utah Supreme Court, to help interpret the law as to whether or not a record is an open public document.[12]

"Digging up Dirt"

As mentioned earlier, the official reason for changing the law was to accommodate new technology and how it has transformed legislative communication. But there was an obvious *unofficial* motive that was brazenly acknowledged by the Republican majority in their statements during the perfunctory "debate" on the House floor. To quote one GOP lawmaker, the new law was passed, in part, to prevent the media from "abusing" GRAMA to "dig up dirt" on legislators.[13] That GOP lawmakers would use the "no-dirt" defense to justify gutting GRAMA suggests that they were afraid that incriminating dirt did, indeed, exist. We are left to wonder if the new restrictive GRAMA law had been in place as early as 2006, whether the public would have learned about the scandals surrounding two of the most powerful leaders in the Legislature, GOP Senate Majority Leader Sheldon Killpack and Republican House Majority Leader Kevin Garn, misconduct that took place or was admitted to within two months of each other, in January and March of 2010, respectively.

---

12 Paul Koepp, "New Law May Not Be Final Say on GRAMA," *Deseret News*, March 6, 2011, p.B1.
13 Paul Koepp, "Senate Votes to Restrict Access," *Deseret News*, March 5, 2011, p.A1.

Sheldon Killpack's DUI Arrest

Sheldon Killpack, who is a member of the LDS Church, was arrested and handcuffed for driving under the influence of alcohol on January 15, 2010, shortly before the start of the annual legislative session. After coming out of a bar, Killpack got in a vehicle with his close friend Mark Walker,[14] also LDS, (who was drummed out of the Legislature in 2008 after his attempt to bribe an opponent to drop out of the race for state treasurer).[15] Killpack refused to take a field sobriety test and his driver's license was suspended for 18 months. Killpack, who, ironically, was the co-chairman of the Senate Ethics Committee, resigned from the Legislature the next day.

The media took the unyielding position that the state must release Killpack's arrest records because the public had a right to know that one of their most powerful legislators had put the public at risk by driving while drunk. But the Utah Department of Public Safety, the Utah Highway Patrol and the Utah Attorney General's office refused to release the four-page arrest report and a three-hour dashboard camera video recording on the grounds the publicity would prevent Killpack from getting a fair trial. The fact that initial arrest records of other crime suspects are routinely released prior to trial fueled accusations by open government advocates that the government was covering up for the former Senate Majority Leader.

The Department of Public Safety and the Attorney General's office petitioned the Third District Court to block the media's demand for Killpack's DUI records. But the judge denied the petition and released the records.[16] The government's apparent stonewalling of the investigation raises questions as to whether there is a double standard in applying the law—one for legislators and their powerful friends—and

---

14 Dennis Romboy and Josh Smith, "Video of Killpack's Arrest Released," *Deseret News*, June 18, 2010, p. B2.

15 Bob Bernick Jr., "News Analysis: Sheldon Killpack and Mark Walker—2 Friends Rise, Fall in Politics," *Deseret News*, January 18, 2010, at http://www.deseretnews.com/article/705359258/News-analysis-Sheldon-Killpack-and-Mark-Walker-2-2-friends-rise-fall-in-politics.html?pg=all (accessed October 7, 2014).

16 Dennis Romboy and Josh Smith, "Video of Killpack's Arrest Released," *Deseret News*, June 18, 2010, p. B1.

another one for everyone else. If the controversial new GRAMA law and its anti-public intent language had been in place in 2010, it would most likely have tied the judge's hands and forced her to rule in favor of the stonewalling government agencies.

Another blatant attempt to invoke the double standard was an apparent attempt by Killpack's attorney to take advantage of friends in high places to gain an unfair advantage for his client. Various media outlets reported that the attorney tried to influence the Attorney General to intervene on his client's behalf. In an email that was made public, the attorney wrote to a friend in the Attorney General's office, "Sheldon thinks you might be able to persuade [Attorney General Mark] Shurtleff to help '[with] the length of [Killpack's] license suspension.' Anything to that?" Shurtleff declined.[17] But how many other attempts by well-connected persons to bend the law are successful and go undetected?

Kevin Garn and the Nude Hot Tub Scandal

In a stunning confession to his House colleagues, their families and onlookers in a packed House chamber on the last day of the Utah Legislature's 2010 session, Republican majority leader Kevin Garn tearfully resigned from office in disgrace because the media was about to expose an 1985 incident in which he persuaded a 15-year old girl to join him nude in a hot tub. Garn was 28, married and a state legislator at the time. The girl, Cheryl Maher, was a student in Garn's LDS Sunday school class.

In 2002, Maher threatened to go public with the tawdry affair during the lawmaker's unsuccessful bid for the Republican nomination for Congress. Garn quietly paid Maher $150,000 in exchange for her agreement to remain silent.[18] But in March 2010, Maher contacted the *Ogden Standard-Examiner*, the legislator's hometown newspaper. The newspaper reported that Maher told them the incident had haunted her and

---

17   Dennis Romboy, "Killpack Sought No Favor, Attorney Says," *Deseret News*, September 4, 2010, p. B1.
18   Marjorie Cortez, "Cheryl Maher Stabbed, Strangled," *Deseret News*, July 13, 2011, p. B3.

she needed to get it out in the open as part of her healing process.[19] Another possible motive might have been Maher's determination to bring Garn down at a time when he enjoyed the perks of power and influence while she languished in a life gone sour.

In his resignation statement, Garn admitted, "One of the consequences of that decision [to lure Maher into the hot tub] was the negative effect it had on this young person's life."[20] Garn's remark proved to be prophetic. Maher led a troubled and tragic life, including jail time for kidnapping her three children in violation of a primary custody order after her divorce.[21] Sixteen months after Garn's expression of remorse, Maher died violently in New Hampshire when she was stabbed and strangled by her boyfriend's 18-year-old son.[22]

Garn's sudden and sensational downfall made him, Utah, and, possibly, by implication, the LDS Church, notorious in the national media. A host of prominent media outlets such as the *Boston Globe, Huffingtonpost. com, the Seattle Times* and *NBC News* ran an *Associated Press* story entitled "GOP Leader's Skinny-dip Confession Stuns Utah." Why is it important to write here about Garn's fall from power in 2010 when the GRAMA law, whether the old one or the new, did not play a role in revealing his hot tub scandal? After all, the scandal came out into the open as the result of Maher's call to the media, not from government records. The answer may be found in an incident in 2006 when police arrested Garn for driving under the influence of alcohol. Unlike Killpack's public arrest and subsequent tug-of-war between the state government and the media,

---

19   Arthur Raymond and Bob Bernick Jr., "House Majority Leader Kevin Garn Admits to Incident with Girl in Past," *Deseret News*, March 12, 2010,at http://www.deseretnews.com/article/700016009/House-Majority-Leader-Kevin-Garn-admits-to-incident-with-girl-in-past.html?pg=all (accessed October 6, 2014)

20   Arthur Raymond and Bob Bernick Jr., "House Majority Leader Kevin Garn Admits to Incident with Girl in Past," *Deseret News*, March 12, 2010, at http://www.deseretnews.com/article/700016009/House-Majority-Leader-Kevin-Garn-admits-to-incident-with-girl-in-past.html?pg=all (accessed October 6, 2014)

21   Marjorie Cortez, "Woman in Garn Hot-tub Scandal Dies," *Deseret News*, July 12, 2011, p. B2.

22   Marjorie Cortez, "Cheryl Maher Stabbed, Strangled," *Deseret News*, July 13, 2011, p. B3.

Garn's 2006 arrest was hidden from public view. The arrest quietly took place during his successful campaign for re-election to the Legislature, an election he likely would have lost had his constituents been made aware of it before they went to the polls. The DUI may never have come to light if not for the media's heightened interest, in 2010, in Garn's past record because of the hot tub scandal. Why was his 2006 DUI arrest kept under wraps? Salt Lake City prosecutor Sim Gill explained that his office did not normally issue news releases about arrests unless his office determines that the media and citizens would have a heightened interest in a specific case.[23] Gill's logic was flawed. Wasn't it obvious that the public would have a heightened interest in this case?

We can only speculate that if Garn's DUI had been made available to the public in 2006, it may have ended his legislative career. With Garn out of the spotlight, Maher may have found him a less tantalizing target and decided not to divulge the hot tub incident. Or, if she had gone public, Garn's status as a private citizen would have made his misconduct less interesting to the media and, consequently, less embarrassing to the state and the Church.

Since the original, public-friendly GRAMA law was, in fact, in place in 2006 and was still unable to pry information of special interest from government control, why would the new, more government-friendly GRAMA have been any worse? Neither version of the law could guarantee the willing compliance of officials to provide public access to government records. But the old law that had intent language that clearly favored the public's right to know, would likely deter some officials from withholding information. It would also provide the legal authority for a court to force the release of pertinent records in the event of a dispute. Under the new law, such transparency and accountability would have been lost, most likely making the withholding of records, such as the Garn arrest, the rule instead of the exception. Is it a stretch to suggest that a lack of transparency would further embolden politicians and other officials to protect themselves and their friends from

---

23   Linda Thompson and Lisa Riley Roche, "Former Utah Lawmaker Kevin Garn arrested for DUI in 2006," *Deseret News*, March 23, 2010, at http://www.deseretnews.com/article/700018666/Former-Utah-lawmaker-Kevin-Garn-arrested-for-DUI-in-2006.html?pg=all (accessed October 10, 2014).

incriminating public scrutiny? As was mentioned earlier, a Republican legislator brazenly admitted that one of their motives for gutting GRAMA was to keep the media from "digging up dirt" on them. How much unreported dirt would it take to seriously undermine Utah's democratic process?

The Infamous GRAMA Hustle

Legislative leaders ramrodded their new GRAMA bill into law a mere two days after making it public and only four days prior to the end of the session. They knowingly cut much of the normal law-making process so the public, as well as most of the lawmakers themselves, would have virtually no time to study, vet or debate it before passing it.[24] Public outrage over the new law was immediate, widespread and raucous, a reaction that took the Legislature by surprise. Media organizations throughout the state and a host of open-government advocates and private citizens fiercely opposed it. The protest made for a rare convergence of opinion that crossed political and ideological lines. For example, the conservative Eagle Forum and liberal ACLU were like-minded in their call for the immediate repeal of the new GRAMA law. A poll done for the *Deseret News* and *KSL* found that over 90 percent of citizen respondents said that restricting access to legislative records would greatly harm the public's ability to monitor the actions of their elected representatives.[25]

No Apologies

Despite being slapped by a rare wave of public rancor, Republican legislative leaders firmly believed, from long experience, that they were, nonetheless, impervious to criticism and the turmoil would quickly run its course. They were alarmingly candid when they said that they had, indeed, accelerated the passage of the law for political expedience and to deny opponents the time and opportunity to analyze and question it. Utah Senate President Michael Waddoups told the media that the

---

24 Paul Koepp, "Senate Votes to Restrict Access," *Deseret News,* March 5, 2011, p. A1.

25 Paul Koepp, "New Law May Not Be Final Say on GRAMA," *Deseret News,* March 6, 2011, p. B1.

Legislature hastily passed the bill on a Friday because he didn't want to provide the bill's opponents an opportunity to pressure senators over the weekend. "It will complicate matters if it has a weekend to fester," he said. Waddoups further justified the fast-tracking because the House and Senate wanted to get it done during a non-election year, giving the voters a year to forget about it before they went to the polls again. "Last year was an election year for all those House members, as well as half the Senate," he said. "So now is the time [to pass the bill]."[26] It was an insolent, nonchalant admission that legislative leaders knew the law would be unpopular and run into the strong headwinds of negative public opinion if the people were given enough time to participate in the normal committee and debate process. His brash confidence that he and his fellow lawmakers would not be held accountable by their constituents is another byproduct of one party having too much power for too long. When a politician's election is virtually guaranteed, there is no incentive to answer to the people. Instead, lawmakers are accountable only to their party bosses.

Rush to Judgment

Senate President Whaddoups even dismissed complaints from his fellow Republican legislators who said they hadn't been given enough time to adequately study the GRAMA bill before being forced to vote on it. He scorned their complaints and said they had already understood its contents and it didn't need to go through the full vetting process. "We really don't have to have a committee meeting [to allow debate on the bill]" he said. "We think we understand it very well."[27]

Many Republican legislators strongly contested Waddoups' remark. They admitted that, once they had actually read it, they found that it was bad legislation. Rep. Kraig Powell (R-Heber City) called the bill an "abomination" and an "atrocious" law and that he was ashamed that he voted for it. He added that he voted for it because he feared retaliation from party leaders had he asked for more time to debate the bill or voted against it. Powell said his leaders threatened to shelve

---

26 Paul Koepp, "Senate Votes to Restrict Access," *Deseret News*, March 5, 2011, p. A1.
27 Ibid.

legislation important to him and his constituents if he didn't cooperate. In a surprisingly candid criticism, he blamed his party's unchallenged dominance of the Legislature for creating a climate of intimidation and entitlement in which party leaders feel free to browbeat dissenters into compliance with their agenda. Referring to HB477, Powell said, "I think it was too much one-party control in our state."[28]

Former Republican Speaker of the House David Clark (R-Santa Clara) said he voted for the bill despite language in it that he found problematic. Party leaders assured him the Senate would make changes to the bill and give the House a chance to amend it before it went to a vote. But the Senate did not make changes to the bill before accelerating its passage. Clark said, "The manner in which this bill was introduced I thought was appalling." Clark belatedly withdrew his support for the bill and said Speaker Becky Lockhart retaliated against him by delaying one of his bills. Lockhart denied it.[29]

The list of GOP lawmakers who voted for the bill but belatedly expressed their regret for voting for it grew quickly once the fury of the public backlash became obvious. But, despite the mass defection of her members, Speaker Lockhart was defiantly unapologetic for her role in cutting corners to slip HB477 into law. "I'm not going to apologize for the House process," she said.[30]

A mere three weeks after the controversial law was passed, legislators were pressured by Governor Gary Herbert (who had quickly realized his mistake in signing it into law) and public opinion to convene a special session to repeal it, which they did. Joining the call to repeal was a powerful coalition of business, religious and community leaders, including the LDS Church. Elder M. Russell Ballard, a member of the Quorum of the Twelve Apostles, co-signed a statement calling for the Legislature to draft a new GRAMA bill based on input from a new 25-member working group. The group was made up of lawmakers,

---

28   Geoff Liesik, "Lawmaker Felt Pressured to Back HB477," *Deseret News*, March 15, 2011, p. A1.

29   John Daley, "Process 'Appalling' to Former Speaker Clark," *Deseret News*, March 19, 2011, p.A1.

30   Paul Koepp, "GRAMA Bill Recalled," *Deseret News*, March 8, 2011, p.A1.

members of the media, the public and representatives from the state executive branch and municipal governments.[31]

Predictably, members of the working group had different opinions as to how much access the public should have to different types of records. For example, John Fellows, general counsel for the Legislature, defended the way in which the proposed but now defeated GRAMA bill was rammed through the process. Fellows argued that certain, potentially controversial bills should remain private from public scrutiny and exempt from open records requests during the deliberative process to spare the legislators sponsoring the bills from embarrassment. As an example, he cited an instance in the 1990s when a Republican lawmaker proposed what became known as the "Bambi Barbeque bill," a measure that would have made it legal to eat road kill.[32]

In 2012, lawmakers unanimously passed a noncontroversial open records law that corrected the deficiencies of the ill-fated 2011 GRAMA bill. The provisions of the new measure were based largely on consensus recommendations from the 2011 working group. As a reflection of its broad base of support, no public witnesses spoke at a House committee meeting on the bill. Lawmakers have used subsequent sessions to fine tune public access to government records, including language that favors openness and public access.[33]

The public uproar against the Utah Legislature's blatant overreach with the GRAMA law was an all-too-rare rebellion against a government that has long considered itself immune from the criticism of a docile, disengaged public. Long-entrenched Republican politicians have virtually no accountability to their constituents and do not fear any meaningful opposition from an impotent minority Democratic Party. Republican candidates are all but assured of election wins in over 80 percent of the legislative districts. They don't have to campaign. They don't have to listen. They don't have to account for their actions. Long

31 Paul Koepp, "GRAMA Panel Meets for First Time," *Deseret News,* March 24, 2011, p. B1.

32 Paul Koepp, "Lawmakers Cite Privacy Concerns," *Deseret News,* April 14, 2011, p. B1.

33 Lee Davidson, "GRAMA: Utah Open Records Bill Signed into Law," *The Salt Lake Tribune,* March 27, 2012, at http://www.sltrib.com/sltrib/news/53795195-78/public-bill-grama-law.html.csp (accessed October 21, 2014).

term, unchallenged one-party rule breeds disrespect for the people and imperils the health of the democratic process their representatives are elected to preserve. Until this gross imbalance of power is corrected and voters restore a true two-party government with effective checks and balances, Utahns can expect more attempts by some members of the majority party to slip ill-advised laws through the system under a cloak. It not only makes for bad laws but also damages the reputation of the state and the image of the LDS Church which is too often closely associated with the excesses of the LDS-dominated Legislature.

The Masters of Meddling

Republicans in the Utah Legislature chafe under federal law. Although the federal government has the authority to govern many aspects of Utah life, legislators resent what they say is an intrusion into issues that ought to be governed by the state. The primary example involves the ownership and use of federal land, which makes up nearly 70 percent of Utah's territory. Legislators in the Beehive State have passed unenforceable laws and non-binding resolutions that demand the lands be placed under state sovereignty because its citizens have a better understanding than the bureaucrats in Washington, DC, as to how the lands should be used and protected. But when Utah's counties, municipalities and other public institutions attempt to exert the same principle of local control over the performance of *their* duties, the Legislature meddles in their affairs by usurping local prerogatives, either through legislation or intimidation. The following section provides a partial list of examples that illustrate how GOP lawmakers, with unchallenged power and virtually no accountability to local voters, have become the masters of meddling.

Zoning and Property Rights in Provo

For many years, Provo City had in place well-established zoning laws that protected renters from unfair practices by landlords. The ordinances also preserved single-family neighborhoods in designated parts of the city. State lawmakers deemed the ordinances unfair to property owners and passed legislation to override Provo's laws. The new law gave owners greater power to determine the uses of their property without regard for the city's long-term vision and planning requirements. State Senator Curt Bramble justified the power play. "Basic questions that we have relate to the role the state can or should take in land use matters generally reserved for local government," he said. Provo Councilwoman Sherrie Hall Everett emphatically disagreed. She said, "There are a lot of [Provo citizens] who say the state shouldn't have their nose in city issues."[34]

Rio Tinto Soccer Stadium

In January 2007, David Checketts, owner of the Real Salt Lake professional soccer team, threatened to sell the team to interests in St. Louis or Philadelphia if Salt Lake County didn't commit $40 million in public funds to help pay for the construction of a new (mostly privately owned) soccer-specific stadium in Sandy, Utah. The funds were to come from the county's hotel tax dollars assessed to hotels as a percentage of revenue they make from tourists.[35]

But Salt Lake County Mayor Peter Corroon, a fiscally conservative Democrat, made the decision not to sign off on the deal. His decision was based on the findings of the county Debt Review Committee which had analyzed the financial projections and voted unanimously to advise the mayor that the risk and cost to taxpayers were too high.[36] Also, the diversion of hotel tax revenue to the stadium would come at the expense of other important projects aimed at promoting tourism, expanding convention capacity and enriching recreational and cultural experiences.[37]

But the Republicans in the State Legislature overruled Corroon's decision and passed a law mandating the transfer of funds from Salt Lake County to the stadium project. Critics of the tax-grab said if the Legislature was so adamant about participating in stadium construction, they should have paid for it out of state revenues. Salt Lake County

---

34 Marc Haddock, "State Zoning Laws Get Airing in Provo," *Deseret News*, July 10, 2010, p. B2.

35 Lisa Riley Roche, Amelia Nielson-Stowell and Leigh Dethman, "Stadium Deal Due by Friday—Or Else," *Deseret Morning News*, February 3, 2007, p. A1.

36 Alex Cabrero and Richard Piatt, "Committee Votes Against Soccer Stadium Tax Revenue," *KSL.com*, January 26, 2007, at http://www.ksl.com/?nid=148&sid=835950 (accessed October 23, 2014).

37 Peter Corroon, email exchange with author, October 26-27, 2014.

Council Chairman Mark Crockett was a vocal opponent of the deal. "If it's truly a state priority, then I'm not sure why it's this county alone that pays for it," he said.[38]

A poll conducted for the *Deseret News* and KSL-TV found that 65 percent of Salt Lake County residents opposed the use of county tax dollars to build the stadium and would have liked to have seen the law repealed.[39]

The vast majority of legislators who voted for the bill didn't live in Salt Lake County and didn't pay taxes there. That they would overrule the decision of a duly elected mayor and county council amounts to taxation without representation, a gross violation of self-government that helped ignite the American Revolution. It also absolved lawmakers of having to account for their vote to their constituents in other districts who might not have approved of *their* tax dollars being used to build a stadium in Salt Lake County.

State and Local School Boards

GOP Legislators have, for years, agitated to make the Utah State School Board and local school board elections partisan contests instead of the nonpartisan elections they are today. They have long been critical of the boards that, in their opinion, have strayed too far from their far-right conservative line. The members of both levels of boards are currently elected by local voters based on a candidate's qualifications and, in the case of incumbents, past performance. Today the members represent a rich, diverse mix of experience and ideas. But politicians at the State Capitol want to make elections partisan so they can attach the potent Republican brand to their hand-picked candidates. They know that once a candidate is associated with the GOP party label, the voters are all but certain to revert to voting the party over the person. Suitability for office would no longer be based on qualifications but on loyalty to party ideology. Instead of having the independence to act on the merits of an

---

38   Lisa Riley Roche, Amelia Nielson-Stowell and Leigh Dethman, "Stadium Deal Due by Friday—Or Else," *Deseret Morning News*, February 3, 2007, p. A1.
39   Amelia Nielson-Stowell, "Most Oppose Real Deal," *Deseret News,* March 12, 2007, at http://www.deseretnews.com/article/660202503/Most-oppose-Real-deal.html?pg=all (accessed October 14, 2014).

issue, party-backed school board members would be beholden to party bosses, who in many cases would have helped to elect him or her. In 2016, despite all of these shortcomings, the Legislature, over the strident objections of Democratic lawmakers, passed into law a bill that makes all State School Board elections partisan as of the 2018 elections. For now, elections for local school boards remain nonpartisan, but for how long?[40]

Utah State Board of Regents

The Utah State Board of Regents is the body that governs public higher education in Utah. It allocates budgets to colleges and universities, approves proposed academic courses and which schools should offer them, and the hiring, firing and compensation of university presidents, among other duties. While the Legislature determines the overall annual budget for higher education, the Board of Regents has historically had autonomy to fulfill its mission.

State lawmakers usurped the Board's autonomy in 2010 when they passed a new law which overrode the Board's prerogative to decide if an expansion of existing engineering programs should take place at the University of Utah or Utah State University. Weber State University had also bid for the program but it would have required setting up a new, expensive program. Consequently, the regents decided, after much deliberation and input from consultants, that Weber State could not offer a cost-effective program. Nonetheless, legislators, without considering the regents' decision, awarded the program to Weber State. Anthony W. Morgan, a highly respected regent, resigned from the Board in protest over what he said was an "unprecedented level of interference [by the Legislature] in academic issues." He accused legislators of usurping the Board's prerogatives for political reasons.[41] The legislators' maneuver prompted

---

40　Whittney Evans, "State Lawmakers Approve Partisan School Board Elections," *kuer.org*, March 10, 2016, at http://kuer.org/post/state-lawmakers-approve-partisan-school-board-elections#stream/0 (accessed January 10, 2017).

41　Wendy Leonard, "Regent Resigns in Protest of Forced Approval of Weber State Engineering Program," *Deseret News*, April 15, 2010, at http://www.deseretnews.com/article/700024642/Regent-resigns-in-protest-of-forced-approval-of-Weber-State-engineering-program.html?pg=all (accessed October 28, 2014).

the *Deseret News* to write a blistering editorial which condemned the "heavy hand of the Legislature" and said lawmakers "steamroll well-executed regional planning processes, ordinances, even votes of other legislative bodies when the political whims dictate."[42]

Mapleton City Hillside Zoning Dispute

The city of Mapleton, located in south Utah County, got embroiled in a land dispute with a friend of and major donor to several Republican state legislators. Radiologist Wendell Gibby had purchased 120 acres on a hillside above Mapleton and wanted to build a lucrative, high-density residential subdivision with lots sized as small as one-third acre. According to a city zoning ordinance, however, his land was in a "critical environmental zone" which required that building lots be no smaller than three acres, a requirement that would have severely limited Gibby's profit potential.[43] Environmental zones are common in cities along the Wasatch Front. They protect hillsides from erosion, mudslides and damage to a sensitive ecosystem with a habitat that feeds and sustains deer, elk, mountain goats and cougars, among other plants and animals.

Gibby filed a lawsuit against Mapleton in an effort to force the city to change its zoning requirements. Mapleton countered with its own lawsuit. Fourth District Judge Derek Pullan ruled in favor of Mapleton,[44] triggering a frenzied response from Gibby's friends in the state Legislature to whom he had ingratiated himself by providing free medical scans and generous campaign donations.[45]

---

42 *Deseret News* Editorial Staff, "In Our Opinion: Legislative Overreach, *Deseret News,* April 19, 2010, at http://www.deseretnews.com/article/700025619/Legislative-overreach.html?pg=all (accessed October 28, 2014).
43 Paul Rolly, "State Legislators Meddle in Mapleton's Affairs to Help Out Development Buddy," *The Salt Lake Tribune,* February 10, 2008, at http://archive.sltrib.com/printfriendly.php?id=8217520&itype=ngpsid (accessed October 27, 2008).
44 Paul Rolly, "Buttars Gets Mad When Friends Lose," *The Salt Lake Tribune,* February 22, 2008, at http://www.sltrib.com/news/ci_8332829 (accessed October 27, 2014).
45 Paul Rolly, "State Legislators Meddle in Mapleton's Affairs to Help Out Development Buddy," *The Salt Lake Tribune,* February 10, 2008, at http://archive.sltrib.com/printfriendly.php?id=8217520&itype=ngpsid (accessed October 27, 2008).

One powerful Libby supporter, Utah Senator Chris Buttars, dangerously crossed the balance-of-power boundary that is supposed to guard democracy from one branch of government usurping too much power from another. Buttars sent a strongly worded letter to Judge Pullan, castigating him for his ruling and that he (Buttars), as chairman of the Senate Confirmation Committee, was embarrassed that he had supported the judge's appointment to the bench.[46] Buttars' letter was a thinly veiled threat that future judicial nominations would be viewed through the lens of a potential judge's political views and allegiance to the Legislature, not for his or her competency and qualifications.

In addition to Sen. Buttars, Utah County lawmakers in the House also rushed to Gibby's defense. They filed bills that would have essentially denied elected city officials from defining hillside protection zones without regard for the city's unique needs and circumstances. The threat of legislative action intimidated Mapleton officials and coerced them into settling with Libby and granting him the zoning designation he wanted. One legislator, Rep. Mike Morley, inadvertently exposed the legislators' hostile, strong-armed tactics when he accidentally copied Mapleton officials on an email he intended to send in confidence to Gibby. In it, Morley threatened to "hammer" city leaders if they try to deviate from the settlement. "If they do [break the deal]," he wrote, "I will hammer them, if not this year, next, but I will hammer them . . ."[47] Morley made his threat during an election year, hence his reference to wait until the next year to hammer Mapleton officials. Perhaps he hoped voters would have forgotten the incident by the following election.

High School Athlete Transfers

The Utah High School Activities Association, a self-governing organization with 149 member public school districts, charter schools and private schools, had been defining and implementing the high school

---

46   Paul Rolly, "Buttars Gets Mad When Friends Lose," *The Salt Lake Tribune,* February 22, 2008, at http://www.sltrib.com/news/ci_8332829 (accessed October 27, 2014).

47   Paul Rolly, "State Legislators Meddle in Mapleton's Affairs to Help Out Development Buddy," *The Salt Lake Tribune,* February 10, 2008, at http://archive.sltrib.com/printfriendly.php?id=8217520&itype=ngpsid (accessed October 27, 2008).

athlete transfer policy for over 90 years. The purpose of the policy was mainly to ensure there was a reasonable opportunity for rough parity among the schools' athletic teams based on size of enrollment and geographical proximity, among other factors. It prevented the more competitive schools from, in essence, recruiting top athletes from outside their boundaries to make their programs more competitive or to sustain existing strong programs at the expense of an athlete's former school.

But the Utah State School Board, which had previously assumed no authority over the association, voted in December 2016 to usurp the high schools' nearly century-old prerogative to govern themselves in this critical facet of the high school experience. That the UHSAA's member schools voted 132–5 to oppose the State Board's takeover is a clear indication the schools have been overwhelmingly satisfied with their association's governance of the policy. Nonetheless, the State Board voted 9–5 to assert control and implement its replacement policy which the UHSAA feared would have made it easier for an athlete to transfer as well as give the State Board power over all future policies and decisions regarding high school athletics.[48]

Among those State Board members who vehemently voted for the hostile takeover was Joel Wright, elected to the Board in 2014. Wright is the same person who interfered in the candidacy of Ned Hill for the presidency of Utah Valley University for which Wright was forced to resign from the State Board of Regents (see *The Ned and Claralyn Hill Story: A Cautionary Tale,* earlier in this chapter). Wright expressed his frustration that the process of debating and deciding on the athlete transfer rule took up so much of the Board's time. A reporter for *The Salt Lake Tribune* quoted him as saying "I'm sick of it. It's distracting us from our [real] mission and it's just making me mad."[49]

---

48   Amy Donaldson, "State School Board Approves New Rules for Athlete Transfers," *Deseret News,* December 11, 2016, p. B1.

49   "12/9/16 USBE Meeting," Utah State School Board, December 9, 2016, video record at http://uvc.uen.net/videos/video/15524/in/channel/84/ (accessed January 10, 2017), and Benjamin Wood, "Utah School Board Loosens Athlete Transfer Rules," *The Salt Lake Tribune,* November 4, 2016, at http://www.sltrib.com/news/4545520-155/utah-school-board-told-to-back (accessed January 10, 2017).

It's clear that Wright would have preferred to dispatch what, to him, was an aggravating matter in a much quicker manner, minimizing what he viewed as unnecessary discussion, which presumably included having to listen to the UHSAA's concerns and suggestions. While he dismissed the athlete transfer debate as a maddening "distraction," it had long been a very important prerogative to the high schools. And if Wright believed the issue fell outside the Board's real mission, why was he so keen to hijack the UHSAA's long-honored stewardship over the transfer rule? The Association's handling of the policy met with very few complaints over many years (only nine of the approximately 2,000 transfer requests had been turned down, a miniscule refusal rate of just .005 percent).[50] This begs the question, What problem was the State Board trying to solve?

(It's important to point out that Wright's meddling in the Ned and Claralyn Hill situation didn't hurt his political career. This is not an uncommon side effect of a political system dominated by one party for too long by office holders and political appointees whose power is almost never challenged or even questioned.)

The State Legislature apparently felt that the State Board's actions didn't go far enough. During its 2017 session, Republicans passed a law dictating how the UHSAA shall structure and run its organization.[51] Instead, why couldn't the Legislature have commended the association for its diligent service for the last nine decades and, rather than summarily stripping it of its authority, offer to serve as an advisory partner to help it update its accounting and appeal processes (which were two points of contention)? The net result of the new law is to subjugate the voices of the many to the demands of the few who are too far removed from the consequences of their actions and cannot possibly have the knowledge or judgment to make decisions that are in the best interests of those who are most affected by them.

---

50 Bob Bernick, "Hughes Set to Take On Utah High School Athletic Transfer Issue," *UtahPolicy.com*, January 31, 2017, at http://utahpolicy.com/index.php/features/today-at-utah-policy/12199-hughes-set-to-take-on-utah-high-school-athletic-transfer-issue (accessed February 1, 2017).

51 "H.B 413 Public School Membership in Associations," *Utah State Legislature*, March 2017, at http://le.utah.gov/~2017/bills/static/hb0413.html, (accessed March 30, 2017).

The list of egregious meddling incidents that exemplify the LDS and GOP-dominated Legislature's (and other state boards' and agencies') eagerness to run roughshod over what should be local matters is too long to mention here. Is it reasonable to conclude that the often domineering and rarely challenged behavior of the supermajority of the Utah Legislature tarnishes the Church's image and violates the self-proclaimed LDS reverence for a healthy, God-prescribed, democratic process?

Where Have All the Voters Gone?

Utah's voter turnout has deteriorated dramatically over the last 40 years, adding yet another peril that undermines the state's democratic process. The decline mirrors a national trend but Utah's voter participation has been worse than the national average, ranking it near the bottom of all states. As unchallenged Republican power in Utah has climbed steadily over the last four decades there has been a corresponding downturn in eligible voter participation. ("Eligible voters" are both registered *and* unregistered residents who meet state voter eligibility requirements. This is an important distinction because state leaders and county clerks seem to prefer to report only the registered voter rates because those rates will be artificially higher than those that include all eligible voters. The statistics I cite below take into account all eligible voters because it is the most accurate reflection of true voter interest and involvement in Utah's democratic process.)

In the early 1960s, the turnout of eligible voters in Utah was nearly 80 percent. But by 2008, Utah was among the five worst states in the country for voter turnout.[52] In the 2010 midterm election (a midterm election is a general election that is held every two years when there aren't races for U.S president or statewide offices), only about one-third of eligible citizens came to the voting booth, ranking Utah next to the last of the 50 states.[53] Utah's eligible voter participation in the

---

52   Sheena McFarland, "Utah Voter Turnout Withers," *The Salt Lake Tribune,* December 22, 2008, at http://archive.sltrib.com/printfriendly. php?id=11284912&itype=ngpsid (accessed January 10, 2015).
53   *Deseret News* Editorial Staff, "Iowa's Strong Turnout," *Deseret News,* December 5, 2012, p. A12.

2012 general presidential election placed it among the six states that set records for low turnout.[54] In 2014, the last year for which complete data is available, only four states had an eligible voter participation rate in the general midterm election of less than 29 percent. Utah was one of them.[55]

Eligible voter participation in Utah's primary elections for statewide office is even lower than it is in general elections. A primary is when two or more candidates of the same party battle each other for the privilege of advancing to the general election. Since 1996, the percentage of eligible Utah citizens who cast ballots in primaries has been under 15 percent. A dismal 6 percent came to the polls for the 2008 primary,[56] which means less than one eligible voter in ten dictated which candidates advanced to the general election. In the 2014 midterm elections, *none* of the GOP candidates for statewide and Congressional offices faced challengers in a primary, further underscoring the lack of competition for public office.

Uncontested Elections

Uncontested elections depress voter turnout. An uncontested election is one in which a candidate is sure to be elected because he or she runs in a lopsidedly Republican district, has a weak Democratic opponent or runs unopposed, which is most often the case. A large percentage of both Democrats and Republicans neglect to register or cast ballots in uncontested elections because they believe their votes will not alter the outcome. They're right.

A senior Republican official unabashedly trumpeted that the overwhelming majority of elections in Utah are not competitive. In May 2013, I received a recorded phone message and a mass-mailed postcard

---

54   CNN Wire Staff, "Election Results 2012: Voter Turnout Lower than 2008 and 2004, Report Says," *CNN Wire,* November 8, 2012, at http://www.abc15.com/dpp/news/national/election-results-2012-voter-turnout-lower-than-2008-and-2004-report-says (accessed January 20, 2015).

55   Adam Brown, "Voter Turnout Just Got Worse," *Utah Data Points,* November 12, 2014, at http://utahdatapoints.com/2014/11/voter-turnout-in-utah-just-got-worse/ (accessed January 3, 2015).

56   Utah Foundation Staff, "Partisan Politics, Polarization, and Participation," *Utah Foundation,* June 2012, p. 5.

from Casey Voeks, Chair of the Utah County Republican Party, encouraging citizens to attend a prospective candidate seminar. The purpose of the seminar was to recruit would-be candidates to run for office under the GOP banner. In his recorded message, Voeks said, "Have you considered running for office? Your chance of being elected to office may be better than you think. Nearly half of [the] seats are uncontested in Utah elections." Republicans routinely win a whopping 75–80 percent of the seats in the state legislature, county commissions and the U.S. Congress by a two-to-one margin or more. All statewide offices, including the governor, lieutenant governor, attorney general and state auditor are dominated by the GOP.

Voeks' promise of noncompetitive races, even when Republican candidates are inexperienced or unqualified, highlights a condition in which Republicans find little incentive to campaign or raise funds. They aren't required to learn about the issues and explain their positions on them, much less listen to the concerns of their constituents. While there is a virtual smorgasbord of valuable ideas in the public square, voters will not be exposed to them, sacrificing their opportunity to select from a variety of real choices.

J. Quin Monson, BYU political science professor and associate director of the Center for the Study of Elections and Democracy, agrees. In a *Deseret News* article, Monson said, "We don't have very competitive elections. Over time that has led to a lack of [campaigning]. We don't have a lot of mobilization activity by parties."[57]

When former State Senator Patricia Jones was a member of the Utah House of Representatives, she asked a fellow legislator (a Republican in a noncompetitive district) if he was ready to campaign for an upcoming election. According to Jones, he said, "I've never done that." She then asked him, "Really? You've never gone door-to-door and you don't send out literature? You don't go out and talk to the public?" He replied, "No, I don't have to."[58] His response is echoed by many Republicans whose elections are all but assured. It has led to complacency and a sense of entitlement in the GOP and has all but removed

---

57 Jamshid Ghazi Askar, "Utah Voter Turnout: A State of Apathy," *Deseret News,* October 24, 2010, p. A1.
58 Patricia Jones, interviewed by author, April 24, 2013.

any incentive for incumbents or candidates to listen to or be accountable to their constituents.

It may be tempting to blame the lack of competitive elections on
Democrats for not fielding viable candidates. But it's nearly impossible
to recruit serious Democratic candidates, even conservative ones, who
are more qualified than their GOP opponents. They know it would be
a waste of time and money to go through the motions of campaigning.
Races in which Democrats do "run" for office are often those who "take
one for the team." They feel the democratic process is better served by
offering the voters at least a nominal choice, no matter the odds against
them. They are often no more than names on a ballot who typically
garner some 15–20 percent of the vote. When better-known Democratic
candidates actively campaign, they capture up to 25–35 percent of the
ballots.

Utah's Caucus/Convention System

The lack of competitive elections and consequent decline of voter turnout has also been blamed, in part, on the "caucus/convention" system
used to nominate candidates for office. Caucuses are grass-roots meetings that take place in March of election years and are usually held at a
school or other public building. Republicans and Democrats hold sep-
arate caucuses. A caucus is where neighbors in the same precinct (the
smallest geographical unit in the democratic process), who are members of the same party, can elect delegates from among them to attend
their party's county and state nominating conventions. They can also
become delegates themselves.

Unfortunately, very few neighbors show up to participate in the caucuses. It leaves the choice of delegates to their more opinionated neighbors, ones who are often inflexible, diehard party activists who do not
represent the more moderate views of a majority of their neighbors
in their precinct. Why is that a problem? Most Utahns are not aware
that delegates elected in their precinct caucuses have historically been
the most powerful people in Utah's political system. Precinct delegates attend their party's nominating conventions where *they* decide
which candidates will be chosen to run for county, state and federal
offices. Because far-right delegates dominate Republican conventions,

it's nearly impossible for moderate-to-conservative candidates (whom far-right delegates snidely refer to as RINOs — Republicans in Name Only) to gain enough support to advance to the primary (if any) and general elections. Instead, far-right candidates consistently get the nod. Since Republicans almost always win general elections in Utah, a Republican candidate who receives the blessing of precinct delegates is all but assured to win office. Thus, the state's unique caucus/convention system empowers a small group of committed party activists to anoint their chosen, like-minded candidates to dominate the Utah Legislature, year after year.

Until 2014, Utah was the only state remaining in the nation where the caucus/convention system was the exclusive method for selecting candidates to run for office. Other states have done away with it because it concentrated too much control over the democratic process in the hands of too few people. In an effort to correct this imbalance in Utah, a broad-based, well-funded citizens group called "Count My Vote" (CMV) called for a change to the election law that would eliminate the caucus/convention system altogether. CMV wanted to replace the system with an open primary election in which any candidate who gathered enough signatures on a petition could have their name placed on the ballot. It would let a candidate take his or her case directly to a broader base of voters without having to pander to and being screened by a handful of extreme delegates. It would increase the chances of moderate candidates to win office.

Not surprisingly, far-right Republican delegates in Utah, as well as party leaders and legislators vehemently opposed such a change. It would dilute their power and control over the state's democratic process. So, CMV leaders began raising funds and collecting petition signatures to put a statewide voter initiative on the ballot to let voters decide if the caucus/convention system should be abolished. CMV leaders believed, and polls supported them, that the initiative stood a good chance of passing if put before the voting public at large. Republican legislative leaders also saw the polls and were afraid they would lose the caucus/convention system altogether. Forced into a corner, GOP lawmakers reluctantly agreed to a compromise: If CMV would call off its initiative drive, lawmakers would pass legislation that allowed for a direct primary path for candidates as well as preserve the caucus/convention system. In other words, candidates would be able to choose from one of two parallel paths, or use both paths, to seek a place on a primary or general election ballot.

Republicans in the Utah Legislature unenthusiastically, and with a fair amount of bitter intraparty conflict, passed the compromise into law in 2014 with the provision that it become effective during the 2016 election cycle. Meanwhile, disgusted hardline state Republican Party leaders and far-right delegates vowed to overturn the law and throw out of office any GOP legislators who voted for it. GOP Party leaders tried to overturn the law in the courts but failed. In September 2016, they abandoned their effort to prevail in the courts and, instead, said they would attempt to get the law weakened or overturned in a future session.[59]

Does it really matter that everyday Utahns do not attend their precinct caucuses? Is it safe for them to assume that any of their neighbors who get elected as delegates at the caucuses will represent their values at the conventions? After all, don't all Republicans think alike? A broad-ranging survey taken in April 2010 by the *Deseret News* and KSL-TV found they do not. In a *Deseret News* article entitled, "Poll: Utah State Delegates out of Step with Most Utahns," reporter Bob Bernick, Jr., wrote that "the poll shows that both parties' delegates are at the far end of the political spectrum—GOP delegates are more conservative than Republican voters while Democratic delegates are more liberal than Democratic voters." The report concluded that, because extreme party delegates are so far out of step with their precinct constituents, moderate voters in both major parties may not be able to find a moderate candidate on the ballot to vote for. In an interview for the article, Kirk Jowers, Director of the University of Utah's Hinckley Institute of Politics and

---

59 Lee Davidson, "Utah GOP Decides Not to Continue Court Battle on SB54," *Salt Lake Tribune,* September 2, 2016, at http://www.sltrib.com/news/4305203-155/utah-gop-decides-not-to-continue (accessed November 28, 2016).

Federal Relations, said the caucus/convention system, "puts way too much power in the hands of a few thousand party delegates."[60]

The predominance of the caucus/convention system in Utah has, for many years, been a key factor in making elections noncompetitive. That so many Utahns see the current system as a stacked deck that foreordains certain delegates and candidates to succeed at the polls has discouraged them from voting in primary or general elections. It has also discouraged them from attending their neighborhood precinct caucus meetings, which, ironically, are the very places where they would have the opportunity to alter the balance of power in their favor.

It's no wonder the current leadership and delegates of the Utah State Republican Party are doing all they can to thwart all attempts to involve more Utahns in the political process. Their grasp on power is dependent on keeping as many everyday moderate Republicans as possible out of the voting booths and limiting the choices of candidates for the few who do bother to cast ballots. The fact that Utah has one of the worst voter turnout rates in the nation attests to the success of far-right Republicans in achieving this objective. It's yet another symptom of an unhealthy democratic process, perpetuated by long term one-party rule by well-meaning but uninformed voters who vote party label over a candidate's qualifications.

Lead-Time Barriers to Voter Registration

Healthy democracies go to great lengths to remove barriers to a citizen's ability to register to vote. But in Utah, there are daunting obstacles that discourage voter registration. In 2012, for example, an estimated half-million residents, about 30 percent of the state's eligible voter population, didn't bother to register for the general election.[61]

---

60   Bob Bernick, Jr., "Poll: Utah State Delegates out of Step with Most Utahns," *Deseret News,* April 28, 2010, at http://www.deseretnews.com/article/700027505/Poll-Utah-state-delegates-out-of-step-with-most-Utahns.html?pg=all (accessed January 23, 2013).

61   Robert Gehrke, "Mitt or Not, Utah Voter Turnout was Paltry," *The Salt Lake Tribune,* November 24, 2012, at http://www.sltrib.com/sltrib/news/55336290-78/2008-ballots-election-making.html.csp (accessed February 18, 2013).

In 2009, then-Governor Jon Huntsman felt an urgent need to confront the problem. He formed the Governor's Commission on Strengthening Democracy to which he appointed 20 prominent Utahns. After a year of work they unanimously recommended reforms they felt the Legislature would need to make to reverse the steep decline in voter participation. One recommendation was to adopt Election Day registration, a change that would increase voter turnout by allowing people to register as late as Election Day rather than face earlier deadlines.[62] Today, people are required to submit mail-in forms to county clerks no later than 30 days prior to the election. People can also apply in-person at a county clerk's office eight days prior to the election or online if they do so no later than seven days prior to the election.[63] But the Legislature rejected the Election Day option and all the rest of the most important reforms recommended by the Governor's Commission.

Data from other states strongly suggest that Election Day registration dramatically increases voter turnout. Minnesota is a long-time user of the practice, having implemented it in 1974. In the 2008 general presidential election, Minnesota's turnout was 75 percent, the highest in the nation. In fact, states with Election Day registration took the top six places. That same year, Utah finished 48th of the 50 states. In 2012, Election Day registration states again swept the top six places, with Minnesota retaining its rank as first in the nation with a turnout of 76.1 percent. Also in 2012, Utah improved its ranking from 48 to 39,[64] an improvement that was attributed to Mitt Romney's presence on the presidential ticket. It was a dismal ranking, nonetheless.

A comprehensive study based on statistics from the U.S. Census Bureau in 2008 was compiled by Nonprofit Vote, a nonpartisan orga-

---

62   Richard Davis, "Lawmakers Ignore Ways to Strengthen Democracy," *Deseret News,* January 9, 2013, at https://www.google.com/webhp?sourceid=-chrome-instant&ion=1&espv=2&ie=UTF-8#q=lawmakers%20ignore%20 ways%20to%20strengthen%20democracy (accessed October 31, 2013).
63   "Registration Dates and Deadlines," *Utah Lieutenant Governor's Office,* at http://vote.utah.gov/vote/menu/deadlines.html (accessed January 2, 2015).
64   Sean Sullivan, "The States with the Highest and Lowest Turnout in 2012, in 2 charts," *The Washington Post,* March 12, 2013, at http://www.washingtonpost.com/blogs/the-fix/wp/2013/03/12/the-states-with-the-highest-and-lowest-turnout-in-2012-in-2-charts/ (accessed December 16, 2013).

nization that works with nonprofits to encourage voter participation. The study found that "turnout in states with Election Day registration is normally 10–12 points higher than in states without it."[65] Since Election Day registration would be likely to encourage more citizens to participate in Utah's democracy, it raises the question of why the Republican supermajority in the Legislature has not enacted it.

The prospect of adopting Election Day registration in Utah remains precarious in the Legislature despite the fact that lawmakers have taken a tentative step to at least evaluate it on a limited basis. They approved a bill that gave county clerks the option to pilot it in the 2014 and 2016 elections. In 2016, only 8 of 29 counties (Salt Lake, Davis, Weber, Cache, Kane, Millard, Sanpete and San Juan) chose to participate in the experiment.[66] Regardless of the results of the pilot (unknown as of the publishing of this book), it remains to be seen whether Republican lawmakers will ultimately give voters throughout the state the option to register on Election Day. They say their hesitation to enact the practice is due to concerns that it would lead to fraud and higher costs.

Is fraud likely to be a problem? Eleven states, including Idaho, Montana and Wyoming, have enacted Election Day registration with rigorous identification requirements and the latest technology to guard against invalid ballots. Maine and Minnesota enacted it in 1973 and 1974 respectively.[67] One would think that after decades of experience, they and other states would have had ample time to rescind the practice if fraud had been proven to be a problem. Also, no other state in the union has reported voting fraud as an issue.

Despite this long record of voter fraud not being an issue, the subject made headlines in the aftermath of the 2016 general election between

---

65   "Voter Participation Gaps in the 2012 Presidential Election," *Nonprofit Vote,* at http://www.nonprofitvote.org/doc_view/417-election-day-registration (accessed December 16, 2013).

66   "Eight Utah Counties Offering Same Day Voter Registration," *Good4Utah. com,* November 3, 2016, at http://www.good4utah.com/news/top-stories/eight-utah-counties-offering-same-day-voter-registration (accessed November 22, 2016).

67   "Same-Day Voter Registration," *National Conference of State Legislators,* August 22, 2013, at http://www.ncsl.org/research/elections-and-campaigns/same-day-registration.aspx (accessed November 7, 2013).

Republican Donald Trump and Democrat Hillary Clinton. Trump won the election in the Electoral College but according to an Associated Press analysis, Clinton won the popular vote by nearly 3 million votes, the widest margin ever by a losing presidential candidate.[68] In an article in the *Washington Post*, Trump is quoted as saying, without evidence, "I won the popular vote if you deduct the millions of people who voted illegally." In the same article, the *Post* provided the results of an exhaustive analysis by the newspaper that examined the voting results of 3,111 counties nationwide and "We found no evidence that could support anything like Trump's accusations."[69]

Would Election Day voting cost more in Utah? Another reason the adoption of Election Day registration faces an uphill battle in Utah is the contention by county clerks that it would add too much work and cost too much. But Zackery N. King, an analyst with the Utah Legislative Fiscal Analyst Office, said the combined extra cost of *all* counties to offer Election Day registration, per election, would be an estimated $131,000.[70] It wouldn't seem to be an unreasonable sum to pay for improved voter participation and to strengthen democracy in a state that usually ranks at or near the bottom of the 50 states in voter turnout.

The state's lead times to register are prohibitive to many prospective voters because many of them aren't able to get time off from their jobs to personally show up at the county clerk's office during government working hours. Others, especially the poor and elderly, lack transportation during the day or don't have access to the Internet. Also, many people don't pay attention to candidates and issues until just before an election, when raucous political posturing and advertising captures

---

68   Steven Porter, "Clinton Wins U.S. Popular Vote by Widest Margin of Any Losing Presidential Candidate," *The Christian Science Monitor*, December 22, 2016 at http://www.csmonitor.com/USA/Politics/2016/1222/Clinton-wins-US-popular-vote-by-widest-margin-of-any-losing-presidential-candidate (accessed January 5, 2017).
69   David Cottrell, Michael C. Herron and Sean Westwood, "We Checked Trump's Allegations of Voter Fraud. We Found No Evidence at All," *The Washington Post*, December 2, 2016, at https://www.washingtonpost.com/news/monkey-cage/wp/2016/12/02/we-checked-trumps-allegations-of-voter-fraud-we-found-no-evidence-at-all/?utm_term=.20aac487ec22 (accessed January 11, 2017).
70   Zackery N. King, phone interview with author, November 6, 2013.

their attention. Others don't realize that they are not already registered until they show up at their polling sites and would welcome the ability to register when they get there.

Registration lead times and other much-needed reforms to boost voter turnout are not likely to happen soon, if ever. During the 2015 legislative session, the House voted down, by a wide margin, the proposal to create a new task force (essentially a re-creation of the failed Huntsman commission of 2009) to recommend ways the Legislature could encourage more voters to register and cast ballots. An article in the *Deseret News* related how Republican Representative Keith Grover of Provo, Utah, was one who opposed the task force. He said forming the task force would be insulting to the voters but he didn't say why. The article quoted another Utah House member, GOP Representative Johnny Anderson (R-Taylorsville), who said it's not the government's business to try to improve voter participation.[71]

The Silenced One-third

A hallmark of a healthy democracy is having an approximate balance of elected representation at all levels of government. Balance is achieved when the values and political positions of a body of elected officials approximate the range and diversity of political and social values across the state's population. Balance ensures that residents who are in a minority, whether by economic class, ethnicity or political ideology, are not summarily disenfranchised (denied a meaningful political voice) by being underrepresented.

There is no such balance in Utah. In the 2014 election, House Republicans boosted their margin to 63–12 (84 percent) and in the Senate it was 24–5 (82.8 percent) making it the second-most Republican Legislature in 88 years.[72] This stark imbalance remained the essentially the

---

71 Lisa Riley Roche, "Voting Task Force Voted Down in House," *Deseret News*, February 19, 2015, p. A4.

72 Adam Brown, "Voter Turnout in Utah Just Got Worse," *Center for the Studies of Elections and Democracy at Brigham Young University*, November 12, 2014, at http://utahdatapoints.com/2014/11/update-the-2015-legislature-will-be-utahs-2nd-most-republican-since-the-depression/ (accessed January 3, 2014).

same as a result of the 2016 election, in which the Democrats took only one seat away from Republicans.

Even though one-third of Utah's voting population routinely votes for Democratic candidates for statewide and Congressional offices (which don't include legislative, county commission or municipal elections), they only win slightly more than 15 percent of the Legislative seats. It gives Republicans the luxury of deciding every major issue in secret, behind closed doors. It's where they decide in advance whether a bill will have a public hearing, which would be the only chance for the silenced one-third to make itself heard.

Supermajority

The reality of a Republican "supermajority" is another reason one-third of Utahns are subject to disenfranchisement. There is no specific percentage of seats required for a party to be called a supermajority. It's a generic and often vague word that means one party holds an excessive number of legislative seats as compared to the minority party.[73] Since the 1980s, Republican legislators have enjoyed the most dominant form of supermajority, virtual one-party rule.

Why is a supermajority significant? If the margin is large enough, it gives the dominant party the power to unilaterally dictate two critical aspects of government—the ability to amend the constitution, and the clout to override a governor's veto (the veto being an indispensable check-and-balance tool to have a healthy democracy) without having to consult, cooperate or compromise with minority lawmakers. Since Republican superiority in legislative seats exceeds the two-thirds vote required by Utah's constitution to make such drastic decisions, they have the unchallenged clout to do so. There is another enormous advantage to having an insurmountable advantage in the Legislature. They can, and often do, meet behind closed doors, without any Democrats invited, to decide the fate of far-reaching issues that impact the lives of all Utahns; budget priorities being perhaps the chief among them.

With virtually no input from Democrats, one-third of all Utahns will continue to have their voices silenced.

---

73   Adam Brown, email exchange with author, March 9, 2015.

Who Benefits from Low Voter Turnout?

In an unhealthy democracy, aggressive special interest groups and entrenched incumbent legislators have the most to gain from poorly attended precinct caucuses, primaries and general elections in a one-party state. Special interest groups include corporations, lobbyists and far-right so-called "watchdog" groups. They form an elite, close-knit network of self-interested power players who favor the status quo because it serves their purposes, financially and politically. Year after year, special interests are able to deepen their roots and extend their mutually advantageous relationships with longtime legislators. In an unhealthy democracy, special interests manipulate the decision-making process in multiple spheres of interest, including education, the quality of air and water, land use and zoning policy, and unchallenged advantages to favored businesses, among others. The status quo is designed to provide special interests advantages not enjoyed by the moderate majority of Utah citizens, whose self-inflicted lack of representation in the political process all but guarantees that their values are largely excluded in the state's power structure.

Special interests are passionate and motivated. They're loud and influential. They're well-organized. They intimidate legislators with their superior ability to conduct partisan call campaigns, pack legislative committee meetings and mobilize like-minded voters. They provide financial and campaign support for compliant incumbents and candidates who promise to push their priorities through legislative sessions. And they and their followers show up at elections. Unless moderate citizens from both parties overcome their apathy and vote, the current plague of one-party rule will perpetuate the power of the special interests at the expense of everyone else.

Conclusion

Utah's democratic process is unhealthy, beset by a multitude of weaknesses perpetuated by the unchallenged, long-term overreach of a dominant LDS Republican Legislature. Entrenched GOP lawmakers, or even unknown Republican candidates seeking an open seat, enjoy little serious competition or no opposition at all in a vast majority of legislative districts. They leisurely dismiss their Democratic opponents as irrelevant. The lack of competition breeds a disdainful disregard for campaigning, an essential ingredient that would otherwise compel candidates to listen and be accountable to their constituents. In a competitive two-party system, on the other hand, an unresponsive elected official faces the very real possibility that he or she will lose their seat in the next election. It promotes broader public participation in the democratic process. It doesn't compromise on the principle that government must be transparent, that proposed legislation be debated in the public square and not railroaded behind closed doors. It imposes severe restrictions on the power of special interests and their lobbyists to bend the Legislature to their will at the expense of the common good.

By researching candidates and issues, casting informed votes, and electing the wisest, most mature and qualified people to office, without regard to party label, Latter-day Saints would help achieve a healthier, more representative government. It would show they are serious about facing the world with the kind of political and cultural diversity that would be inviting to prospective converts and friends of the Church of all political stripes, not just a self-selecting population for whom a criterion for joining the Church is whether or not it meets the de facto political requirements so visible in Mormon culture. Such diversity could only boost the Church's prospects of being looked upon with greater favor around the world. But it won't happen if Latter-day Saints don't show up to participate in the political process and cast informed votes for those who truly represent their values.

Chapter 12

The Church Gets Blamed

"It hurts the Church to be linked to any political bent. I've had several meetings with the General Authorities and they're concerned about that."[1]

— *Patricia Jones, Former Utah State*
Senator and LDS Church member

The Utah State Capitol is just up the hill from the Church's world-wide headquarters in Salt Lake City. Given its close proximity to Capitol Hill and its perceived influence, for good or for ill, over the state's political affairs, the Church is closely associated with, and often blamed for, extreme or embarrassing behavior coming from the Legislature. It would be improper to presume to know what Church leaders are thinking or what motivates them. But well-informed, highly respected observers of the Church and the Utah political scene believe LDS authorities and their proxies are privately concerned about the political imbalance in Mormon culture at large and in the Utah Legislature in specific. Church leaders have taken steps, some subtle and some overt, that could be construed as encouraging Latter-day Saints and their elected representatives to migrate from the far-right and closer to the moderate middle of the political spectrum. In this chapter, I discuss how and why the Church's image and worldwide missionary program are exposed to negative publicity and why it's important to portray its

---

1   Patricia Jones, interviewed by author, April 24, 2013.

171

doctrine, policies and practices as compassionate, politically neutral and welcoming to people of all cultures and political persuasions.

The Power of Perception

Influential Utahns, both Republicans and Democrats, acknowledge that the Church's "blame-by-association" with far-right Mormon Republican office holders is real. As a long-time Utah legislator, former Senator Patricia Jones has, on numerous occasions, talked directly to LDS Church leaders. She said they expressed to her their worries that the steady drift of Church members and elected officials further to the political right has caused tension in the Church and put its reputation at risk.[2]

Rich McKeown, who was the chief-of-staff for former three-term Republican Utah Governor Michael Leavitt, agreed that when extreme conservative ideology draws negative publicity to Utah, it's likely to damage the Church's reputation. "Utah and the Church are often synonymous in the eyes of people," he said. "When nutty things happen in Utah, both Utah and the Church get attribution."[3]

Jim McConkie is an attorney in Salt Lake City and nephew of the late LDS Apostle Bruce R. McConkie. He's a former Assistant U.S. Attorney in Utah and served as an assistant to Utah Congressman Gunn McKay in Washington, DC. When asked if the Church is perceived as being synonymous with Utah's far-right political culture, he said, "I absolutely agree with that. It doesn't help the Church to be thought of as Republican."[4]

Cancelling Sean Hannity

Sean Hannity's daily three-hour radio program was, for nine years, a top-rated program on KSL Radio, a powerful, Salt Lake City-based, 50,000 watt station owned by the LDS Church. Hannity was controversial for his combative attacks against Democrats and liberals. Despite Hannity's high ratings, senior executives at KSL decided to cancel the show effective October 1, 2010. The official reason given for the cancellation was that the station wanted to free up air time for more locally

---

2 Patricia Jones, interviewed by author, April 24, 2013.
3 Rich McKeown, interviewed by author, June 29, 2011.
4 Jim McConkie, interviewed by author, July 13, 2011.

produced programming.[5] But a reliable source (who asked to remain anonymous) with intimate knowledge of the internal discussions that led to the decision, said the real reason was executives were concerned that Hannity's listeners, a large share of whom were Latter-day Saints, might mistakenly believe the Church endorsed Hannity's extreme, inflammatory right-wing political views.

Trouble in the Missions

It stands to reason that the Church's unintended right-wing image would hamper the reach of its worldwide missionary program. LDS proselytizing efforts do not fare well among liberals in the U.S. or with people in liberal-leaning societies, most notably in Europe. One rebuttal to this view says the Church *does* preach the gospel to liberals so it isn't the Church's fault they're not listening. But if missionaries have a reputation (deserved or not) as messengers of an ultraconservative, anti-liberal Church, they are not likely to get past the liberals' doors to preach the gospel. Furthermore, if only conservatives are willing to listen to the missionaries, their conversion becomes a self-selecting (some might call it a "self-inflicting") process in which their percentage continues to grow and dominate Church membership. It creates a de facto political and cultural screening process which frustrates the Church's commitment to preach the gospel to "every nation, kindred, tongue, and people."

The Church's reputation as a predominantly conservative denomination is causing image problems across the Atlantic. Author Richard Lyman Bushman said, "Latter-day Saints in England and Europe are partly offended, partly amused, by the American right wing. It looks silly in Europe. It seems so extreme, so unable to cope with real life, caught up in an ideological illusion of how society works."[6]

In an op-ed in the *Deseret News*, Richard Davis agreed that LDS proselytizing is likely to struggle in the more liberal parts of the world, such as Europe. He said the Church's conservative image "may discourage

---

5   Gina Barker, "'Sean Hannity Show' to Leave KSL Radio Oct. 1," *Deseret News,* July 1, 2010, at http://www.deseretnews.com/article/700044877/Sean-Hannity-Show-to-leave-KSL-Radio-Oct-1.html?pg=all (accessed March 8, 2012).
6   Richard Lyman Bushman, interviewed by author, August 1, 2012.

investigators of varying political views from investigating the Church and it may encourage people to leave the Church when they assume they don't belong on [account of] political grounds."[7]

Republican LaVarr Webb said LDS authorities are worried that the Church's association with right-wing politics has had a negative impact on its standing in the world and, by implication, its attempts to bring the gospel to others. "[Church leaders] want it to be an international Church and operate in countries with a wide variety of . . . governance ideologies and my impression is they don't want to be branded as a far-right, ultraconservative church . . . and so what happens in Utah I do think reflects on the Church."[8]

Concern over blame-by-association in the mission field is not a recent phenomenon. In the mid-1960s, Apostle Mark E. Petersen, then-president of the West European Mission, became alarmed when a fellow member of the Quorum of the Twelve, Ezra Taft Benson, who also served in Europe at the time, spoke openly about his far-right political views. Benson's comments were not well-received by the Europeans. Petersen wrote to Hugh B. Brown, First Counselor in the First Presidency, that he "wished there was some way to keep Elder Benson out of politics." Petersen told Brown the publicity was hurting the Church.[9] In recent years, the Church has adopted a policy that forbids General Authorities from making comments or engaging in activities that could be construed to be political in nature.

American Exceptionalism

Prominent LDS politicians have further risked the Church's missionary program by associating it with right-wing dogma in the form of so-called "American exceptionalism." Professor Philip L. Barlow, the Leonard J. Arrington Chair of Mormon History and Culture at Utah State University, said American exceptionalism, a label used almost

7   Richard Davis, "Being LDS Does not Limit One's Political Persuasions," *Deseret News,* January 16, 2013, p. A13; and Richard Davis, interviewed by author, July 7, 2011.

8   LaVarr Webb, interviewed by author, June 8, 2011.

9   Gregory A. Prince and Wm. Robert Wright, *David O. McKay and the Rise of Modern Mormonism,* Salt Lake City: The University of Utah Press, 2005, p. 303.

exclusively by conservatives, "has come to suggest that the United States is not only distinct from, but superior to other countries." He said the term has become more prevalent among U.S. politicians over the last 30 years.[10]

Those who embrace American exceptionalism usually equate it with patriotism when it is not. It's more accurately defined as nationalism. There's a big difference between the two. Patriotism is considered to be a positive quality in a people: a love for, devotion to and defense of one's country. But nationalism is a form of arrogance, a belief that one's country is superior to others and has the right and obligation to impose its economic, governmental and cultural norms on others. In its most virulent form, nationalism is a threat to international cooperation and, too often, a catalyst for war. Using Barlow's definition, then, American exceptionalism is another name for nationalism.

Author George Orwell (*Animal Farm, 1984*) also drew a clear difference between nationalism and patriotism. "By 'patriotism' I mean devotion to a particular place and a particular way of life, which one believes to be the best in the world but has no wish to force it on other people," he said. "Nationalism, on the other hand, is inseparable from the desire for power. The abiding purpose of every nationalist is to secure more power and prestige . . . for the nation."[11]

Mormons Linda and Richard Eyre publish a popular weekly column in the *Deseret News*. In their column of July 12, 2012, they expressed the same concern as Orwell that there is a troubling tendency to equate patriotism with nationalism. They wrote, "Something troubles us. It is the confusion between patriotism and nationalism. We occasionally hear [so called] 'patriotic' people talking about how much better Americans are than other peoples. It was nationalism, not patriotism, that infused Adolph Hitler's Germany and started World War II," they wrote. "Real patriotism is essentially another word for thankfulness. Being truly

---

10   Philip L.Barlow, "Chosen Land, Chosen People: Religious and American Exceptionalism among the Mormons," *The Review of Faith and International Affairs*, Volume 10, Issue 2, 2012, at http://www.tandfonline.com/doi/full/10.1080/15570274.2012.682511 (accessed September 22, 2014).

11   George Orwell, "Notes on Nationalism," *Polemic*, May 1945, at http://orwell.ru/library/essays/nationalism/english/e_nat (accessed September 22, 2014).

thankful for our freedoms, for our heritage, for our constitution and for this extraordinarily beautiful land does not [mean] . . . pride or exclusivity — it brings humility and the desire to share what we have and to expand and export our freedom and opportunity to others. It seems that patriotism can branch in two different directions. One is toward gratitude and humility and responsibility; the other is toward pride, conceit, privilege and prejudice. When it goes that second way, it is nationalism rather than patriotism."[12]

To get a perspective on how conservatives' interpretation of American exceptionalism is linked more closely to nationalism than patriotism, one only has to look to the furor caused by conservative media over comments made by President Barack Obama during a NATO press conference in Strasbourg, France, April 4, 2009. During a question and answer session, Ed Luce of the *Financial Times* asked the president if he subscribed to "the school of American exceptionalism that sees America as uniquely qualified to lead the world." The president responded, "I believe in American exceptionalism, just as I suspect that the Brits believe in British exceptionalism and the Greeks believe in Greek exceptionalism."[13] The president continued, "The United States remains the largest economy in the world. We have unmatched military capability. And I think that we have a core set of values that are enshrined in our Constitution, in our body of law, in our democratic practices, in our belief in free speech and equality that, though imperfect, are exceptional." He went on to say, "The fact that I am very proud of my country

---

12   Linda & Richard Eyre, "Mormon Parenting: The Difference Between Patriotism and Nationalism," *Deseret News,* July 12, 2012, at http://www.deseretnews.com/article/865558979/Eyres-The-difference-between-patriotism-and-nationalism.html?pg=all (accessed December 9, 2016).

13   It seems clear that President Obama's use of the term "American exceptionalism" in his response to Luce's question is meant to convey a sense of patriotism, not nationalism, which is the opposite of the definitions I provided at the beginning of this section. Unlike nationalism, Obama described a world in which many nations, not just the United States, have the right to patriotically celebrate the virtues of their societies and where no nation, including the U.S., attempts to forcefully impose its economic, social and cultural values on other nations. It seems reasonable to assume that Obama knew the difference between patriotism and nationalism but chose not to take time to lecture on the point, instead using the same term that Luce used to frame his question.

and I think that we've got a whole lot to offer the world does not lessen my interest in recognizing the value and wonderful qualities of other countries, or recognizing that we're not always going to be right, or that other people may have good ideas, or that in order for us to work collectively, all parties have to compromise and that includes us."[14] In other words, Obama was exhibiting the quality of humility, a trait most Americans would probably agree is rare in politics and foreign policy and is extolled, at least in word, as a universal principle of all religions.

Infuriated conservatives pounced on Obama's NATO speech, selectively taking it out of context or omitting parts to make the case that the president's foreign policy was damaging America's global credibility and weakening the nation's security. The Heritage Foundation, a conservative think tank, derided him in an article as a liberal "apologist." The writers criticized Obama for, as they chose to interpret it, undermining American prestige. They asserted that Obama's comments debased America's greatness by denying its superiority in values and its inherent right to decide worldwide foreign policy by "apologizing for [America's] past 'sins.'"[15] They assailed the president's comment that Brits and Greeks believe that their nations (and, by implication, other nations) are also exceptional. In another attack on Obama's NATO remarks, Ramesh Ponnuru, Senior Editor at *The National Review,* distorted Obama's words when he wrote, "While acknowledging that America has been a force for good, [Obama] has all but denied the idea that America is an exceptional nation."[16]

Writings and comments by Mitt Romney and Utah's Republican U.S. Senator Mike Lee convey the impression that the LDS Church

---

14   Office of the Press Secretary, *The White House,* April 4, 2009, at http://www.whitehouse.gov/the-press-office/news-conference-president-obama-4042009 (accessed July 18, 2012).

15   Niles Gardiner and Morgan Lorraine Roach, "Barack Obama's Top 10 Apologies: How the President has Humiliated a Superpower," *The Heritage Foundation,* September 2, 2009, at http://www.heritage.org/research/reports/2009/06/barack-obamas-top-10-apologies-how-the-president-has-humiliated-a-superpower (accessed July 18, 2014).

16   Ramesh Ponnuru, "The Obama Administration's Assault on American Identity," *The National Review,* March 8, 2010, at https://www.nationalreview.com/nrd/articles/339276/exceptional-debate (accessed August 29, 2014).

is an advocate of American exceptionalism, and, by association, the Republican nationalist belief that America is superior to other nations. During his 2012 bid for the presidency, Romney (whose every word reflects on the Church) joined the chorus of ridicule disparaging Obama's NATO remarks. In his book *No Apology*, Romney fumes that the president's belief that nations other than America also had a rightful claim to seeing themselves as exceptional, "Is another way of saying [Obama] doesn't believe [in American exceptionalism] at all." The Mormon candidate performs another remarkable deception when he accuses the president of viewing America as being in decline and that Obama "Sees his task as somehow managing that decline." He further writes that the president was "eager to note all of America's failings, *real* and perceived (italics added), and reluctant to speak out in defense of American values."[17] It's revealing that Romney admits, perhaps without meaning to, that America does, indeed, have "real" failings, but a president who publicly acknowledges them is to be rebuked for being candid.

U.S. Senator Mike Lee, a Mormon whose far-right political ideology is widely publicized throughout the U.S., also forged a close link between Mormonism and American exceptionalism. During Romney's campaign, Lee said, "Mormons sort of have an extra chromosome when it comes to American exceptionalism. Mormons do have an added dose of belief in American exceptionalism."[18]

Prominent conservative journalists and politicians, inside and outside the Church, have portrayed Obama, Democrats and liberals as less patriotic and less American than conservatives, an undeserved charge that invokes unwelcome memories of the prosecutorial excesses of Republican Senator Joseph McCarthy during the Cold War. Even today, it's a hurtful stereotype held by many Republican Church members toward LDS Democrats. But which view is the most constructive and gospel-like? The Democratic view that President Obama's NATO speech

---

17   Mitt Romney, *No Apology*, New York: St. Martin's Press, 2010, pp. 42-43.
18   Paul Bedard, "Mitt Ally: Mormons Have Extra Dose of Patriotism," *Washington Examiner,* June 12, 2012, at http://washingtonexaminer.com/mitt-ally-mormons-have-extra-dose-of-patriotism/article/722021 (accessed August 27, 2014).

shows gratitude for what is good about America but also recognizes the right of other nations to see themselves as exceptional (i.e., patriotism)? Or the Republican view that America is superior to other nations (including its allies) and has the right to impose its economic, cultural and security model on the rest of the world (i.e., nationalism)?

One couldn't fault the peoples of other nations, including those who might otherwise have been candidates for conversion to the LDS Church, for being offended at Republican claims that America is superior to their own nations and values.

Same-sex Attraction

LDS leaders have been increasingly active in signaling that, with the exception of the Church's unwavering opposition to gay marriage, they favor a more liberalized, compassionate stance on same-sex attraction than has historically been the case. Recent changes in Church policy toward the LGBT (lesbian, gay, bisexual and transgender) community have influenced Mormons to be more welcoming of and compassionate toward their LGBT brothers and sisters, both inside and outside the Church. Also, it seems likely the liberalization of Church attitudes toward them may help the missionary program be more successful in societies where differences in sexual orientation are more accepted.

The Evolution of Church Attitudes toward Lesbians, Gays, Bisexuals and Transgenders

In his 1969 book, *The Miracle of Forgiveness*, LDS Apostle Spencer W. Kimball, rightfully considered by Mormons as a man of goodwill and genuine love for his fellow man, nonetheless reflected the conservative religious views of his day that same-sex attraction was a crime against nature, whether or not it was sexually consummated. Kimball spurned the notion that homosexuality could have biological origins. He said such claims were "as untrue as any other of the diabolical lies Satan has concocted" and referred to those who made such claims as "weaklings." He reminded Church members, however, that the Lord loves the homosexual and that same-sex attraction is curable and can be forgiven. He urged them to be helpful and sympathetic so the homosexual among them "is no longer low and degenerate."[19]

Mormon Apostle Boyd K. Packer was also a highly esteemed Church leader devoted to conservative Christian principles and the welfare of mankind. Like Kimball, however, Packer forcefully denounced homosexuality. In his address at the priesthood session of General Conference, October 2, 1976, Packer implied there are occasions when one was justified in using physical force when confronted by homosexuality. As an example, he related a story about an experience he had while visiting a mission. He said he was approached by a missionary who felt guilty and wanted to confess that he'd punched his companion. The missionary explained that when his companion made homosexual overtures toward him, he knocked him to the floor. During his talk at the priesthood session, Packer related how he told the missionary, "Well, thanks. Somebody had to do it." The apostle went on to tell his listeners, "I am not recommending that [violent] course to you, but I am not omitting it. You must protect yourself."[20]

Nineteen years after Elder Packer's talk from the pulpit at General Conference, Apostle Dallin H. Oaks offered softer counsel. In the October 1995 *Ensign*, he advised, "Our doctrines obviously condemn those who engage in so-called gay bashing—physical or verbal attacks on persons thought to be involved in homosexual or lesbian behavior."[21]

Today, LDS leaders no longer believe that gays and lesbians exclusively choose their sexual orientation. Instead, they believe it to be a complex combination of influences, still not well understood, of nature (being born that way) and nurture, a learned behavior resulting from traumas in their lives. They also understand that having an attraction to one's same gender is not the same as sexually act-

---

19   Spencer W. Kimball, *The Miracle of Forgiveness,* Salt Lake City: Bookcraft, 1969, pp. 78, 82, 84, 85.

20   Boyd K. Packer, "To Young Men Only," *Priesthood Session of General Conference,* October 2, 1976, http://www.lds.org/bc/content/shared/content/english/pdf/language-materials/33382_eng.pdf?lang=eng (accessed February 23, 2013).

21   Dallin H. Oaks, "Same-Sex Gender Attraction," *Ensign,* October 1995, at http://www.lds.org/ensign/1995/10/same-gender-attraction?lang=eng (accessed August 4, 2013).

ing on that attraction. The Church recently went online with a website devoted to same-sex issues. The website, *Love One Another: A Discussion on Same-Sex Attraction* advises Mormons that "The attraction itself is not a sin, but acting on it is. Even though individuals do not choose to have such attractions, they do choose how to respond to them." The website adds that Mormons who are attracted to the same gender and who remain chaste "can continue to enjoy full fellowship in the Church, which includes holding the priesthood, carrying out callings, and attending the temple." General Authorities emphasize that Latter-day Saints have a responsibility to reach out to all of God's children, "including our gay and lesbian brothers and sisters."[22]

The posture of LDS leaders toward same-sex attraction has evolved significantly compared to 50 years ago, with most of the liberalization taking place only in recent years. The evolution has not gone unnoticed by rank-and-file Mormons, who are adjusting their views to align with those of their leaders.

The Church Supports Legal Protections for the LGBT Community

On November 10, 2011, the managing director of the Church's public affairs office, Michael Otterson, made a rare appearance before the Salt Lake City Council. He read a letter from Church leaders in support of the city's proposed anti-discrimination ordinance that would protect citizens from being denied housing, employment or public accommodations because of their sexual orientation. Otterson said, "The Church supports this ordinance because it is fair and reasonable and does not do violence to the institution of marriage." He added that the Church's support came with the caveat that the rights of organizations, such as faith-based private universities, must have the right to restrict hiring and housing to those who are not in harmony with their beliefs. With the Church's unprecedented stamp of approval, the City Council unanimously passed the ordinance.[23]

---

22   MormonsandGays.org Staff, "Love One Another: A Discussion on Same-sex Attraction," *Church of Jesus Christ of Latter-day Saints,* at http://mormonsandgays.org/ (accessed August 1, 2013).
23   Aaron Falk and Scott Taylor, "LDS Church Backs S.L. Gay Protections," *Deseret News,* November 11, 2011, p. A1.

A month after Otterson's statement, a poll by Dan Jones & Associates found that a striking 73 percent of Utah households favored a statewide law patterned after Salt Lake City's ordinance, a result that was undoubtedly much higher than it would have been prior to Otterson's remarks. Jones reported that the findings were consistent with respondents in every county across the state.[24] The Salt Lake Chamber of Commerce also came out in support of a statewide law. The Chamber said that with the law, the state would be more competitive in attracting new businesses, many of which embrace equal rights for their LGBT employees.[25]

But the Republican political supermajority in the legislature, about 80 percent of whom are Mormons, showed how out of touch they were with their Church, the business community and public opinion. The Utah Senate killed the proposed statewide law during their 2012, 2013 and 2014 sessions by refusing to publicly debate or vote on it. In 2013, Stuart C. Reid, a Republican representing Utah Senate District 18, wrote an op-ed in the *Deseret News* in which he explains that he voted against the proposed law on the grounds that homosexuality is immoral and undeserving of legal protection.[26] In 2014, Republicans, *in a closed meeting,* agreed to overwhelmingly reject the bill.[27]

Finally, in 2015, lawmakers passed a statewide anti-discrimination law to protect the rights of LGBT people while excluding some organizations and individuals from having to comply with certain aspects of it if it violated their religious convictions. Why did the law pass in 2015 when the Legislature had rejected it the previous three years? Was the passage of the bill due to a genuine change of heart on the part of

---

24 Jasen Lee, "Utahns Favor Housing, Job Rights," *Deseret News,* December 19, 2011, p. B1.

25 Dennis Romboy, "Anti-discrimination Bill is Introduced," *Deseret News,* March 7, 2013, p. B1.

26 *Stuart C. Reid, "With SB262, Utah is at a Crossroads,"* *Deseret News*, March 12, 2013, p. A8.

27 Dennis Romboy, "Senate Won't Vote on Anti-Bias Bill," *Deseret News,* March 12, 2013, p. A1; Robert Gehrke, "Senator Says Attorney in Gay Marriage Case has Conflict of Interest," *The Salt Lake Tribune,* February 6, 2014, at http://archive.sltrib.com/printfriendly.php?id=57500631&itype=cmsid (accessed February 21, 2015).

lawmakers? Some individual legislators may have indeed experienced such a change. But the Legislature was made up mostly of the same members who had rejected the bill the previous three years. Given that a majority of voting constituents in most districts is likely to be LDS, it raises the question of whether a significant number of legislators acted more out of political self-interest than compassion.

The argument that passage of the bill was mostly the result of political expediency is supported by the introduction of a major new variable into the process: the emphatic involvement of senior Mormon leaders in favor of it. Elders L. Tom Perry and D. Todd Christofferson, whose brother is openly gay, are members of the powerful Quorum of Twelve Apostles. They publicly and unambiguously wielded what most observers agreed was an unprecedented display of clout in the legislative process. The Church authorities joined local LGBT leaders and supportive lawmakers in writing and promoting the landmark bill,[28] strongly suggesting it was an essential step for a society to be in compliance with God's command that all His children be treated with dignity and respect.

Yet there were Mormon legislators who grudgingly voted for the bill even though they didn't want to. Bowing to Church pressure, Republican Senator Mark Madsen of Saratoga Springs appeared to speak for his like-minded colleagues when he complained, according to an article in the *Deseret News*, about the Church allegedly using coercion to compel him and other legislators to vote for a bill he felt imposed a [nondiscrimination] standard he did not agree with.[29]

Gay Youths and the Boy Scouts

Another example of Church authorities successfully urging moderation regarding gay rights was their support for the admission of openly gay youths into the Boy Scouts of America. It represented a major change to the Boy Scouts long-standing policy to bar homosexual boys from belonging. The Church is the largest sponsor of scouting in the U.S.,

---

28 Natalie Gochnour, "Best of Utah Demonstrated in Balanced SB296 Compromise," *Deseret News,* March 6, 2015, p. A15.
29 Dennis Romboy, "Compromise Passes Senate," *Deseret News,* March 7, 2015, p. A1.

with more than 430,000 scouts representing 38 percent of all scouting units. As such, it had a major impact on the change, which was passed by the 1,400-member National Executive Board, on May 23, 2013, by an impressive margin of 61 to 39 percent. Implementation of the new policy would be voluntary and left to the discretion of each council and troop.[30] Gay scouts in LDS-sponsored units are expected to live by the same doctrinal law of chastity as heterosexual scouts.

The Church's decision to admit gay Scouts was in stark contrast to the results of a survey of Scout leaders in the Great Salt Lake Council conducted in March 2013, two months *before* Church leaders announced their support for the policy change. Prior to Church guidance, the survey found that 83 percent of Scout council leaders in Utah, the vast majority of whom were almost certainly LDS, were *opposed* to admitting openly gay Scouts.[31] After LDS authorities weighed in with their more liberal, compassionate position, it appears that a majority of LDS Scout leaders on the Salt Lake Council fell into line and supported Church leaders. This is another example of how Church members and the leaders of some of its programs had drifted to a right wing position and how LDS leaders used their authority to urge the Saints to move to the middle of the political spectrum where they would adopt a more compassionate and inclusive spirit for all of God's children.

Unauthorized Immigration

For years, Republicans in the Utah Legislature have been turning up the volume in their attacks on unauthorized immigrants, thousands of whom are Mormons, who came to live in Utah and other states. Using inflammatory language, they have clamored for severe laws that focused exclusively on punishment. They have refused to consider moderate provisions such as a guest worker bill, a bill that was backed by Church leaders, which would permit undocumented residents to legally remain in the state to work and support their families.

---

30   Benjamin Wood, "Boy Scout Troops to Welcome all Boys," *Deseret News*, May 24, 2013, p. A1.
31   Benjamin Wood, "Scout Executive: 'We're Here to Serve all Boys,'" *Deseret News*, May 21, 2013, p. B1.

Actions and statements by LDS General Authorities suggest they may have become alarmed by the superheated invective directed toward the immigrants, the vast majority of whom are Latinos, especially from Church members. They issued numerous statements urging Mormons to adopt a more liberal, compassionate approach. The statements seem to have had the desired influence on rank-and-file members, if not on their legislators.

Before the Church went public in favor of a more humane approach, a *Deseret News*/KSL-TV poll showed that 70 percent of Utahns wanted the state to adopt an Arizona-type law that was focused exclusively on enforcement and punishment.[32] However, *after* the Church called for a kinder balance between compassion and enforcement (what people of faith would refer to as mercy and justice), a poll by Dan Jones & Associates found that public opinion had done a dramatic turnabout with 55 percent now supporting a more benevolent stand. The poll also exposed a big difference between Democrats and Republicans with regard to which party's values were closest to the Church's position: 68 percent of Utah Democrats wanted to see more balanced, moderate laws compared to 58 percent of Republicans.[33] Many Republican legislators refused to budge, however, and were openly irked at the stand taken by the General Authorities. Others saw their Mormon constituents quickly shifting on the issue and were more cautious, quietly choosing to dampen, if not reverse, their rhetoric.

The Church Embraces LDS Latinos

The Church has strongly communicated its long-established commitment to a welcoming, loving posture toward immigrants, despite their undocumented status. The First Presidency has said that the immigration status of its members "should not by itself prevent an otherwise worthy Church member from entering the temple or being ordained to

---

32   Arthur Raymond and Bob Bernick, Jr., "Arizona's Tough Law is Popular with Utahns," *Deseret News,* April 30, 2010, p. A1.

33   Dennis Romboy, "Utah Compact Recognized; Poll Shows Utahns Like it, Too," *Deseret News,* February 16, 2011, at http://www.deseretnews.com/article/705366875/Utah-Compact-recognized-poll-shows-Utahns-like-it-too.html?pg=all (accessed March 8, 2012).

the priesthood."[34] They released a related declaration which said the U.S. should secure its borders within the law, but that "the Church opposes . . . mass expulsion or mistreatment of [unauthorized immigrant] individuals or families" who have already entered the country.[35]

President Dieter F. Uchtdorf, Second Counselor in the First Presidency, joined 13 other faith leaders from around the country in March 2013 to discuss immigration reform with Democratic President Barack Obama. Uchtdorf said, "He [Obama] was talking about his [immigration] principles, and what he said was totally in line with our [LDS] values."[36]

While he was a General Authority, Elder Marlin K. Jensen, now an emeritus member of the Quorum of the Seventy, spoke at an interfaith forum on immigration at Westminster College, Salt Lake City. In response to a question from the audience, he said, "The Church's view of [an immigrant] in undocumented status is akin . . . to a civil trespass. There's nothing inherent or wrong about that status."[37] An editorial in the LDS Church–owned *Deseret News* said, "Crossing the border illegally is a minor offense, on the order of a speeding ticket."[38]

In another article, the newspaper's editorial staff criticized Republican U.S. Senator Mike Lee for his uncompromising resistance to federal immigration reform. According to the editorial, Lee said he would not

---

34 Mormon Newsroom Staff, "Responsibility of Church Members: Avoiding Being Judgmental." June 10, 2011, *Church of Jesus Christ of Latter-day Saints,* at http://www.mormonnewsroom.org/article/avoiding-being-judgmental-immigration (accessed November 26, 2012).

35 Mormon News Room Staff, "Immigration: Church Issues New Statement," *Church of Jesus Christ of Latter-day Saints,* June 10, 2011, at http://www.mormonnewsroom.org/article/immigration-Church-issues-new-statement (accessed March 19, 2012).

36 Matt Canham, "Mormon leader, Obama's immigration matches LDS Values," *The Salt Lake Tribune,* March 9, 2013, at http://www.sltrib.com/sltrib/politics/55974230-90/church-faith-immigrants-immigration.html.csp (accessed March 12, 2013).

37 Dennis Romboy, "Debate resumes over illegal immigrants' status in the LDS Church," *Deseret News,* Feb 15, 2008, at http://www.deseretnews.com/article/print/695253342/Debate-resumes-over-illegal-immigrants-status-in-LDS-Church.html (accessed November 26, 2012).

38 *Deseret News* Editorial Staff, "A Sad Day for Utah," *Deseret News,* July 1, 2009, p. A12.

support any reform that offers amnesty, which is the code word Republicans use to deride immigration reform that isn't exclusively punitive. Lee's rejection of compromise solutions, such as the guest worker program advocated by the Church, fell under his label of amnesty. The editorial board admonished the senator to moderate his position: "We hope Lee would avoid rejecting such solutions out of hand," the editorial said. "Our immigration system ought to include avenues to accommodate [undocumented workers] who want to cross our borders simply to seek a better life."[39]

Rapid Growth of LDS Latinos

The conversion of Latinos to the LDS Church in the U.S., including those who have crossed into the country without government documents, has undergone rapid growth. A Pew Research survey found that LDS Latinos make up 7 percent of Mormons in the U.S. and their numbers are growing. Spanish-speaking LDS congregations country-wide have increased from 403 in 2001 to close to 800 as of 2012, according to the Church.[40] There are over 100 Spanish-speaking wards and branches in Utah alone, where some estimates say between 50 and 75 percent of the members are undocumented. Among them are stake presidents, bishops and branch presidents.[41]

Fractured Families

There are numerous personal stories of hardship and pain that chronicle incidents that show how zealous law enforcement officials, prosecutors and judges in Utah have forced Latino families, many of them poor, to endure the bitter trial of grief and separation and how it drives them even deeper into financial hardship. President Dieter F. Uchtdorf

---

39   *Deseret News* Editorial Staff, "Fewer Deportations," January 22, 2013, *Deseret News*, p. A8.

40   Russell Contreras, "Latino Mormons Speaking out Against Romney," *The Washington Times,* Feb 20, 2012, at http://www.washingtontimes. com/news/2012/feb/20/latino-mormons-speaking-out-against-romney/?page=all (accessed February 21, 2012).

41   Peggy Fletcher Stack, "LDS Missionaries: Undocumented Immigrants walk fine line when spreading their faith," *Salt Lake Tribune,* July 10, 2009, at http://www.sltrib.com/lds/ci_12787617 (accessed February 21, 2012).

said "It is heartbreaking when you read some of the stories about how families are impacted by this issue."[42] A press release from the Church's Mormon Newsroom says, "Families are meant to be together. Forced separation of [immigrant] working parents from their children weakens families and damages society."[43] A few of those stories are treated in more detail below.

The Lindon Raid

In February 2008, Brett Tolman, Republican U.S. Attorney for Utah, authorized a surprise law enforcement raid on a manufacturing company in Lindon, Utah. Tolman's objective was to root out Latino employees who were in the country without legal papers. Immigration and Customs Enforcement (ICE) agents arrested 57 workers, made them turn over their cell phones, strapped bands on their wrists, and forbade them from notifying their families for two hours. Bail was set for $7,500 cash or bond as they waited to face criminal charges.[44]

The workers' families were devastated. Tearful, frightened wives and mothers, most of whom were already at the bottom of the economic ladder, despaired over who would now earn an income to provide for the basic needs of their families, many with young children. One man was raising a 12-year old daughter by himself. A mother didn't have the money to feed her crying three-and-a half year old daughter, much less post bail for her husband. Another, reduced to the role of sole breadwinner, struggled emotionally to know how she would support her two children, ages four and six.[45]

Tolman was quoted as saying he understood that many of the workers arrested have families and that his office would show "compassion"

---

42   Joe Walker, "LDS Official Discusses Immigration with Obama," *Deseret News,* March 9, 2013, p. B1.

43   Mormon Newsroom Staff, "Church Supports Principles of Utah Compact on Immigration Reform," *Church of Jesus Christ of Latter-day Saints,* November 11, 2010, at http://www.mormonnewsroom.org/article/church-supports-principles-of-utah-compact-on-immigration (accessed March 19, 2012).

44   Deborah Bulkeley, Sara Israelsen-Hartley, Laura Riddle and Geoff Fattah, "50 Lindon Workers Nabbed in Federal Immigration Raid," *Deseret News,* February 8, 2008, p. A1.

45   Ibid.

for those who were affected.[46] The co-authors of an op-ed in the *Deseret News*, including this author, denounced Tolman's claims that he was showing compassion. "By compassion, Tolman must have meant separating husbands and fathers and their paychecks from their terrified wives and children," they wrote.[47]

It's unclear whether the leaders of the Utah Legislature knew in advance of the Lindon raid. But it's highly unlikely that a major federal operation on their turf, especially one that would generate headlines, would be executed without the advance knowledge and encouragement of state lawmakers.

Isaac Lugo

In another incident, sixteen-year old Isaac Lugo became a ward of the state six months after his undocumented father, a single parent, was led away in handcuffs and deported. His father's crime? An unpaid parking ticket. While in the Weber County jail, Isaac's father did not tell authorities about his son who was hiding in their Ogden apartment. The father feared that Isaac, who came to the U.S. when he was seven years old, would be arrested because he didn't have legal papers either. Isaac fended for himself for a month by living off their savings. Family friends eventually noticed that the father was missing and called the Department of Child and Family Services, which placed Isaac in a foster home.[48]

The Hyrum Raid

The Swift & Co. meat packing plant in Hyrum, Utah, was raided by federal agents in December 2006. About 150 workers without legal papers were rounded up and jailed. Several days later, according to the former director of the Multicultural Center of Cache Valley, a seven-year old boy called the center to ask if anyone knew where his parents were. The boy refused to give his name or whereabouts, apparently having been

---

46 Ibid.

47 Richard Davis and Larry Brown, "Legislators Fall Short on Humanity," *Deseret News*, February 15, 2008, p. A16.

48 Elizabeth Stuart, "The Children Left Behind," *Deseret News*, November 15, 2011, p. A1.

warned that giving out such information could lead to separation from his home and family. The former director said that the raid, even after several years, is still taking its toll on those who were traumatized.[49]

Maria and Kids

A Latino Latter-day Saint mother, Maria, has lived illegally in the U.S. for over 20 years. Her five children are U.S. citizens because they were born in the country. But her husband's illegal status was discovered when he was pulled over for driving with an expired license plate. He was jailed for three months, a time considered by many critics to be inhumane and unjustly long, then deported to Mexico. Maria's LDS ward paid her mortgage but she struggled to pay her bills. She was left to care for her children in a crowded, deteriorating home. She hadn't talked to her husband since he was deported because they couldn't afford the call. She could take her children to Mexico to rejoin her husband, but she feared for their safety in a country they barely know and where lawlessness and poverty are rampant.[50] Since her husband was deported, Maria has kept a low profile to avoid being deported herself, but she can't find a job for fear of being found out.[51]

The Correa Family

The Correas are an LDS family from Argentina. They came to the United States without permission in 2000 and eventually settled in American Fork, Utah. They left their home country to escape anti-Mormon and anti-American prejudice. Because he worked for an American company in Argentina and was LDS, his house was vandalized with graffiti that said, "Go away Yankee Mormon," among other threatening messages. A bomb threat aimed at his company compelled him to take his wife and two children to America, despite their illegal status.

---

49   Marjorie Cortez, "Effects of Hyrum Raid Still Linger after 6 years," *Deseret News*, December 12, 2012, p. A1.
50   Doug Robinson, "Deported Husband is Missed," *Deseret News*, December 6, 2011, p. B1.
51   Doug Robinson, "The Readers Speak, Reach Out to Family," *Deseret News*, December 20, 2011, at http://www.deseretnews.com/article/700208553/The-readers-speak-reach-out-to-family.html?pg=all (accessed December 28, 2011).

The Correa family flourished in their adopted country. Claudio and his wife Debora became well known as exceptional stained glass artists, whose faith-inspired work is found in LDS temples and other buildings around the world. Their two children were honor students. They paid taxes and had a clean record, not even receiving as much as a traffic ticket in the ten years they spent in America.

In October 2010, U.S. Immigration and Customs Enforcement (ICE) agents somehow discovered Claudio's undocumented status, arrested and incarcerated him in the Utah County jail. The Correas appealed to the government to grant an asylum waiver. The law permits a waiver if there are extraordinary circumstances, but a judge denied their appeal on a technicality that they had not filed the petition within the required 12-month period after having arrived in the country. In December 2010, the family was deported.[52]

These tragic stories of devastated families and dashed dreams are but a few of the hundreds of similar stories in Utah driven by a relentless campaign by conservative Utah lawmakers to enact punitive enforcement-only laws. The keystone of their argument for jailing and deporting immigrants, most of whom fill important needs in the local economy, and wrenching their families apart, is that they have broken the law, a law that LDS leaders call the equivalent of trespassing. They treat a complex challenge as a black-and-white situation in which there are no compromises or mitigating circumstances. Critics of the anti-immigrant faction argue that the punishment is excessive for the transgression and runs counter to the admonishment of LDS leaders that "families are meant to be together," including immigrant families.

In the last few years, Utah lawmakers have taken a lower profile on the immigration issue, not only because of Church influence, but also because they want to wait until Congress enacts nationwide reform, a prospect that remains frozen by the unyielding opposite positions of the two major parties. Democrats insist there should be a path for immigrants to achieve guest worker permits so they can work in the country

52   Dennis Romboy, "Deportation May Shatter Life of Argentine Artists," *Deseret News,* October 27, 2010, at http://www.deseretnews.com/article/700076566/Deportation-may-shatter-life-of-Argentine-artists.html?pg=all (accessed January 16, 2012).

and, if they meet rigorous financial, time and language requirements, an opportunity to eventually achieve citizenship. On the other hand, Republicans are holding out for punitive enforcement-only legislation.

LDS Church Leaders Called Corrupt

Many conservative Mormons and their hardline GOP legislators refuse to accept the Church leadership's more liberal, compassionate approach toward undocumented immigrants. Among them is Ron Mortensen, a member of the LDS Church and co-founder of the Utah Coalition on Illegal Immigration. Mortensen is an influential, oft-quoted voice for conservatives who oppose legislation that would include a humane approach. Mortensen and his followers refer to such immigrants as felons, an accusation that is representative of the anti-immigrant faction in Utah and the nation at large. He also condemns Church leaders for, as he says, knowingly abetting corruption on the immigration issue.

Mortensen wrote a lengthy article for the Washington, DC–based Center for Immigration. In it, Mortensen complained that General Authorities are blatantly interjecting mercy (compassion) into the debate at the expense of justice. "Mercy is emphasized over justice and the [Church's] press release gives the distinct impression that the Church is moving to the left and closer to a social justice position," he wrote. "Advocates for illegal aliens, including the Church's public affairs group and senior Church leaders, place compassion (and corruption) ahead of the rule of law."

Mortensen's contention that "the Church is moving to the left" on immigration reinforces the fact that Church leaders find themselves more closely aligned with the values of Mormon Democrats on this issue than with the powerful bloc of far-right conservative Utah legislators. In a surprising and candid admission, Mortensen concedes that the Church's missionary effort is likely to be harmed by the strict enforcement-only laws favored by Republicans.[53]

---

53   Ron Mortensen, "The Mormon Church and Illegal Immigration," April 2011, *Center on Immigration Studies,* at http://www.cis.org/mormon-church-and-illegal-immigration (accessed November 26, 2012).

Signs of Stress in Latino Missionary Work

Former Republican Utah Governor Olene Walker said the Republican Party's swing to the hard right on immigration was a "big mistake in Utah." She said the Church's support for the Utah Compact, a document that urges moderation regarding the treatment of undocumented immigrants, and the guest worker bill was meant to send a very public signal to the LDS faithful that undocumented immigrants deserve to be treated in a more civil, respectful manner.[54]

Rich McKeown commented on the effect of Utah's uncompromising LDS legislators on immigration. "What you begin to sense when you hear legislators pontificate in a very extreme way—about deportation, about arrest—they begin to collide with the principles they claim to advocate for the Church," he said.[55]

An example of how signs of trouble are emerging for the LDS missionary program in Latino communities took place in Arizona, a state with a significant Mormon population. Then-Arizona State Sen. Russell Pearce, widely known to be a devout Mormon, was the architect of the toughest anti-immigrant bill in the nation. The *Arizona Republic* reported that Kenneth Patrick Smith, president of a Spanish-speaking LDS congregation, said missionaries have had doors slammed in their faces since the new law was enacted. The newspaper cited the following example: "Jose Corral was a fourth-grade teacher and a legal permanent resident from Mexico who was preparing to be baptized into the Church. On learning that Sen. Pearce was a Mormon, he told the missionaries not to come back because he considered the law to be hostile to immigrants and Hispanics."[56]

A prominent Latino leader in Utah came back from a visit to his native Peru and reported that the nasty tone of the immigration debate in Utah and the U.S. has spawned a negative view of Americans and, by association, Mormon missionaries in Peru and other Latin American

---

54 Olene Walker, interviewed by author, November 13, 2012.

55 Rich McKeown, interviewed by author, June 29, 2011.

56 Daniel Gonzalez, "Arizona Immigration Law Fallout Harms LSD Church Outreach," *Arizona Republic,* May 18, at 2010 http://www.azcentral.com/ arizonarepublic/news/articles/20100518arizona-immigration-law-mormon-church.html (accessed February 16, 2011).

countries. He said his son recently returned from an LDS mission in the Dominican Republic and the people there wanted to bring up the immigration issue to the missionaries. He said, "[The people] are angry. It's very disruptive [to the missionary effort]."[57]

The arrest of an undocumented LDS missionary at a U.S. airport has made Latino LDS parents afraid to send their children on missions where air travel is required. "Many, many Latin people are now forbidding their sons [and daughters] from going on missions," said Cecelia Carmona, an undocumented single mother who has sent six children (including the arrested missionary) and a grandson on missions and is also a returned missionary herself. She said, "All of this is affecting proselytizing for the Church in our original countries."[58]

Mitt Romney and Latino Self-Deportation

Mitt Romney's nomination as the Republican candidate for the U.S. presidency in 2012 made him the most visible Mormon in the world. His anti-immigrant remarks during the campaign alienated both Mormon and non-Mormon Hispanics and further reinforced the perception around the world that the Church, through blame-by-association, is insensitive to their hopes for a better, safer life for themselves and their children.

During a Republican primary debate in January 2012, Romney said his administration, if elected, would take measures to deny jobs for undocumented workers, making it impossible for them to provide for their families. He said it would force them to "self-deport." He said undocumented immigrants who are denied employment will "decide they can do better by going home [to their native countries] because they can't find work here . . . "[59] The reason immigrants take significant physical and legal risks to come across the border, often with their

57   Paul Rolly, "LDS Church has Duty to Protect Missionaries," *The Salt Lake Tribune,* May 7, 2011, at http://www.sltrib.com/sltrib/opinion/51758464-82/church-latin-lds-missionaries.html.csp (accessed May 12, 2011).

58   Peggy Fletcher Stack, "LDS Missionaries: Undocumented Immigrants Walk Fine Line when Spreading their Faith," *The Salt Lake Tribune,* July 10, 2009, at http://www.sltrib.com/lds/ci_12787617 (accessed May 12, 2011).

59   Lucy Madison, "Romney on Immigration: I'm for 'Self-Deportation,'" *CBS News,* January 24, 2012, at http://www.cbsnews.

children, is to escape poverty, political instability, war and persecution in their home countries. It's hardly a situation any reasonable person would describe as "better." Romney's comments raise the question of whether Hispanics in the U.S. and around the world believe that a fervent anti-immigrant stance is typical of all Mormons. Is it feasible that such comments and actions associated with Romney and other prominent Church members are negatively impacting the Church's image and missionary program both in the U.S. and abroad?

A Higher Law

LDS leaders counsel Church members to extend a welcoming hand of fellowship to undocumented Latter-day Saint immigrants. Yet many Latter-day Saints are still critical of the policy. They say their leaders are violating the Twelfth Article of Faith, which requires Mormons to obey the laws of the land. They insist the Church has been wrongly approving the baptism of such immigrants into the faith, allowing them entry into its temples, calling them to leadership positions and sending them on missions. But Church spokesman Mark Tuttle defended the Church's policy against such criticism. "I wonder how they'd feel about the second great commandment, to love thy neighbor as thyself," he said.[60]

There's a long history of civil laws being cast aside when people feel compelled to comply with a higher moral law. Perhaps the most powerful example of such defiance is chronicled in the life of Jesus Christ. We learn in Luke 13:10–15 of the King James Bible how Jesus defied Pharisaic law when He healed a crippled woman on the Sabbath, incurring the anger of the ruler of the synagogue. An account in Mark 3:1–6 tells how He healed a man who had a withered hand, also on the Jewish day of rest. When the Pharisees confronted Christ over his alleged heresy, he angrily rebuked them for "the hardness of their

---

com/8301-503544_162-57364444-503544/romney-on-immigra-
tion-im-for-self-deportation/ (accessed May 13, 2011).
60   Dennis Romboy, "Debate Resumes over Illegal Immigrants' Status in LDS Church," *Deseret News,* February 15, 2008, at http://www.deseretnews.com/article/695253342/Debate-resumes-over-illegal-immigrants-status-in-LDS-Church.html?pg=all (accessed August 9, 2013).

hearts," provoking the priests to report his crime to the Herodians. Another example in Mark 2:23–27 reports how Jesus and the disciples plucked ears of corn on the Sabbath. The priests demanded of him, "Why do they on the Sabbath day that which is not lawful?" Jesus rebutted, "the sabbath was made for man, and not man for the sabbath." Why did Jesus justify breaking the laws of the land when he knew his actions would stoke the flames of persecution and put himself and his disciples in mortal danger? He was demonstrating an eternal principle that, when the laws of men conflict with the laws of God, the higher laws take priority.

There are many acts of law-breaking that are revered in America. The Founding Fathers committed treason when they incited the American Revolution and faced a noose if they failed. The colonial protesters who instigated the Boston Tea Party in December 1773 illegally heaved British tea into the harbor by invoking the higher law of self-governance against the oppressive rule of a British king. The courageous men and women who ran the Underground Railroad to spirit slaves north across the Mason-Dixon Line broke the laws of the land and faced severe penalties if caught. Mormon pioneers were well aware that they violated the Twelfth Article of Faith and federal law when they languished in prison rather than abandon polygamy and their wives and children. Latter-day Saints hallow these examples of illegal acts. But many Church members selectively rail against the transgressions of their undocumented Latino brothers and sisters who are guilty, according to Elder Marlin K. Jensen, as quoted earlier in this chapter, of no greater crime than a "civil trespass" regarding which there is "nothing inherent or wrong."

Conclusion

It seems clear that the Church's overall image is being compromised by its association with the far-right political behavior of many LDS politicians and members. In contrast, it appears that Mormon leaders have strongly signaled that Church members and their legislators should adopt more liberal attitudes toward the LGBT community, unauthorized immigrants, and, it should be presumed, other disadvantaged minorities. The Church leaders' appeal for moderation, if heeded, would reduce resistance to Mormon missionaries and help chip away at barriers to the Church's quest for assimilation into mainstream American culture. But too many Utah GOP legislators, along with powerful LDS politicians on the national stage, are often out of step with public opinion and the counsel of their own ecclesiastical authorities. In order to influence us to forge a more civil, compassionate society, LDS leaders are appealing to our God-given natures to welcome others in a spirit of love and respect as we would hope to be welcomed were we in their circumstances.

Chapter 13

The a la Carte Candidate

"It seems to be part of our nature as human beings to make assumptions about people, politics, and piety based on our incomplete and often misleading experience."[1]

— *Dieter F. Uchtdorf, Second Counselor in the First Presidency,
Church of Jesus Christ of Latter-day Saints*

In their First Presidency "Letter Encouraging Political Participation, Voting in US," of October 5, 2016, the highest Church officials state that "Principles compatible with the gospel may be found in various political parties, and members should seek candidates who best embody those principles." In the same message, they urge the Saints to "spend the time needed to become informed about the issues and candidates you will be considering."[2] The First Presidency does not issue such statements lightly, only when they want to make a significant change or reinforce a critical Church value. So why does the President of the Church and his most senior counselors feel compelled to issue essentially the same message prior to every state and federal election and instruct ward bishops to read it to all their members? It seems obvious

---

1   Dieter F. Uchtdorf, "What is Truth?" *LDS Church Educational System Devotional*, January 13, 2013, at https://www.lds.org/broadcasts/article/ces-devotionals/2013/01/what-is-truth?lang=eng (accessed November 17, 2014).
2   Mormon Newsroom Staff, "First Presidency Letter Encouraging Political Participation, Voting in US," *Church of Jesus Christ of Latter-day Saints*, October 5, 2016, at http://www.mormonnewsroom.org/article/first-presidency-2016-letter-political-participation (accessed November 22, 2016).

that it's because they are worried that Church members are not working hard enough to become informed about the issues and the worthiness of all candidates, not just Republican ones. If so, why does that worry them? Might it be because the immense political imbalance in Mormon culture is having a detrimental impact on the Church, the feelings of a significant minority (Democrats) of Church members, its worldwide missionary program, and its attempts to gain acceptance in mainstream American culture? Does it foster a general negative perception that the Church's stated compassion for the poor and other vulnerable minorities is more rhetoric than reality when it comes to public efforts to alleviate the plight of the poor?

The Church leaders' appeal for Latter-day Saints to become more knowledgeable about candidates and issues applies to all Mormons throughout the U.S. But I have, as before, used Utah as an example of why their message is critically important in a state in which the behavior of the LDS Republican-dominated state legislature, for good or for ill, is a major determinant of how *all* Mormons and their Church are perceived in the U.S. and around the world.

In this chapter, I introduce the concept of the "a la carte" candidate and ways for Church members to comply with the LDS General Authorities' guidance that votes should be cast on the basis of a careful review of a candidate's qualifications, not his or her party label.

Many good restaurants have menus that offer a choice between a ordering a meal that already has its contents determined in advance (I'll call it the "full meal" option), and an "a la carte" option that allows you to mix-and-match foods to customize a meal to fit your specific tastes. The full meal option is the quicker, easier way because it minimizes the amount of time and effort you have to spend to decide. The a la carte approach, on the other hand, requires more time, thought and effort but it helps you select the foods that are best suited to your culinary values and tastes.

You have the same options when voting for candidates for public office. An a la carte candidate is one whom voters select from among a menu of candidates with different values and qualifications. It requires more time, effort and thought to choose candidates via the a la carte method, but it's much more likely to result in the election of candidates who best represent your values. It means you have studied the candidates and formulated an informed opinion before arriving at the polls. On the other hand, voting for candidates using the "full party" option (what I referred to as the "full meal" option in the restaurant example), is easier and more convenient than a la carte, but too often results in the selection of Republican candidates who are less qualified than their Democratic opponents. Many Republican candidates are entrenched politicians whose reelections are all but automatic in the vast majority of legislative districts (many run unopposed), giving them license to promote legislation that is corrosive to the democratic process (as in the proposed GRAMA bill referenced in Chapter 11, *The Perils of Unchallenged Power*). It also frees them to develop cozy, self-serving relationships with special interests and dodge the responsibility to know and be accountable to their constituents.

Many voters using the non-selective full party option take advantage of what is called "straight-ticket" voting. The straight-ticket option is when voters are allowed to check a single box at the top of the ballot. It tells the voting machine to automatically cast a vote for all the rest of the candidates of the same party on all pages. It lets voters skip having to view each page on the ballot and lets them avoid having to consider each candidate on his or her merits and positions.

The stranglehold that the LDS Republicans have in the Utah Legislature gives them the power to design voting ballots that encourage straight-ticket voting, a design that takes advantage of the GOP's dominant brand and the tendency of Utah voters to cast ballots based on party affiliation. It's a practice that most states have abandoned in order to encourage a more a la carte style of competition in elections. In fact, Utah is one of only 11 states on a declining list of states that still offer straight-ticket voting.[3]

Do Mormons invest more faith in their Church leaders' exhortation to become informed voters than they do in their near-automatic loyalty to the Republican Party? One wonders, because in the November 2014 election, nearly half of Utah voters used the straight-ticket voting

---

3 "Straight Ticket Voting States," *National Conference of State Legislatures*, January 7, 2015, at http://www.ncsl.org/research/elections-and-campaigns/straight-ticket-voting.aspx (accessed March 4, 2015).

option, up significantly from 40 percent in 2012. Sixty-three percent of straight-ticket voters cast their ballots for Republicans.[4] It appears that the Republicans' stubborn defense of the practice is having the desired effect of allowing voters to ignore the Democratic candidates' worthiness for office. What are Republican Party leaders afraid of? Are they worried that informed voters might cut into their huge advantage in the State Legislature and congressional delegation? It's yet another symptom of an unhealthy democracy being imposed by one-party Republican rule and all its perils, for both the state and the LDS Church, that follow in its wake.

Wasted Candidates

Utah politics are overflowing with examples of how voters have shunned moderate-to-conservative Democratic candidates even after these voters privately told the candidates they were the superior candidates over their Republican opponents. The voters admitted they were under tremendous pressure, overt or understood, from their families, friends and neighbors to reject Democrats out-of-hand because of their Democratic Party label. Here are several examples of stories people have told me:

A highly respected former LDS bishop and stake president ran for the Utah State House of Representatives as a Democrat in the district in which he had held his senior ecclesiastical offices. One neighbor told him he should be the one voted into the legislative office and had all the right qualities to be successful but he belonged to the wrong party. Others told him they had always admired him but they couldn't support him because they were Republicans. Also, he said his own family members became cooler toward him once they learned of his party affiliation.

A school teacher was a former GOP member of the Utah House of Representatives who was muscled out of office in the caucus/convention system by his own party leaders because they deemed him too moderate. Utah County Democratic Party leaders asked him to run as

---

4 Bryan Schott, "The Straight Ticket Conundrum," *Utahpolicy.com*, January 7, 2015, at http://utahpolicy.com/index.php/features/today-at-utah-policy/4448-bryan-schott-s-political-bs-the-straight-ticket-conundrum (accessed March 4, 2015).

a Democrat but he refused. He said his family would be upset if he ran as a Democrat even though his values had not changed.

An accomplished university professor challenged the Republican incumbent for a seat in the U.S. House of Representatives. She was a registered Republican but ran as a Democrat because she believed her Republican opponent was too extreme in his far-right positions. Her moderate values had not changed, but her friends and colleagues were dismayed that she ran as a Democrat.

A popular two-term mayor of a Utah County city ran as a Democrat for the county commission and was soundly defeated. Since mayoral elections are non-partisan, party affiliation was not a consideration when he easily won two elections to the mayor's office. But when voters learned he was a Democrat, his popularity vanished. A longtime friend of the candidate said he couldn't vote for him because several generations of his (the friend's) family had been Republicans and would not approve.

A well-liked educator and former mayor of a fast-growing city in Salt Lake County announced he was running for Congress as a Democrat. He had served as an LDS bishop, stake president and mission president. Despite his impeccable Church service throughout his adult life, one or more bishops whom he had ordained when he was stake president told him they were disappointed that he would run as a member of the Democratic Party.

The list of examples in which family, friends, and colleagues refused to consider voting for a qualified Democratic candidate because of their party label is too long to mention here. It is a disturbing symptom of a culture in which its voters have surrendered the balance, diversity of thought, transparency and accountability so essential to a healthy lawmaking process.

How Can I Find the Best Candidates?

To the average citizen who doesn't follow local, state or national politics, candidates or issues, it can be daunting to use the a la carte method to find out which candidate is most deserving of his or her vote. But it's a lot easier than you think and can be done in only four or five hours, possibly less, to become well-informed. Here are a few things you can do:

Candidate Websites

Nearly every candidate has a website. You can find the link to their website on campaign signs, in their literature, or by searching on the Internet. Start a file for campaign literature and read through it rather than tossing it into the recycling bin. It takes very little time to review the competing candidates' qualifications, experience and positions on key issues and decide which ones you feel will do the best job representing you. I have even called or exchanged email with candidates to ask them to clarify their qualifications and positions on issues. Most of them are happy to respond.

Neighborhood "Meet the Candidate" Socials

Many candidates are featured at neighborhood socials at someone's home to talk to voters. They'll usually let you know about it on their website or literature. For example, I attended one for a candidate for the Utah House of Representatives where I had an opportunity to meet him on a personal level and ask questions I might not have been able to ask in a larger group. If you want to become informed, take advantage of these socials.

Neighbors' Opinions

Another option is to ask for the opinions of your neighbors, fellow church-goers, friends or family members. Some of them are bound to be well-informed and most would be more than happy to let you know what they think (sometimes way too enthusiastically). It's best to pick reasonable people of differing opinions so you can weigh their points of view and decide for yourself.

Sample Ballots

How can you find out which candidates are running to represent you in your local, state and federal voting districts? You can find that information on a single document. It's called a sample ballot and, if you don't already receive one in the mail from your county clerk, you can go online to get the one that applies specifically to your district. It can be done with just a few keystrokes. The state website will ask for your address and then email a printable sample ballot to you that will tell you all the candidates and issues you will have the right to vote on. If you don't have access to the Internet, a call to the state office that presides over elections will get you a sample ballot through the mail. Many states have a Secretary of State whose website links you to sample ballots. Other states will take you to their official voter's information center. Utah's sample ballots are available on the Lieutenant Governor's website.

Conclusion

The Church's image, members and mission suffer as an unintended consequence of its blame-by-association with an LDS Republican-dominated Utah State Legislature and its often-extreme far-right behavior. This extraordinary domination in Utah and other states is made possible because so many Latter-day Saints choose the Republican Party label over the candidates' qualifications when casting ballots on Election Day. But if voters were to select candidates via the a la carte approach, it would almost certainly result in a significant increase in competition for public office and inject much-needed balance, transparency and accountability into the democratic process.

It appears to be important to LDS Church leaders that Church members vote only after closely considering the merits of candidates and positions, regardless of party label. In the First Presidency's pre-election missives to the general Church population in the U.S, they strongly advocate what meets, in essence, the description of the a la carte approach to filling public offices with the most qualified candidates, whether they are Democrats or Republicans. For, as President Uchtdorf counsels, it behooves us not to form opinions about "people, politics and piety" before we've made an honest effort to challenge our own assumptions with knowledge.[5]

---

5   Dieter F. Uchtdorf, "What is Truth?" *LDS Church Educational System Devotional*, January 13, 2013, at https://www.lds.org/broadcasts/article/ces-devotionals/2013/01/what-is-truth?lang=eng (accessed November 17, 2014).

Conclusion

Building a More Civil, Compassionate and Spiritual Society

Today, there is an enormous political imbalance in the LDS Church in the U.S., where many of the 70 percent of American Latter-day Saints are advocates of a strident strain of Republican ideology. It's a phenomenon that has caused unintended consequences which have put the Church's reputation and its worldwide mission at risk. These unfortunate consequences have distorted Mormon culture, threatened the reach of the Church's missionary program and strained member unity. It has conveyed a perception to the world that the Church and its members, despite all their good works, are not doing enough to compassionately, and without judgment, sustain the poor through the funding of government anti-poverty safety nets. The imbalance has promoted an unhealthy democratic process and, through blame-by-association, undercuts the Church's image and its attempts to gain greater acceptance in mainstream American society. These perceptions cast a shadow not only upon Mormons in Utah and other states with large concentrations of Church members, but also upon its members around the world.

There's no firm evidence that actions by LDS Church leaders are motivated by a desire to mitigate the risks of this imbalance to the Church. But in interviews for this book, people who have had private conversations with General Authorities believe that LDS leaders recognize and are concerned about the downside of having the Church associated with a single political party. That, along with their official statements in recent years, could easily be seen as an attempt to urge the Saints to adopt more moderate, compassionate beliefs, most notably regarding the hotly contested social issues of undocumented immigration and same-sex civil rights in housing, jobs, and public accommodations. Church authorities have engaged in unprecedented efforts, directly or indirectly, to influence Utah's Republican legislators to pass laws that are more compassionate and sensitive toward the human rights of minorities. It's not unlike the time when, for more than 70 years from the Church's founding into the early 1900s, the Saints were a vulnerable minority in pursuit of a better life, a time when they would have welcomed compassionate treatment from their neighbors and the governments under which they lived.

How did this political and cultural imbalance, with its unintended injury to the Church, come to be? It wasn't always this way. In the early days of the Church, founder Joseph Smith and his fellow LDS authorities were divinely inspired progressives (still known today as progressives or liberals) who mandated — it wasn't voluntary — the redistribution of members' wealth through significant contributions of money and goods to the poor. Members who failed to do so were told that they had surrendered their rights to the full blessings of God. Early Mormon progressives fought for government reform, much like progressives today who fight for the protection of minority rights under the U.S. Constitution, the fair application of laws in the criminal justice system, the rights of workers to labor in safe environments for a fair wage, responsible stewardship over the environment, opportunities for quality education for all, consumer protection from exploitation by big business, access to affordable healthcare for the poor, and other major fairness and quality-of-life issues.

The progressive character of the early Church would, over many decades, be gradually supplanted by today's overwhelming LDS allegiance to the Republican Party. The seeds of this evolution would not be sown until the Church began its quest to gain statehood for the Utah Territory, which was realized in 1896. Statehood would not have happened had Church leaders not met the demand of the GOP, which held power in Congress, to elect a Republican congressional delegation to send to Washington, D.C. To meet that condition, Mormon authorities engaged in an aggressive campaign to convert a critical mass of Church members from the Democratic Party, which until then had enjoyed considerable support in Utah, to the GOP, which had been among the most antagonistic of the Church's adversaries. Ironically, Church leaders at the time had to work hard to convince members that they could be a Republican *and* a good Mormon.

But Mormon loyalty to the Republican Party, as commanding as it is today, did not grow without disruption. In the 1930s and 1940s, Church members, along with the rest of the nation, overwhelmingly entrusted Democrats during the administration of Franklin Delano Roosevelt to guide the U.S. through the perilous times of the Great Depression and World War II. After the war, however, the balance of power shifted to the Republican Party. The Republicans persuaded many Americans that their ideology was a stronger bulwark (compared to the Democrats), against a growing Cold War threat from Russia and China, godless communist states who were openly committed to destroying America's freedoms. The Republican message found fertile ground in the hearts and minds of religious conservatives, including Mormons, who were terrified that the menace of communism would spread across the globe and stamp out their constitutional right to practice religion as they pleased.

The fusion of Mormon religious doctrine with Republican political ideology gained momentum in the 1950s, when Senator Joseph McCarthy became the Republican face of a reckless, often unconstitutional, campaign to purge U.S. institutions of alleged communist spies and sympathizers. Republicans brazenly and falsely accused Democrats of being soft on communism because the Democrats openly despised McCarthy's disdain for the rule of law and fought to protect the constitutional right of every individual to due process. McCarthy went so far as to demonize Democrats as the party of traitors. By associating the GOP with anti-communism and patriotism, as well as his attacks on mainstream and liberal clergy, McCarthy's methods further bonded Republican ideology with conservative religious denominations. In all probability, McCarthy's caustic campaign influenced LDS Church leaders and members to move even further to the political right, not just to express their true beliefs, but also to make sure there wasn't any doubt as to the strength of their anti-communist and patriotic credentials. Even today, there's an undercurrent in the Church, expressed in both overt and subtle ways, which sometimes seeps to the surface, that Mormon Democrats are not as spiritual or patriotic as LDS Republicans.

The acceleration of the march of the LDS Church to the political and cultural right , along with other conservative religions, took place during the 1960s and 1970s when the Vietnam War and Watergate scandal helped undermine respect for authority and morals and ushered in the sexual revolution and the civil rights era. These vast, seismic shifts in social values coalesced into the culture wars of the 1970s, further widening the chasm between the secular and the religious. It worsened the animosity between Democrats and Republicans, further polarizing the nation into the hardened, uncompromising positions we see at all levels of government today. People treated party labels as being more important than qualifications as they voted for candidates for public office.

But many years ago in Utah, people were not as quick as the rest of the nation to embrace party labels as the primary criterion with which to examine a candidate's worthiness. Rather, they applied the "a la carte" approach and evaluated candidates by how well they represented their values. They discerned that not all Democrats thought alike, that Utah Democrats were independent from other Democrats across the nation. They were valued for how well they aligned with the people's beliefs. This was especially important to Mormons who wanted to elect upstanding representatives who would act in harmony with their religious beliefs. For example, Latter-day Saints ignored party labels and sent Democrats Calvin Rampton and Scott M. Matheson to the governor's mansion for an unbroken string of 20 years, from 1965 to 1985 as a much-needed counterbalance to a growing Republican majority in the Utah Legislature. From the early 1960s to the late 1970s, Utah Democrats and Republicans split the two seats in the U.S. Senate. The seats have been monopolized by Republicans ever since. During the same period, Democrats were successful in securing seats in the U.S. House of Representatives, something that has become increasingly rare in recent years.

The splitting of votes across party lines is practically unheard of in Utah today. This is true despite the fact that many current Democratic candidates hold the same values as former governors Rampton and Matheson. A great many Utah Democrats still defy the national Democratic Party and believe in being socially moderate and fiscally conservative, including a commitment to keep government out of debt by exercising "affordable compassion" to meet the considerable needs of the vulnerable among us. Again, not all Democrats think alike and a discerning electorate would see that and strengthen the health of our democratic process by voting accordingly.

If Democrats and Republicans in Utah share many of the same values as one another, does it matter which party is in power? Yes. It would make a huge difference. Democratic candidates in Utah are often more tempered, qualified and experienced to hold office than their Republican opponents but are ignored by voters because of their party label. Having these moderate Democrats in office would provide wiser, better-informed decision making in the Legislature. And it would result in a greater balance of power and constrain the temptation of some Republicans to overreach the bounds of good government. It would also minimize the risk that the Church would be harmed through blame-by-association because of the excesses of an unfettered supermajority party.

Is it possible that LDS Church authorities have the need for greater political balance in mind when they regularly issue pre-election challenges from the pulpits for Latter-day Saints to carefully study the candidates and issues before voting, regardless of a candidate's party affiliation? Are they worried that being perceived as a partisan church is compromising its image and making it less attractive to prospective converts who have a wide variety of political views?

What can Latter-day Saints do to correct the extraordinary, problematic cultural and political imbalance in which so many Church members favor an uncompromising brand of Republican ideology that they equate with gospel values? How can they avoid hurting the feelings of and alienating fellow Latter-day Saints who affiliate with the Democratic Party?

Mormon Republicans could boldly reassess their assumptions and beliefs so that their inherent goodness can shine through to the world instead of being smothered under a stifling association with a strident political belief system. They could adopt the a la carte approach, not only to elect the best candidates, but also to selectively choose from among the best elements of all ideologies to guide them. They could be less judgmental of and more compassionate toward the poor and downtrodden among them by supporting government anti-poverty programs, not just private charities. They could be more sensitive toward and accepting of those who do not think the same as they do about how the land should be governed, while recognizing that they can still be unified under the gospel.

Latter-day Saints have the power to help reshape the cultural and political landscape, not just in Utah, but across the U.S., in a way that still represents their deepest religious beliefs. By doing so, they could become ambassadors for a more civil, compassionate and spiritual society, a model of empathy and good will, and a bright light unto the world for all of God's precious children.

Appendices

Appendix A:
Definitions of Basic Political Terms

Except for the section below entitled *Left vs. Right vs. Moderates*, the following definitions are based on the work of Thomas E. Patterson in his book *The American Democracy*.

Ideology

Patterson wrote that an ideology is "a consistent pattern of political attitudes that stems from a core belief or set of beliefs." There are two main competing political ideologies that are broadly referred to as "liberal" and "conservative." Each ideology is subdivided into two smaller categories called "economic" and "social."[1]

Economic Liberals

Economic liberals generally believe that government should play an expansive role in funding social welfare programs to assist disadvantaged and vulnerable people who lack the opportunities and financial means to afford the basics of life as well as the education and training to compete for jobs. They say the poor will become self-sufficient only after those basic needs are met. Economic liberals are stereotyped by conservatives as being fiscally irresponsible "bleeding hearts" who are willing to go into debt to fund government safety nets at the expense of a balanced budget.

Economic Conservatives

Economic conservatives generally want to keep government as small as possible and let free enterprise market forces produce wealth and

---

1   Thomas E. Patterson, *The American Democracy (Ninth Edition)*, New York: McGraw-Hill, 2009, p.158.

jobs that would then "trickle down" (as this economic ideology is often called) to the poor to lift them out of poverty so they can become self-sufficient. Economic conservatives are stereotyped by liberals as being callous toward the needy and prioritizing the financial cost of helping them ahead of the human costs of poverty.

Social Liberals

Social liberals want government to stay out of legislating what are commonly called social values such as abortion and same-sex marriage, among others. They believe it should be left to each individual to choose what Patterson defines as "unconventional or new values."[2]

Social Conservatives

Social conservatives see it as government's role to be actively involved in people's lives by protecting and promoting, through legislation if need be, what are called "traditional" moral values, standards that are typically embraced by religions.

Hybrid Ideology

It's uncommon to find someone who is purely liberal or purely conservative in their economic and social beliefs. In fact, political scientists have estimated that no more than one-fourth of Americans describe themselves as having consistent beliefs across all four categories.[3] I call this blending of values a hybrid ideology.

Left vs. Right vs. Moderates

Perhaps the most common terms used to label a person's political beliefs are "left" and "right." Left (also called "left-wing" or "progressive") is used to characterize liberals. Right (used interchangeably with "right-wing") refers to conservatives. Democrats are usually lumped together in the liberal left while Republicans are generally portrayed as members of the conservative right. The terms "left" and "right" are oversimplified terms that are convenient categories but inadequate to describe the complexity of hybrid ideologies held by many

---

2 Ibid.
3 Ibid.

Americans. For example, there are Democrats who are not purely liberal and Republicans who are not purely conservative. Many of these are called "moderates," people who exist roughly at the center of the political spectrum and tilt toward one of the two major ideologies. Sometimes, moderates are also referred to as center-left or center-right. In contrast, the terms "far-left" (also called ultra-liberal) and "far-right" (synonymous with ultra-conservative) describe those who are at the extremes of the political spectrum. At the risk of adding more overgeneralization, moderates are normally seen as being willing to compromise while the far-right and far-left are characterized as being passionately entrenched in their beliefs, unwilling to listen to anyone else's views and quick to pick confrontation over civil discourse.

Appendix B:
Interchangeable Words

Throughout the book I freely substitute certain words with others that essentially have the same meaning. For example, Mormons, Latter-day Saints, LDS, Saints and Church members are used interchangeably to mean members of the Church of Jesus Christ of Latter-day Saints. Mormon Church leaders are sometimes referred to as the First Presidency (the top three governing apostles), General Authorities and Church officials, authorities or hierarchy. I also switch between Republican, GOP, conservative, and various degrees of the political right. Democrat can be synonymous with progressive, liberal and various degrees of the political left.

Index

About the Author

Larry Alan Brown was born and raised in Lancaster, New York, a suburb of Buffalo. He earned degrees at Michigan Technological University and Brigham Young University. At Michigan Tech he was the associate editor of the university newspaper and later worked as a reporter at the *Buffalo Courier-Express,* a major daily newspaper.

Brown enlisted in the U.S. Navy as an officer during the Vietnam War where he saw action aboard the aircraft carrier USS Oriskany. While on active duty, he sailed aboard two aircraft carriers and as the navigator on a guided missile destroyer homeported at Pearl Harbor, Hawaii. He loved adventuring into ports of call in Europe, Scandinavia, the Far East and Africa.

The author made his career in the computer industry where he published a book about program management. He and his family moved from California to Utah where he published several humor articles in the *Deseret News,* served as a member of the city council and planning commission at the municipal level and assisted in the campaigns of numerous political candidates.

Brown is a convert to and active member of the Church of Jesus Christ of Latter-day Saints (Mormon). He enjoys backpacking in the remote canyon country of Southern Utah. He and his wife Tammy raised four daughters (where he and the family cat bonded as the only males in the household) and have seven grandchildren.

Visit the author at www.larryalanbrown.com.

Photo by Bryant Livingston Photography